What Hydronics Taught Holohan

A Memoir of Life in the Heating Industry

DAN HOLOHAN

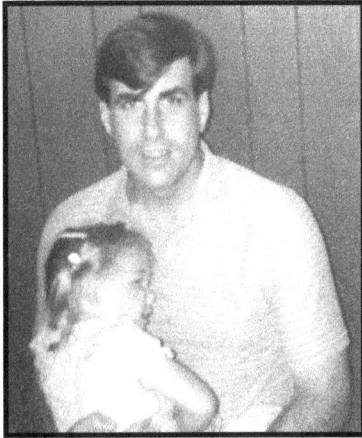

For Erin

"Young and *stronger*, and . . . even more beautiful!"

A way a lone a last a love a long the . . .
riverrun, past Eve and Adam's, from swerve of shore
to bend of bay, brings us by a commodious vicus of
recirculation back to Howth Castle and Environs.

James Joyce, *Finnegan's Wake*

Preface

For the past twelve years or so, I've had the privilege of working closely with my dad, Dan Holohan. Given all he's taught me, though, I think I was his apprentice long before that. For some reason, the older I get, the smarter he gets. Life's funny that way, isn't it?

My dad used to show a video during his seminars of my three sisters and me opening up pumps and valves under the Christmas tree. Who needs Barbie when you've got a compression tank? After all, Barbie wasn't going to keep our home cozy while we were out playing in the snow. Her "dream house" lacked a mechanical room! Plus, the thought of doing a heat-loss calculation on a house that's missing an entire back side made me shudder more than a Long Island winter.

My dad began his career working with my grandpa, Big Ed Holohan, at a NY-based manufacturers' representative. While he worked he'd listen to the old-timers who stopped by and they became teachers of a lost art. They'd tell stories about old heating systems they'd come across. They'd also pepper in tips and tricks they'd learned on the job. My dad wanted to learn even more, so he went to the library and poured over books about how heating systems (particularly steam- and hot-water heating systems) were invented and how they'd evolved over time. He wanted to preserve this history, so he began writing books and teaching.

Years later, my dad and mom, The Lovely Marianne, built HeatingHelp.com. I grew up right alongside the family business. It was my turn to listen and learn. And when they retire in 2016, they'll pass the torch and I'll take over HeatingHelp.com. I hope to make them proud.

My apprenticeship was filled with stories. And my dad never lets the truth get in the way of a good story. My grandpa was the same way. I think the people and their stories are a big part of what attracted them to the heating industry in the first place. At the end of the day, this business is about people, right? That and the fact that, as my grandpa would say, people are always going to need heat, especially in the winter.

You'll meet my grandpa, among others, later in this book and I think you'll like him. I was very young when he passed away suddenly, but he lives on in my heart and through the stories we tell. I think of my grandpa often. I think about the many generations that have made this industry great and how fortunate I am to be a part of it. It saddens me to hear that fewer young people are entering the trades. I wonder if hearing these stories might change their minds.

Over the years, I've gotten to know my dad as a father, friend, and colleague. I cherish the time we've spent together, the laughs we've shared, and all that he's taught me. *What Hydronics Taught Holohan* contains stories that my father told me. I share them with you because stories are meant to be passed on. And these are great stories, told by a great man, but I'm just a little biased. I hope you enjoy them as much as I did.

Hug your dad.

Erin

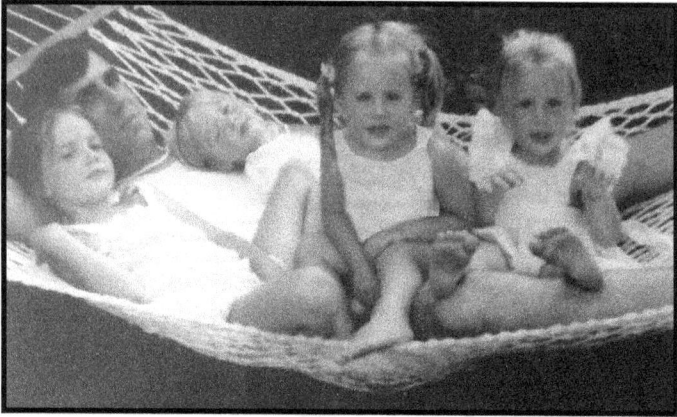

Nine by Twelve

On the afternoon that I was born, and thirty or so miles east of the place where I was born, men were leveling Long Island potato fields and laying out the building plots of what was to be our future neighborhood.

You would grow stronger here, but I didn't understand that at first.

They built our house and the one across the street first. These were the model homes. Young families would drive out from New York City on the weekends to see if this town they called Bethpage would be a good fit for them. A mile away sprawled Grumman, where thousands of workers had built war planes, and where other workers would someday build the Apollo Lunar Module. Jobs were plentiful in Bethpage.

Our neighborhood was next door to Levittown, which had gone with copper-in-concrete radiant heat for its 17,000 single-family houses because this was the least-expensive way to warm people and heat water. The once-model home in which I now sit also had radiant heat glowing from its slab. The model across the street had a basement, so they used steel convectors there, fed from diverter tees in a one-pipe hydronic loop.

I gave this some thought in 1977 when your mother and I looked at what was to become our home. The family that was selling the house was the second to own it, and they had abandoned the leaking radiant tubing in favor of Slant/Fin baseboard in 1970. They were asking $36,000 for the place. It had no garage and the property measured just 50 feet by 100 feet. We talked them down to $35,500 and signed the papers.

It was a Cape Cod house. On the first floor was a living room, a small dining room, a galley kitchen, a master bedroom, such as it was, one bath, and another bedroom that measured nine feet by 12 feet. A peaked roof upstairs allowed for two additional bedrooms with slanted ceilings. Each had an electric in-wall heater that rattled and smelled like potential death. We moved in and then had you and your three sisters in just three years.

Kelly, as you well know, arrived first. She was in the bassinet in our bedroom for months and then moved into the nine by 12 room in which I now write. I painted the room yellow and put alphabet stickers on the walls. I hung stuffed animal from the ceiling by fishing line so Kelly would have her very own Macy's parade every day. I changed diapers on a table that's right behind where my office chair is now.

Meghan arrived two years later. She moved into Kelly's crib and Kelly graduated to a big-girl bed that was to the right of where my desk is now. We had our master bedroom back, such as it was.

Thirteen months later, you and your twin, Colleen, arrived. Kelly and Meghan moved upstairs into one of the bedrooms with the slanted roof and scary heater. I had those replaced with a baseboard zone.

A few months later, your Aunt Judy, married for just one year, learned that her husband couldn't keep his vows, so she moved into the other slanted-roof bedroom upstairs. Rusty, the cocker spaniel, and the only other male in the house, decided to run away. He was always a smart dog.

Judy stayed with us for about two years and then moved out. You and Colleen moved upstairs and the nine by 12 room downstairs became my office when I worked for the manufacturers' rep, and then the World Headquarters of Dan Holohan Associates, Inc., when we started that company in 1989.

We dormered the house when you all got bigger and put all the bedrooms upstairs. We also added a second bathroom. I hung a Men's Room sign on the downstairs bathroom, which confused some of our visitors during the holidays.

When your grandma got sick, your Aunt Missy, who has Down syndrome, moved in with us. We figured what's one more potato in the pot?

When I moved into nine by 12 with all its memories, I painted it dark green, the color of peace. I hung book shelves on every available inch of wall, and filled them with old books. I set my brown-wood desk against the West-facing wall because that's where my reader most likely is. Behind me is a sliver of Long Island and thousands of miles of steel-grey Atlantic.

You all grew like corn and went through all the things that girls will go through. You had the advantage of each other, though. No one was allowed to have a problem alone. You stuck together. Still do.

When we started our business, our only goal was to put the four of you through college. We did that and followed up with fancy weddings, and then, when you all married good men, we decided that we were done baking. You were women complete.

Every story I have ever written, I've written from this desk, in this tiny room where so much has happened. And this is what I learned from this room:

When you have just one child, you think that you are in charge of that child's future. You think nurture is the most important thing and you weigh each decision you make carefully. You go to bed each night feeling a bit guilty about what you did, or what you didn't do, with the kid that day.

When the second child arrives, you wonder how you could possibly love this child as much as you love the first, but love is malleable and it molds itself between you and that other child, and years later, you wonder how you could have ever have had those thoughts. And you continue to think that nurture is most important. The guilt goes on.

But when you and Colleen arrived, fraternal twins that look nothing alike, magic arrived with you. We cared for you both as infants as we had cared for Kelly and Meghan before you. We treated you two exactly the same, but you didn't respond to us in the same way. Colleen was quiet and smiling, a puddle of peace. As she grew, she did what we asked her to do. Don't run into the road, even if a big dog is chasing you. Don't climb on that; you'll fall. Eat all your food.

You, however, nurtured the exact same way from the moment you and your sister arrived at home, were a maelstrom. Colleen would whimper a bit and wait for us to change her. You would tear off your diaper and throw it at us from your crib. Colleen would lift her leg to try to climb out of her crib. We'd say no, and she would sit down. You, who walked at nine months, would toss your leg over the crib rail and fall to the floor. I'd gasp, admonish you, and put you back. You'd do it again. I'd put you back. You'd do it again. And again.

I realized I wasn't going to win this battle of wills. I got out of your way.

You and Colleen taught me that it is our *nature* that guides us so much more so than nurture. Parents are there to keep us from destroying ourselves when we are small, but we are who we are from the start, and we will be who we will be, no matter what.

You took jobs after college and were never happy with any of them. You had ideas of how you might do things better. Your bosses didn't want to listen to your suggestions, so you'd get another job. The same thing would happen.

You'll remember the year your sister, Meghan, was involved with World Teach, and living in that small village in Costa Rica, teaching school. We all traveled there to visit with her during Easter week. You and I found ourselves having breakfast at a Denny's one morning in the capital city of San José. You were unhappy with the latest job.

"You can't work for anyone," I said. "You're an entrepreneur. You have to build something on your own."

At first, you didn't believe me. It's your nature to question things, but time passed and you started your own business, doing graphic design, and writing, as I do. You thrived.

Our business grew to become HeatingHelp.com and I needed you more and more because you're simply better at things Internet than I am. We retained you and our business bloomed. We could not have done any of this without the guidance of this strong woman who once refused to stay in the crib that used to be right over there next to where my desk is now in this nine by 12 room. I glance over and I can still see you.

I'm going to continue to write, but this business we call HeatingHelp.com is now yours, my daughter. And thinking back to the days when you climbed out of your crib again and again to get at the world, I realize that this transition from father and mother to daughter is natural. We nurtured you as best we could, but you were born with many questions, a powerful will, and a fierce determination.

I will always be there for you, but it's time, once again, for me to get out of your way. And as I do, I leave you with this love letter of a book. It expresses my love for this thing we call Hydronics, sure, but most of all it expresses my love for you and your magnificent spirit and determination. You will do well.

So here, Erin, my precious daughter, is what Hydronics taught Holohan.

Hydronics taught me to be curious

Temperature's a big deal in the hydronics biz. Everyone talks about it. Outdoor temperature, indoor temperature, water temperature, mean-radiant temperature, outdoor-reset temperature. It never ends, and most of us don't even say the word, Fahrenheit. It's just assumed.

Which made me curious.

I learned early on that most of the scientific concepts we take for granted nowadays started as an idea that some guy in a room came up with one day. Take temperature, for instance. Before we had thermometers no one knew exactly how hot or cold it was outside. You'd go outside in July and say, "Boy, it's hot today! It must be, what..." And there you'd get stuck because that guy in the room hadn't yet given you the concept of temperature. You couldn't say that it was 98 in the shade because Fahrenheit hadn't shown up yet. All you could do was mop your brow. Think about it; we base so much of what we do on the temperature inside and outside of our buildings. Isn't it strange to imagine a time before Fahrenheit?

Speaking of whom, I get very confused when I'm in Canada and Europe and someone on the TV tells me it's going to be a lovely 25 degrees on that day. I'm reaching for my overcoat until I realize he's talking Celsius, not Fahrenheit.

And actually, he's not even talking Celsius (even though we often call it that) because we don't use the Celsius scale nowadays. Anders Celsius was the guy that dreamt up that one. It was 1742 and he decided to make the boiling point of water zero degrees Celsius and the freezing point of water 100 degrees Celsius. Hey, why not? He was

Anders Celsius and he could do what he pleased. His scale, right?

No one uses Celsius as he intended it. We use the Centigrade scale, but Celsius often gets credit, even though he had nothing to do with turning the scale upside-down to get to Centigrade. Doesn't seem fair, does it?

In the U.S., most of us are still swearing by Gabriel Fahrenheit. Gabe was a German merchant and the first guy to make a mercury thermometer. This was also a long time ago, 1721 to be exact. He had to come up with a scale to go along with his new thermometer, of course, and he needed to have fixed points on that scale, so this is what he did. He used as zero degrees the temperature of the coldest stuff he could imagine, a mixture of salt and sal-ammoniac. The other fixed point was the normal temperature of the human body, which he called 24 degrees Fahrenheit. He could do this because he was Gabe Fahrenheit. Who's going to argue the Fahrenheit scale with Gabe Fahrenheit?

Anyway, on this original Fahrenheit scale, water freezes at 8 degrees Fahrenheit and boils at 54 degrees Fahrenheit. Gabe took his thermometer around and showed it to people who had no concept of temperature measurement (now there's a sales job for you). I like to think that someone told him what to do with his thermometer, which led to the invention of a different sort of thermometer, but I digress.

As luck would have it, some of the people mentioned that the mercury moved very quickly past the numbers on the original Fahrenheit scale, so Gabe decided to give the scale more numbers. He did that by simply multiplying everything on his original scale by four and that's why, nowadays, water freezes at 32 degrees Fahrenheit and boils at 212 degrees Fahrenheit. The normal temperature of the human body is actually 96 degrees Fahrenheit, but we now call it 98.6 because Gabe is currently on the other side of lawn and not in a position to protest.

The fun part of this (at least for me) is that this guy just made it all up. He could have called it anything and we would have gone along because he was Gabriel Fahrenheit. You could do the same if you were willing to work as hard at it as he did. Go ahead, establish the Erin Scale or the Haskell Meter. Knock yourself out. History will remember you forever.

Think of it. What makes a foot a foot, a yard a yard, a meter a meter? Someone just made all of this up at some point and worked really hard to convince the rest of us to go along. Why is a troy pound different from an avoirdupois pound? And isn't it amazing that people in different countries can get things done when it comes to engineering?

You say poTAto. I say poTAHto. But how do we all say hydronics?

There was a guy named Delisle who was also into thermometers. He introduced the Delisle scale (ever hear of it?) in 1724. He was following on the heels of Gabe Fahrenheit and he, like Celsius, decided to call the boiling point of water zero degrees. He also figured that 100 degrees Delisle should be the temperature of the cellar in the Paris Observatory.

But on what day? Hmm.

In spite of that wacky decision, the Delisle scale became the one that Russia chose to use for many years. They eventually switched to the Reaumur scale. René Antoine Ferchault de Reaumur sold alcohol (not vodka) thermometers and the boiling port of water was 80 degrees on his scale. Much of France still uses this scale. How about that?

Isn't it amazing that we all managed to get where we got?

So who invented the Centigrade scale, which most of the world agrees is the most sensible scale of all? Well, that grand accomplishment goes to Carl Linnaeus, a Swedish botanist. Oh, and he's the guy who also established the modern binomial system (genus plus species) for naming plants and animals. The Centigrade scale was just something he came up with in his spare time.

Imagine that.

And what about the sacred British thermal unit?

When I was growing up in the heating industry, I read trade-magazine articles by John Woodworth, who worked for the Hydronics Institute. He was an engineer and I respected and admired him. In later years, we became friends through my own magazine writing, and when he retired in July 1999, he sent me a very worn copy of Thomas Tredgold's, *Warming and Ventilating of Public Buildings*. The First Edition of this book arrived in England in 1824. The copy John gave me was a Third Edition, published in 1836. He included a note:

Dan, I think you should have the enclosed book, rather than have it rot in a Hydronics Institute cabinet.

Regards,

John Woodward

For which I will always be grateful. What a treasure this was! I have many old books in my collection, but this was probably the first written specifically about warming and ventilating public buildings. In it, on page 24 are these words from Mr. Tredgold:

"In order to compare the effects of different kinds of fuel, some convenient measure of effect should be adopted: not only for the purpose of lessening the trouble of calculation, but also to render it more clear and intelligible. I shall, therefore, without regarding the measures of effect employed by others, adopt one of my own, which I have found useful in this and other inquiries of a similar nature.

"I take as the measure of the effect of a fuel, the quantity, in pounds avoirdupois, which will raise the temperature of a cubic foot of water one degree of Fahrenheit's scale."

What we have there is the British thermal unit. It came from the mind of Thomas Tredgold, a railroad engineer who dabbled in heating and ventilating public buildings. What's delightful about the definition, though, if the business about the *cubic foot* of water. These days, a Btu is the amount of heat required to raise one *pound* of water one degree on the Fahrenheit scale, not one cubic foot.

Mr. Tredgold goes on in his book to give examples of how much fuel it would take to bring a cubic foot of water to a boil from several different temperatures. He explains about latent heat, and how we have to add a lot of that to get water to change from liquid at 212°F to steam at that same temperature. I keep smiling about that change from one cubic foot to one pound of water, though. I figure it got changed for one reason, and one reason only.

Mr. Tredgold left the building.

But what does it matter? He was just making this up as he went along, the same as the guys with the temperature scales were dreaming it all up. So, once he was dead, what was the big deal about changing it? I mean if everyone agrees that a pound of water is easier to work with than a cubic foot of water, right? So why not?

And that's how the sacred British thermal unit came to be.

And since the British had kicked the snot out of Napoleon in 1815, I suppose they felt just fine naming this unit of heat measurement after their country. They were the victors, and to the victors go the degrees,

The French weren't buying it, though. And neither were the Germans.

Which is understandable.

Today, even the British don't use the British thermal unit.

Want to start a scientific movement?

Just make up a new term and gather a group around it. Can't miss.

More and more curious

The more I learned, the more I began to realize that a lot of people in the hydronics industry didn't know certain things, but they were afraid to admit that they didn't know, and the older they got, the more they were afraid to ask.

So one day, during a steam seminar, I did an experiment. I was talking to a group of mostly engineers, and I mentioned that I had been on a problem job with a contractor and we came across a Farquhar Flange. I was putting on my Fahrenheit/Tredgold hat here.

I waited a moment but no one said a thing.

"Do you all know what I'm talking about?" I asked. Many heads nodded, which was delicious because I had no idea what a Farquhar Flange was. The name had just popped into my brain and slid down and out of my mouth.

"You've seen these?" I said.

Heads nodded.

"What color was yours?" I asked one of the nodders.

"I think it was red?" he said.

And there you have it. One of the best things that Hydronics taught Holohan is that when people in this business don't know something, they will never let that stand in their way.

Old joke:

First guy: "You ever drive a Henway?"

Second guy: "What's a Henway?"

First guy: "About two pounds!"

Rim shot! Tip your wait staff!

Only in the hydronics business, the second guy would just say, "Henway? Sure, I rented one from Hertz last summer."

Keep smiling, Erin. It is, as we both know, a *very* funny industry.

Hydronics taught me
about industry people

I've been thinking about the tens of thousands of contractors I've met in my travels since 1970. I love these people (some more than others) and their tenacity. There's not much they won't take on (for better or worse). Here's a short list of things I've found that most of them have in common. It's what makes them so special, and forever fascinating.

Most aren't engineers. Contractors think in pictures; engineers think in numbers. Question members of either group and they'll tell you that this is true. A good contractor can look at an empty room and visualize all the mechanical equipment to come in its proper place. They'll know what will fit and what won't, what will be in the way of something else when it comes to service. An engineer will need a blueprint for this, and chances are the down-the-road-service aspects of the job won't show up on those blueprints.

Consider that engineers write most of the technical books and instruction manuals for hydronic-heating systems, and being engineers, they write for engineers, using lots of numbers. That's why contractors don't read those tomes. Contractors are visual and kinesthetic. Engineers are digital. Big difference.

Most contractors love stories. I learned this early in my career by listening to them talk about the jobs they did. They'd weave people stories into the mechanical equipment like a gorgeous tapestry. It's not just about the heating system to the contractors. It's about the wacky things the people in the buildings do to those heating systems. Want to reach contractors? Do it through story.

Many are dyslectic. This has come up many times on the HeatingHelp.com site, and in the thousands of seminars I've done. So many contractors have told me that they can't read well. Some can't read at all. The trades attract these people because it's tactile. You feel it, and again, you think in pictures. I've had wholesalers complain to me about contractors who constantly call to have them explain something again and again, or size something again and again. Some of these wholesalers view those contractors as being stupid. I see those contractors as people coping with dyslexia. The letters are upside-down and inside-out. And engineers are writing the words.

This is widespread challenge in our business. If you realize that and help those contractors they'll love you for it.

Many hate math. There are mathematical formulas in the heating world, and even lots of numbers in something as simple as a heat-loss calculation. There are even more numbers on the financial side of the business. You can't put a wrench on any of this.

Again, it's pictures vs. numbers. If you're presenting information in a purely mathematical way, don't be surprised if many contractors just ignore what you're saying and try to work around you. That's why they ask you for rules of thumb. How many Btu per square foot of space? That's why they oversize equipment. Over-sizing seems safe to them. That's why they base the price of their job on what the other guy is charging.

They hate math.

Most love challenges. And this is a great thing. They love being able to fix the system that the other guy couldn't fix. Hydronics isn't just a job to many of them; it's a blood sport. "Get outta my way, kid. I'll show you how it's done." And most of the time, they will.

Most build knowledge like a brick wall. Those bricks at the base? They could be something that their father or grandfather told them, or something that their first boss mentioned. That first brick goes down and everything else rests upon it. And if that first brick is a strong one, the wall will be fine. But if that first brick is faulty, so will the wall be faulty. I have told the story about where the circulator belongs in a hydronic heating system thousands of times, yet each day, contractors will argue with me about this because it's not how their pappy did it. Understand what's going on here and be gentle in how you teach people. And please be patient. There are a lot of bricks in that wall.

Most make up their minds and stick with it. This, too, has to do with the teachers. It might have been a grandfather, father, mother, or some old guy at the shop where the contractor first worked. An idea got pounded into the contractor's head and reinforced over the years. It's not going to come out of that head easily. If you need to change someone's mind, persuasion works better than arguing. For instance, whenever I talk go contractors about pumping away from the compression tank, I tell them that if they do it that way, they will never again have to bleed air from a radiator. And since not having to bleed air from radiators is in the contractor's best interest, most are willing to give it a try. And once they do, they believe me, and they trust me to tell them more.

Don't argue. Talk about what's in it for them.

Most are loyal to products. In this industry, when a new product arrives, it had better be as gee whiz as the iPhone, or way cheaper than what the contractor is currently using. This is because they like to stick with what works for them. If they buy a product, get used to it, and it's not bringing them callbacks, they'll buy it again and again and not want to try anything new. You can try to change their minds but what they're doing works for them. If you talk to them about saving energy, they'll be thinking that it's the customer's energy and not theirs. They're looking to save the energy required to go back and fix a product that's not working as it should. So to get their attention, you'd better be much cheaper, or iPhone incredible. And if you're that much cheaper, chances are your product won't last, so you'll lose them forever. And let's face it, being iPhone incredible doesn't happen very often.

Some will defend the problem product rather than be wrong about their decision. This is human nature. We choose, and sometimes poorly. But then an amazing thing happens. We feel stupid that we're having a problem with (fill in the blank), but if we admit that the product is just plain lousy, that means that we were stupid to buy it in the first place. So we will defend the faulty product and try to make it work. We make excuses for it. We'd rather live with it than admit we were wrong. It's human nature.

Many let politics lead them. I once had a conversation with a heating contractor who insisted on plastering his work truck with political bumper stickers. I mentioned that this could be costing him business because America is basically divided between those who lean right and those who lean left these days. I asked him why he would go out of his way to probably lose half of his potential customers by tipping his hand, politically.

"Some people are not going to like you right from the start when they see your truck moving around town," I said. "They'll never hire you if they see you as what they consider an extremist. They won't want to listen to you when you show up at their house to fix their heating system."

"I don't care about those people," he said. "I gotta be me."

"So you're only going to work for people who agree with your politics?"

"No," he said. "I'll work for those idiots, but I'm not changing my truck. I gotta be me. If they don't like it, tough."

He worked from his house, which was okay as long as he didn't keep his truck in his driveway. Zoning laws didn't allow that, but he didn't want to pay for a garage so he parked in his driveway. This is working-class neighborhood and lots of tradespeople do that. Most of the time, the neighbors don't complain because they're, well, good neighbors. Most people just want to get along.

But this contractor decided to go beyond the signs on his truck. He covered his lawn with cardboard political signs, most of which called anyone who disagreed with his positions idiots. And in today's America, that would be about half of his neighborhood.

So some of his neighbors called the town to complain about his truck in the driveway. An inspector showed up and that was that. He now had to pay to park his truck somewhere else, and I suppose the lesson here is that if you poke someone with a stick, there's a good chance they're going to poke back.

Then the Great Recession came down on him and he promptly went right out of business.

"What happened?" I asked.

"People are cheap," he said.

He had to be him.

Isn't it amazing what can happen once you make up your mind, declare anyone who disagrees with you to be the enemy, and then refuse to budge?

Here's something to consider. A few years ago, three researchers from the Wharton School at the University of Pennsylvania, and Duke University published a paper in the *Proceedings of the National Academy of Sciences*. It was about how labeling products can affect that product's sales. I found this fascinating.

In the first study, they interviewed 657 people, divided more or less in half by gender. They asked the people to fill out a questionnaire that they had designed to reveal both the person's political leanings and their energy-saving-product purchasing habits. They learned that the more conservative a person was, the less likely they were to buy a product that the manufacturer touted as being friendly to the environment. But if the manufacturer labeled the product as one that saved money, the conservatives went for it.

How about that? Oh, and just the opposite applied to the liberals, who were all about saving the planet.

Then the researchers did a second study. This time, they interviewed 210 people. They gave each person $2 to purchase a light bulb. The choice was between an incandescent bulb and a more-expensive, energy-saving bulb. Both bulbs looked the same, but the researches advertised the higher-priced bulb two ways. First, they claimed that the more-expensive bulb would save the user money because it used less electricity. Then, they changed the ad, claiming that the more-expensive bulb was good for the planet.

The liberals were willing to buy the more-expensive bulb regardless of how it was advertised. The conservatives would buy the bulb that would save money, but not the bulb advertised to be good for the environment. Even though it was the same bulb.

Finally, the researchers made the price of both bulbs the same and found that all of the folks surveyed went for the special bulb, regardless of how it was advertised.

The researchers' conclusion was that folks who see themselves as conservatives weren't really against buying green products. They were, however, conditioned to link green products to liberals, and that's why they instinctively shy away from products advertised that way. It's good to save money, they say, but it's bad to agree with liberals.

And that brings us to Energy Star products, as designated by the U.S. Environmental Protection Agency. Right up front on those Energy Star labels you will see how much greenhouse gas that product will save, and how using that product protects our climate. But now that you know about that survey, do you think it's possible that the Energy Star label might be turning off a good portion of the buying public?

Yeah, so do I.

And how about advertisements in magazines? If a manufacturer focuses on how good his energy-saving boiler, circulator, or you name it is for the planet, does that cause a kneejerk reaction in conservative-minded readers. Maybe they'll just flip the page, but not before muttering something nasty about Al Gore.

Everything seems to be getting greener these days and manufacturers are stretching the limits to explain how and why their products are greener than the other guy's products. But when we all stress the good of our planet instead of the potential for saving money on fuel and electricity, are we losing half our potential customers right from the start. I wonder.

I keep thinking about that contractor who went out of business because he didn't care what people thought about his political views. They could either agree with him or take a hike. Half of them took that hike and that was enough to turn that guy belly-up when the economy tightened up.

And to think that was his choice. What about his family?

Gosh.

Contractors and customers

Some of this is going to seem crazy, and some of it may even seem scary. It scared me when I first learned about it, but it's key to understanding what makes this business tick, though. Not everyone sees things the way you see them, or the way I see them, and if we try to force other people to see things our way instead of their way, we're not going to get where we're trying to go. And nothing happens until somebody sells something.

So try this experiment with me. Read these brief descriptions of three heating systems and then decide which one you'd like to see in your own home. Which would feel the best to you? Take your time deciding.

System # 1 The heating system in this home is a joy to look at. It's obvious that a craftsman put it together. Look at the way those pipes line up. Everything is so plumb and level! And notice how clean all of those joints are. The boiler room is well lit and everything is clearly labeled. You'll be proud to show this one to your friends and neighbors.

System # 2 All I can say about the heating system in this home is that it is so whisper-quiet that you'll barely know that it's running. It purrs along with such precision that you'll probably forget that it's there on most days. Such quiet comfort! There won't be any clanging radiators in this home, no ticking radiators, nothing to go bump in the night. Just peace, quiet and comfort.

System # 3 A company with a solid reputation for quality assembled the heating system in this home. This system is tough as nails, and smart, too. The company that installed it stands behind their work with the integrity that comes from many years of doing business in the neighborhood. Ask around. Your neighbors will tell you about these people. We think they're the best we've ever seen. When you buy this home you're putting yourself in very good hands when it comes to the heating system. Feel comfortable in your decision.

Okay, did you pick one?

Which house would you buy, all else being equal?

But before you choose, know that you can't go wrong because, in each case, I'm describing the same house. The only thing different about your three choices is how I chose to describe each one.

Surprised? This has to do with a relatively new area of psychology called neurolinguistic programming. I know that's a mouthful, so the psychologists who study how people process language, just call it NLP. If you pay close attention to what people are saying and *how* they're saying it (and isn't that a dying art in a world filled with people who would rather stare at screens than listen) you'll be able to shift your own speaking style to match the other's person's style. Do this and that person will pay closer attention to what you have to say.

I stumbled upon this in my reading and it's very powerful stuff. Each of us has a preference for the way we receive and give information. That's why you chose that particular heating system over the other two, even though all three were the same. We each have a preference for language that is either Visual, Auditory, or Kinesthetic.

I used visual words to describe System #1. I know you were seeing it in your mind's eye. If you liked the way that that description looked, you are probably a visual person (and I know you are because you have made your living as a graphic designer). If you and I were getting together to see which heating system would best meet your needs, and I spotted that you were using expressions such as, "I see what you mean," or, "That's an interesting way of looking at things" (terms you use often), I'm going to pick up on those Visual expressions that you're using, and as we continue to chat, and I'm going to mirror your NLP preference by using more visual words. If you re-read this paragraph you'll see that I'm doing that right now.

See what I mean?

Now listen to this: System #2 sounds best to people who favor the Auditory style. With this one, I used words that tuned in on how things will sound when the system is purring along. The person that chose this one, is probably an Auditory person (which happens to be what I am). Auditory people prefer to read about products rather than look at pictures or videos. I want to hear you describe it. I want to listen to stories told by others who own the product already. This person loves to read testimonials.

If I was speaking to you (see how I'm doing it right now?), and you said something like, "I hear you," or "Let me say something about that," or, "What do others have to say about it?" I'm going to tune-in on those words and begin to speak in a more Auditory way. And as I begin to match your speaking pattern you will be listening more closely to me, and you'll start to think that we're on the same wavelength. You'll be much more receptive to what I have to say because I'm speaking your language.

Literally.

Ever notice how you just like some people more than others? That's NLP at work. It's natural in all of us, and most of the time, you're not aware that it's going on, and that's what makes NLP so potent in business. People buy from those they like.

Okay, here's how I feel about System # 3. This is the best one for those who are Kinesthetic. These are people who like to give and get information through touching things, and deciding how they feel emotionally about things. A Kinesthetic will come up with expressions such as, "I'm feeling really good about this," or "This worries me, " or "Let me point out something that I think is important here," or "How are you going to back up that claim. Let's cut to the chase." All of these expressions relate to feelings, and that's the best way to communicate with a Kinesthetic. These are people who want to touch things and feel things, and many hydronic installers are Kinesthetics, which is why they prefer hands-on training to books and brochures, or engineers talking with numbers and formulas.

You've watched me teach. Notice how I always used photographs and diagrams instead of PowerPoint slides with bullet points? That was my way of reaching the Visuals in my audience. I removed as many words as I could from the slides and used instead as many visual images as possible. I do this because I realized that I had in my audience a mix of people and I wanted to reach them all. So I combined the three NLP preferences into one presentation. I used stories to appeal to the Auditory people. I used photos for the Visual folks, and I described in detail what it felt like to be on that job, or to watch this or that action take place. That last was for the Kinesthetic people.

Why do we find some speakers boring and others interesting? The boring ones are most likely sticking to the NLP style that appeals to them, not to you or me. The same goes for salespeople. If you're more interested in the way that new car is going to *look*, and the salesperson insists on talking about how *quiet* it is, or how tight the steering *feels*, you're not going to get along with that person. You're probably going to buy from someone else. People buy from people they like.

Oh, and there's one more thing. When you're having a conversation, always watch the other person's eyes because eye movement will reveal the other person's language preference. All the eye movements I'm about to describe are from your point of view as you're looking at the other person. Ask a question and watch the eyes.

If you're with a Visual person, her eyes will quickly glance upward and to the right when she is remembering something. When constructing an image, she will look up and to the left. It's involuntary. It's fascinating once you know to look for it, and it happens every time.

Now speak to an Auditory person and watch as he glances to the right side when remembering something (not up, just to the right), and to the left side when he is putting something into words (again, from your point of view). This person is sort of looking at his own ears, which helps you to remember that this is an involuntary action of an Auditory person.

Finally, a Kinesthetic person's eyes will always flash downward and to the right when he or she is having internal dialogue, like trying to recall something. And he or she will look downward and to the left when describing how something felt. Most of the installers in the hydronics business that I've met are Kinesthetic people. Ask about a problem job they're dealing with and they'll look down and to the right for an instant. They can't help but do that.

Lefties sometimes do just the opposite, so note which hand they're using when picking up a pen, or notice on which hand they wear a watch.

One more and then we'll move on. Ronald Regan was a very popular and charismatic president. For years, Peggy

Noonan wrote his speeches. In one of those, she wrote, *"For those who yearn to be free, America is not just a word, it is a hope, a torch shedding light to all the hopeless of the world."*

Beautiful, hopeful words, but can you see the NPL in there? Kinesthetic, followed by Auditory, followed by Visual, all written to appeal to a majority of Americans. It worked. Twice!

Words are powerful, and how we use them can make them even more powerful.

People buy from people they like.

And other industry people, who happen to be dead

Erin, there are *so* many of them. You know all those books in my office. That room used to be your bedroom, yours and your sisters. So much has taken place in this nine by 12 room. The people in those books have spoken to me through the decades, as they will to you. Their story is America's story, and also the story of other countries where the Dead Men tinkered with metal and water and fire, and invented wonderful machines that kept people warm and alive.

Here are a few of the people who have traveled with me through the years. I've enjoyed their company very much, and I'm delighted to be able to keep them alive for you and others.

John Mills, who liked to experiment

This fellow did so much, but he was also a bit eccentric. He was there at the start of hydronics. He worked with the H.B. Smith Company as a freelance inventor and engineer from 1873 until 1897. He was forever experimenting, learning, and sharing what he learned with others.

Between 1888 and 1890, he wrote a two-volume text called, *Heat, Science and Philosophy of its Production and Application to the Warming and Ventilating of Buildings.* It was one of the first serious books about heating and this magnum opus became an important resource for boiler- and steam engineers in the years that followed. I have a copy of it and it's a great read.

John Mills invented the boiler that carried his name, and Mestek, the successor company to H.B. Smith, continued to make that boiler until just a few years ago. John Mills also realized that if a tall building was to have a one-pipe-steam system, it would be best to send the supply main straight up to the top of the building, then turn it horizontal and go around the perimeter of the attic, and finally, downfeed all the radiators so that the steam and the condensate would be traveling in the same direction. They called this the Mills System and it worked beautifully.

I remember going to a fancy building on Central Park West in Manhattan, where I saw a Mills System that had 12-inch screwed pipe. It was something to marvel at because a 12-inch screwed tee is a lot bigger (and heavier) that you think. I thought about John Mills that day, and about the men who installed that big pipe to his design. I try to imagine what sort of wrenches those guys owned, where they stood to get the leverage, what size their arms were. Those guys left echoes of themselves in that building.

John Mills also experimented with heat loss, and he developed a quick method for figuring out the load in a building. They called it (not surprisingly) the Mills Rule.

Contractors loved the Mills Rule because it was so easy to use. Before long, they nicknamed it the 2-20-200 Rule and I'll explain why in a minute. Most of the size-it-quickly rules of thumb that followed John Mills' rule evolved from this method. They were all fine for their time, but not so good nowadays because we build better than they did.

Consider what sort of windows they used during John Mills' time. Most likely, they were leaky. And what about insulation? Do you think they used fiberglass batts back in the day? Do you think they used anything at all inside those walls? Not from what I've seen, and not from what I've read. The heat loss of a building was much greater back then, and the Mills (2-20-200) Rule was appropriate for that sort of construction. Not so good nowadays.

Here's what I mean. Take any building and size a new steam boiler using the Mills Rule. The first thing you're going to do is measure the square footage of all the glass in the building. Once you have that number, divide it by 2 (that's the 2 in the 2-20-200 nickname for the Mills Rule). Okay, now set that aside for a moment.

Next, measure all the cold surfaces in the building. A cold surface is any wall, floor, or ceiling that doesn't have heat on its other side. In a two-story house, the first floor walls are cold surfaces if they face outdoors. It's warm on one side of those walls and cold on the other side. If a wall faces another heated room, you wouldn't measure that wall for heat loss.

You'd probably measure the ceiling on the second floor of this building because that ceiling faces the attic space (which is unheated), but you wouldn't measure the ceiling on the first floor of that building because that faces the heated second floor. The same goes for the floor; you'd count it if it was over a cold crawlspace or an unheated basement, but not if it was over a heated basement. Make sense so far? Good.

Okay, once you've measured all the cold surfaces, divide that number by 20 (that's the second number in the 2-20-200 nickname). Put it on the back burner for a minute; we have one more measurement to make, and this has to do with the air that's inside the building. The air is constantly changing because of infiltration. Old buildings were drafty (many of them still are). Measure the cubic feet of air by multiplying the length, times the height, times the width of each room. Now add those numbers together and divide the total by 200 (the third number in the 2-20-200 nickname of the Mills Rule).

The grand total you come up with will be the required square footage of Equivalent Direct Radiation (or E.D.R. for short) for the building. One square foot of E.D.R. for steam will give out 240 Btuh when there is 70-degree air on the outside of the radiator, and 215-degree steam on the inside of the radiator. That temperature of the steam is significant because 215-degree steam is steam at about 1-psi pressure, so what the definition of E.D.R. is telling us is you don't need pressure greater than 1-psi inside the radiator, even on the coldest day of the year.

For hot-water heat, when the average water temperature is 170-degrees, the value of E.D.R. drops to 150 Btuh per square foot. This is because hot water isn't as hot as steam.

The Dead Men used the Mills Rule for both steam- and hot-water systems.

But here's the problem with the Mills Rule. We've upgraded the windows and even the insulation in many of those old buildings. The radiators are now oversized, based on the current heat loss of the renovated building. That can cause money to flow out through those new windows if people are going to be cracking them open to be comfortable. If you used the Mills Rule, or a similar shortcut, to figure the radiation for a modern building, you'll probably wind up with enough radiation to heat three buildings. That's the problem with using sizing shortcuts from more than 100 years ago. They didn't keep up with the times, and I think John Mills would agree, were he around today. He'd be using a computer to size his systems. He'd probably be writing the software. Or building the computer.

Sometime in 1905 or 1906 (and this was in Westfield, Massachusetts), Mr. Mills wandered into town, dressed shabbily and looking penniless. J.R. Reed, who ran the H.B. Smith Company at the time, saw him and said, "John Mills, I always warned you of this. Didn't I say that if you kept on at the rate you were going that you would surely scratch a poor man's pants?" He then gave Mr. Mills a check for $5,000 and said, "You are not going to give this money away, or use it for any more experimenting."

John H. Mills never again appeared in Westfield. He died in 1908. And my guess is that he never did stop experimenting. I wish I could have met him, but I do hear his words through his book.

Meet Denis Papin

I was thinking about how the things we take for granted came to be, and what life would have been like had they not appeared when they did.

Take the lowly relief valve, for instance. This is something most people in the hydronics industry would rather not touch because, as with everything else, once you touch it, you own it. Most of the contractors I know will just look at that lowly valve and assume it will do its job when and if the boiler ever goes berserk. Otherwise, let's let sleeping dogs lie.

I was reading a magazine that is more than 100 years old the other day and came across this delightful little story. Listen to this:

"The first safety valve was invented in 1681 by Denis Papin, a Frenchman, who was born at Blois, France in 1647. He commenced his experiments on the phenomena of steam in July 1676, at London under Robert Boyle, the distinguished Irishman who founded the Royal Society of London."

(That's the guy who gave us Boyle's Law. He plays a huge part in hydronics.)

"About 1780, Papin brought out a little steam apparatus called, "Papin's Bone Digester," for softening animal bones for 'cookery, voyages at sea, confectionary, chemistry, and dyeing.'

"England's Charles II ordered Papin to make a digester for his laboratory at Whitehall, and the invention excited much interest. By means of this steam-pressure cooking machine, delicious jellies were made from beef, mutton and other bones. Enormous strength was needed in the machine to stand the high pressure generated, and Papin found that he could only make his machine successful by contriving a mechanical device that would release pressure at a certain point and thus prevent explosion.

"This he finally worked out during 1681 in the first steam-pressure safety valve; then his machine could be utilized without fear. A hundred years later, James Watt and others made use of his invention in connection with a steam-powered engine, and later in the 18th Century, Watt and other inventors made use of a similar apparatus utilized for heating purposes.

"Papin was one of the great benefactors of the human race. Living in the age of Pascal, Newton, Boyle, and Leibnitz, he partook liberally of the spirit of progress, which was a work in those days to free the human race of its shackles imposed by ignorance of natural laws, and may well be said that Papin 'built better than he knew.' He was both a prophet and executor of mechanical progress, and his memory is one of the sacred treasures of the power- and low-pressure, steam-heating industries."

So, because the King of England liked jelly, we now have relief valves. Isn't that delicious? There's a sketch of the device in that old, yellowed magazine. The relief valve sits atop a big, closed kettle. The relief valve is a long lever attached to a pivot point. There's a plug connected to the lever, very close to the pivot point, and this sits in a hole in the boiler. The lever reaches out several feet and had a movable weight near its end. You could move the weight this way and that to adjust the relief pressure.

And all for the sake of jelly.

In my files, I have a sketch of the first hot-water heating system, which also has a neat connection to food. The man who first came up with the idea of central, hot-water heating was Jean Simon Bonnemain. The sketch I have is from 1777 and it shows a big, enclosed kettle sitting atop a fire. This was the boiler. Coming out of the top of the boiler there is a large pipe. It goes all the way up to the top of the building and then laces its way back and forth across each floor of the building and all the way back to the top of the kettle. There are no radiators. The big pipe enters the top of the boiler through a dip tube, much like the dip tube that cold water uses to enter a water heater. There's a second pipe that runs from the kettle to the top of the building, and at the top of this pipe there is a funnel. This is how you fill the system. Go get yourself a bucket and start climbing stairs. Oh, and one more thing, connected to the top of the main heating pipe, there's a second pipe that rises up and then loops over into the top of an open tank. This gives the heated water a place to go, should it expand too much. This was the world's first gravity system and Jean Simon Bonnemain used it to warm chickens for the Paris poultry market.

How about that?

Bonnemain's open tank got me thinking about how far we've come. Today, we have these wonderful, pressurized tanks that take up so little space in a boiler room, but as with relief valves, most of us take those tanks for granted. We see them on just about every job and don't give them much thought.

Jelly and chicken - two inspirations for modern hydronic heating.

Go figure.

And then there's Hugh J. Barron, and his Irish temper

You may never have heard of Hugh J. Barron. He was an Irishman by birth and a steamfitter by trade. He served with the Fighting Sixty-ninth. He became an independent contractor at one point and then a salesman. He was long a member of the Master Steamfitters Organization, where he and others prepared and read lengthy papers on the technical aspects of this at-the-time-new art called steam heating.

In 1894, the Master Steamfitters Organization invited David Nesbit, an English heating engineer, to deliver a paper to the group. Mr. Nesbit traveled across the Atlantic for this, but when he arrived, those in charge of the Master Steamfitters Organization insisted that he deliver the paper in 10 minutes or less. They had grown weary of all these long-winded presentations and callously put into place what I suppose was their version of Twitter. Mr. Nesbit was, and quite understandably, upset.

But not as upset as the Irishman, Hugh J. Barron. He went nuts. He immediately abandoned the group and got together with 15 like-minded heating professionals who wanted to learn more than could be taught in 10-minute chunks. They formed a new organization and called it The American Society of Heating and Ventilating Engineers. Today, we know that group as ASHRAE.

Don't mess with the Irish.

I have one of those lengthy papers that Mr. Barron delivered to the Master Steamfitters Organization before they made their ill-fated Twitter decision. He titled it, A Look Ahead, and presented it at their June, 1893 meeting. It rolls on for 14 typewritten pages. His intent was to predict what would take place in the heating business during the following 75 years, but he begins his talk by looking backward 75 years. He tells the story of how the hydronics industry began, and a wonderful story it is.

And then, when he turned toward the future, I was amazed at how much he got right. This was one prescient Irishman. He predicted that radiators would quickly evolve into "poems in art." When we look at those ornate Victorian beauties that appeared around the Turn of the Century we have to tip our hats to him. He sure got that one right. He also said that the steam radiators will be connected with a single pipe, and that pipe would be hidden within the walls. At the time, there was only two-pipe steam, and most of the pipes stretched unsightly through the rooms. He also said the radiator supply valve would be replaced with a foot valve so Victorian ladies would be able to control the heat without having to bend down. This, too, arrived shortly thereafter. "Let the radiator man study beauty," he said. "His business is an artistic one." And isn't that a lovely way to look at business?

He said that the natural development of architecture would lead to hot-air heating by indirect steam or hot water. These are the systems that have huge iron radiators suspended within ductwork in the basement, and ducts running upward within the walls to end in floor grills. This system arrived and most worked with natural convection alone, but Mr. Barron predicted that at some point, fans would become part of that system. He also predicted that electric-resistance coils would replace steam heat in many buildings.

"Cast fittings will disappear and be succeeded by malleable and wrought fittings, and also by steel fittings," he said. "Screwed joints will, to a great extent, disappear and be replaced by electric welding. The exhaust steam from engines that is now thrown away in cities will be saved by having one large central pipe. Steam for heating will be taken from this." Consider the steam-based, district-heating systems of cities such as New York and Philadelphia.

And then there was this prediction: "There are impending changes in the relation of the jobber. Very soon, every contractor will buy from the jobber only, and no manufacturers will sell directly to consumers or contractors. Every article and specialty will be distributed by the jobber. Specialization will be carried so far that no jobber would think of manufacturing and no manufacturer would think of jobbing. They could not make it pay. Margins of business will be too close and business will be too well organized to allow anything of that kind. Specialization is now carried very far in our particular business, but it will be carried much further. Where specialization is carried to its extreme, as in the production of one simple article, competition becomes very fierce; so fierce in fact that it destroys itself by reducing profits to such a point as to make the carrying on of business undesirable."

From there, he goes on to sing the praises of a radiator trust that was forming at the time. The members of that trust called it The Carbon Club and it operated along the lines of Standard Oil. If a company that was not a member of the club bid on a job, The Carbon Club's members would band together and put that company out of business by offering the client ruinously low prices for the work and the material. They changed the industry by doing this and they prevailed, even though their very existence violated the Sherman Antitrust Law.

Mr. Barron says, "The trust, to my mind, is merely a step in the march towards economic democracy. I have spoken of product and cost; it means a great deal more than that; it means minimizing of profits also. Roughly speaking, today, net profits in business are 20, 10 and 5 percent. The first figure being the maximum profit, the middle figure the mean profit, and the last, the point at which business is done, the lowest or minimum profit. I believe that these profits will gradually go down in the next hundred years to 7-1/2, 5, and 2-1/2 percent or very close to those figures. There are those who consider the trust the greatest evil that menaces us at present. I think they are mistaken. Good and evil are only relative terms. Let us have faith that it only hastens the good time that is coming."

The U.S. government disagreed with Mr. Barron and they busted the radiator trust. The Carbon Club changed their ways and went through a few name changes in the years that followed. They eventually emerged as the Institute of Boiler and Radiation Manufacturers.

Hugh J. Barron died on April 6, 1918 as his old regiment fought in The Great War. He was 62 years old. He helped found ASHRAE and encouraged the nascent I=B=R. He believed in learning, teaching, and sharing. He saw the future well and he did not suffer fools. He was one tough Irishman.

A bit more about The Carbon Club

You know how I have that stack of *The Metal Worker*, a weekly trade journal that carried all the news, good and bad? I have every issue for 1899, which was important year in the history of hydronic heating, and a very wacky one as well. Many of the oddball devices that I've seen in basements over the years – the things that made me scratch my head in wonder – appeared as new product introductions in that wonderful magazine during that fin de siècle year. Reading through those 52 issues is like getting into a time machine. And there's a certain peace in that. There's no uncertainty in the past.

This was the year of The Carbon Club, an association of boiler manufacturers who got together in the spirit of what they called "cooperative competition," a concept that would send you to slammer if you tried it nowadays. But The Carbon Club guys were brazen in their very successful efforts to control not only the prices, but also the supply of boilers. They did all of this for what they saw as the good of the industry. Oh, and there was also a shortage of cast iron that year and these guys wanted to make large profits. And as I said, they did all of this in spite of the Sherman Antitrust Law, which had been in effect for a decade. How's that for ballsy?

Here's a brief article from *The Metal Worker*, which appeared on July 15, 1899. Listen:

"A meeting of the Carbon Club will be held in New York on next Monday, when the reports of the Membership Committees will be made. While the desirability of securing all manufacturers as members is apparent the condition of the iron market and the outlook is more important. The minimum price schedule adopted on June 20 has been found to contain some defects, and while these will be open for correction it is probably also that a further advance will be made in the list. This, if done, will be due to the price and scarcity of iron, with the strong probability that the price of iron has not yet reached the top. Some manufacturers, both outside of the club and members, have

arranged for their iron supply for the year, but as it could not be replaced except at the market prices, the price of boilers should be arranged in accordance or a radical advance would be necessary in boiler prices made by any manufacturer when his iron supply was exhausted and must be replaced at the much higher cost. This has been clearly pointed out, yet there are manufacturers who are holding to the former low prices, preferring to selfishly reap whatever benefit can be derived from being on the outside rather than to do their share to build up the market on a sound business basis. Should their example be generally followed demoralization and a year without a profit would result. Sometimes severe measures are necessary to open the eyes of the selfish. The Carbon Club is now strong enough to seek out the customers of such manufacturers and apportion them to the members with the instruction that prices must be quoted to them low enough to secure their trade. This would be drastic and not without its drawbacks, and it is to be hoped that cooperation can be secured by a more commendable method. Some members of the Carbon Club who were formally regarded as price cutters frankly state that though they suffered at the first advances they have now benefited by adhering to the course pursued and feel sure that others can be equally benefited by adopting the same course, whether members of the club or on the outside. The club, as far as can be learned, has been perfectly reasonable in all of its actions, and no considerable objection has been offered by the contracting trade."

How about that? You're a selfish manufacturer if you lower your price to get business, and if you persist in that wackiness of trying to get more customers by dropping your price, the entire membership of The Carbon Club will seek out your customers and steal them from you by basically giving away the stuff and driving you out of business. So there.

The "selfish" quickly got into line, and as I think about it, I realize that this was the boost the fledgling hydronics industry probably needed at the time. A very nice profit was guaranteed all manufacturers, and the contractors went along with it. The building owners paid their price and hydronics grew. All boats rose with the tide that they forced, but who knows how it would have gone if The Carbon Club hadn't broken the law?

This is the other thing that The Carbon Club did that year, and this forever changed the way we size hydronic systems. They waited until the very end of the century for this, and it makes me smile every time I read it. Here you go. This was in the December 23, 1899 issue of *The Metal Worker*:

"A meeting was held of the Carbon Club at the Murray Hill Hotel, New York, December 18 and 19, with a large attendance of the members. Several applications were received from manufacturers and some new members were elected. The recommendations of the Committee of Boiler Ratings, which were discussed at the November meeting, were taken up, and after some minor changes, were adopted. This is virtually a standardization of the home heating boilers made by the members of the club, and with the uniform rating and uniform prices many of the perplexities of the trade are removed. All boilers are now rated on a proportion of 100 for steam and 165 for water, with steam at 2 pounds pressure or water at 180 degrees at the boiler. The rating now includes all mains, returns and risers as heating surface, and the surface exposed in them must be added to the surface required in the radiators to determine the boiler power needed. It is only necessary for

the trade to understand that the mains must be considered to avoid purchasing a boiler that is too small. If a boiler shows the 2 pounds steam pressure or 180 degrees temperature in the main when at work, the rating will be considered verified by the manufacturers. The new list also divides boilers into two classes. A uniform rating has been agreed upon for tank heaters on a basis that they will heat 130 gallons of water for every 100 feet of surface that they are rated to carry, and their prices have been rearranged so that concessions are made to the buyer on some sizes."

What we have here is the agreement between all the boiler manufacturers of the time that a hot water boiler should be 65% greater in capacity than a steam boiler serving the same building. You see that today when you look at the difference in the value of Equivalent Direct Radiation for steam and hot water radiators (240 Btuh per Sq. Ft. EDR for steam and 150 for hot water)

They also agreed that no steam heating system from that day forward should need more than 2-psi pressure at the boiler to heat the building. This was a very significant decision because it put a stop to what was becoming a very dangerous situation. Contractors had been using boiler pressure as a competitive edge. They were sizing systems with as much as 60-psi pressure at the radiators. Higher pressure means smaller radiators and pipes, but the problem is, all steam-heating systems have to start at 0-psi pressure, and at the lower pressure, the extreme steam velocity moving through the small pipes would suck the water out of the boiler. This caused boilers to either dry-fire or explode. The Carbon Club put a stop to that wackiness. They did it by standardizing pipe-sizing charts that would allow for one-ounce of pressure drop over 100 feet of travel. They leveled the playing field for all the contractors.

At that meeting, they also recognized that there is a piping pick-up factor, which must be recognized by contractors when they size a boiler, lest they undersize a boiler, which would be very bad for the manufacturers. They established a standard for heating domestic hot water. And finally, they let the proof be in the pudding. If a contractor could heat the entire building with a boiler that contains no more than 2-psi pressure, or 180° hot water, then he picked the right boiler for the job. If it couldn't do that, then the problem was on him.

Simple.

Maybe those days weren't as wacky as I thought they were.

And just because you're dead, doesn't mean you can't chat

Erin, one of the nicest things about books is that the authors live on long after they're under the grass quilt. I was having a conversation with one the other day. A Mr. Ara Marcus Daniels, who is quite dead, but still sitting on my bookshelf and willing to chat with me.

We were talking about early heating systems, Ara and I. I had questions and he had answers. We both had time on our hands and I figure that when you want to know stuff about how things began, it pays to ask someone who was there at the start.

Here's how it went:

Dan: Nice to finally get a chance to chat, Ara. I've been reading your stuff for years and you've taught me a lot. I'm not sure you'd like the way the business has gone since you left the building. There are more furnaces than boilers in America these days. And in some parts of the country, they think radiators are ugly. They cart them away to the junkyard. What do you think about that?

Ara: Well, it's 1930, where I am right now and will always remain, and radiators have been around for at least 75 years. These days, comparatively few appreciate them and the opportunity to improve and enhance them is perhaps as great today as at any time in their history.

Dan: You got that right. It's a constant struggle. Hey, I'm wondering who the first person in the U.S. to use radiators was. You have any idea?

Ara: Who can say when the first so-called "radiator" was used in this country? I've searched the records of the United States Patent Office and found not less than 750 patents during the last 87 years. That's an average of more than eight claims per year.

Dan: That's a lot. Which came first, the steam- or the hot-water radiator?

Ara: It was hot water. In 1837, Joseph Nason, who established the Nason Manufacturing Company in 1841, went to England and identified himself with a Mr. Perkins, the inventor of the Perkins hot-water system of heating, which at that time was well-known and recognized throughout England. Mr. Nason superintended the erection and installation work of this system in London and elsewhere.

Dan: Tell me about that system. What made it unusual?

Ara: It was a closed system constructed almost exclusively of three-quarter-inch pipe. The boilers were of the box-coil type, made in one continuous length without fittings, other than couplings. The radiators were of similar coils with no fittings or valves. There was an expansion tank near the top of the system, but no safety valve.

Dan: Yikes! No safety valve. What would Denis Papin say? That sure must have made life interesting. So you're saying the earliest radiators were just pipe coils?

Ara: Yes, and they carried about the sides of the rooms, probably first in greenhouses. The coils were continuous from the boiler through the rooms and back to the boiler. The water would cool down along the way.

Dan: Pipe that small must have slowed the water. I mean the system had mostly three-quarter-inch pipe. Imagine the friction in runs that long. And there were no circulators at the time to help out.

Ara: Yes, they soon found they needed pipes with larger diameters, which were bulky and not nice to look at. This made it difficult to sell. They also realized that the radiation surface had to be large enough to dissipate all the heat that came out of the boiler. The radiators were the safety valve.

Dan: That must have been pretty risky. You have to keep everything running full-blast all the time. Were there any valves?

Ara: After a time, they started to use a three-way valve that could divert the water from a main line into the radiating coils. They used one of these valves on the supply and another on the return to each radiating coil. They'd direct the flow from the main into the coil, and then on the return side of the coil, they'd use the second three-way valve to send the water back into the main.

Dan: So it was a one-pipe system with the radiator coils positioned off the single main. It must have been difficult to keep track of all those opening- and closing valves, especially since this was a manual operation.

Ara: It was. They had to open and close the valves in a certain order. If they didn't, everything went awry. So they eventually got around this by using just one three-way valve on the supply to the coil, and then piping the return from the coil to a separate return pipe.

Dan: So that was the beginning of two-pipe, hot-water heating. I've often wondered how that came to be. Did they change the size of the pipe as they moved away from the boiler and shed load?

Ara: Strangely, no. They thought that they had to keep all the pipes the same size so that there would less resistance to flow. The water, of course, wants to flow to the highest point and that was presenting problems with heating the lower floors. After a while, they solved this problem by feeding the vertical main into the bullhead of a tee and taking the coil off the run side of that tee. The other side of the run extended a foot or so horizontally before turning vertically again to get to the next floor up.

Dan: So the rising hot water would sort of slam into the bullhead tee and be forced to go both left and right rather than straight up to the top floor.

Ara: Exactly.

Dan: Such a simple solution. Do you know where the first hot-water system in the U.S. was?

Ara: I do. I mentioned earlier Mr. Nason. When he returned from England he installed a closed system with radiating pipe coils in the counting room of the Middlesex Mill in Lowell, Massachusetts. This was in 1841. He imported all the pipe from England.

Dan: So here we have our very first heating contractor!

Ara: Indeed, and it's interesting to observe as the art progresses that the hot-water circuits, in these better and improved systems, were treated in much the same way as plumbers treated circuits for domestic water supply in their best work. Each flow- and return line was valved at the bottom with a small draw-off line for emptying the circuit.

Dan: And how about steam heat?

Ara: Steam-heating apparatus, in all its detail as used in America, is peculiarly American and its origin is credited, so far as I'm informed, to Joseph Nason.

Dan: And the radiator as we know it today? Well, I mean in 1930, which is where you are right now and forever will be.

Ara: The radiator probably owes its birth to the use of tapered thread on the ends of pipe. The original radiator, possessing characteristics resembling today's radiators, consisted of a row of wrought-iron pipes screwed into a cast-iron base, with the upper end of the pipe closed by welding a metal button onto it.

Dan: I still see those in old buildings. We call them Nason radiators. Speaking of which, any idea who came up with the name "radiator"?

Ara: To Mr. Nason, credit is given by some to the coining of that word as it's used today to design that part of the hot-water and steam-heating system by which structures are warmed through standing radiation. Unquestionably, Mr. Nason is the father, if not the grandfather, of our present systems of warming buildings as the art is practiced today. Much of his time was spent also in the development of fittings, valves, etc, for he took out patents for cast-iron fittings, malleable fittings, tapered joints, screwed- and flanged valves, the angle valve, globe valve, stop cock, as well as for much of the machinery needed for their manufacturing.

Dan: Well, that certainly makes me feel I haven't done much with my time in this business.

Ara: Well, someone has to tell the stories.

Dan: And somebody has to remember. Thanks, Ara.

And finally, John Bartlett Pierce (and what might have been)

Erin, you and I have walked through Bryant Park many times, especially around the holidays when the place is filled with craft booths, hot cider and thousands of people. There used to be a reservoir in this spot that provided all of New York City's water, but that's long gone, replaced by the main New York City public library and this jewel of a park.

Alongside the park (and I've pointed this out to you before), right on West 40th Street, is the 36-story Bryant Park hotel. It's a City landmark now, a gorgeous tower made of black stone, designed to look like hard coal. Gold-leafed bricks dance across its crenellated roof, and they're there to simulate fire. This is because the Bryant Park Hotel used to be the American Radiator Building. It stands as a monument to the once-great promise of hydronic heating in America. The sprawling main floor was once a glamorous showroom for radiators and boilers. People came from all over to look at the elegance of radiators and the wonder of boilers, as they now look at luxury cars in showrooms. Central heating was new then, and it was a wonder.

The American Radiator Company eventually blended into American Standard, and that company replaced the radiators and boilers in the huge showroom with plumbing fixtures. The radiators and boilers got flushed.

Then the Japanese bought the building and kept it vacant for years. That was sad to watch. In 1998, after a small carousel and great lawn replaced the homeless in Bryant Park, a developer bought the building and turned it into this crazy-expensive hotel. There's a small, bronze plaque near the front door that feebly whispers what once was. Few stop to read it.

John Bartlett Pierce was born in Emden, Maine, about 65 miles west of Bangor. It gets very cold there. He was born on June 2, 1843 into two of the state's oldest families. They had money, so he attended Westbrook Seminary. He survived the Civil War, and went to work at age 25, as a clerk in a New Hampshire hardware store. Five years later, he moved to Buffalo, New York and opened a hardware store, where he began to dabble in the installation of steam- and hot-water boilers and radiators, a very new business at the time.

In 1880, he built a small factory in Buffalo, where he made steel boilers. In 1882, he opened a second factory, this one in Westfield, Massachusetts, where he made cast-iron radiators. He and other hydronics pioneers did so well with these boilers and radiators that they decided to merge their efforts into the American Radiator Company. John Bartlett Pierce was the first Vice-President of that grand American conglomerate, and he remained a Director until he died in 1917.

I was in Hartford, Connecticut at a convention a few years ago. There's a beautiful carousel there and I wish I had known of it when you and your sisters were small because there's a sign on the carousel's fence that reads, *Every carousel has a lead horse. Can you find ours?*

I looked and it was true. I told you about this and you were as delighted as I was, but you were a woman by then. I hope we'll get to share many lead horses with Bridget as she grows, and I hope that my sweet granddaughter will pass on the secret to her own children long after I'm gone.

The lead horse in the tiny Bryant Park carousel has blue ribbon and a floral wreath, which makes it quite special. I was sitting in Bryant Park, watching the parents put their kids on that tiny gem, and I mentioned to some of them about the lead house.

"It's the white one over there. You can't miss it."

The parents and the children were as delighted as I was. As the kids rode, I told some of the moms and dads about the American Radiator building, which is right there across the street. I explained about the black stone and the golden roof, designed to look like fire in a boiler.

"Oh, really?" they'd say, and then turn away.

Hydronic history is not for everyone.

The American Radiator Company was the lead horse in the hydronic heating business for decades. They were instrumental in researching and engineering so many of the things we today take for granted. I can't pass that building without remembering all of this. They changed America.

In his will, John Bartlett Pierce left a million dollars in company stock to 400 of his employees who had "demonstrated keen business ability, combined with a fine sense of honor, a high quality of integrity, and a conscientious and loyal devotion to the performance of duty." The residue of his estate, which was considerable, established the John B. Pierce Foundation, "whose object shall be the promotion of research, educational, technical or scientific work in the general field of heating, ventilation and sanitation, for the increase of knowledge to the end that the general hygiene and comfort of human beings and their habitations may be advanced."

Isn't that wonderful? The author of the Pierce Memorial brochure wrote, "Within a decade we shall all better appreciate the vision and scope of this remarkable, affectionately conceived plan of Mr. Pierce's for the broad and general advancement of the whole heating and ventilating industry."

Isn't that great? There exists today this huge fund, established nearly 100 years ago to research better ways to heat, ventilate and plumb buildings. So if we ever wanted to, say, figure out whether a building with a hydronic heating system provides more comfort than, say, a building heated with a furnace, we should be able to go to the John B. Pierce Foundation and get the money to do that research.

Isn't that fabulous? I got so excited when I learned about this that I went scrambling after the Foundation. Hey, I've sat through enough blah, blah, blah at association meetings where someone always stands up and cries the blues about the research we could be doing, if only we had the money. Blah, blah, blah.

So I went looking for it and found it on their Web site. Their Mission Statement is, "To conduct basic research on the interactions between physiological systems and the stresses imposed by the modern environment, with the goal of optimizing these interactions to improve human health and comfort."

Isn't that grand? It's sort of what the late, great John Bartlett Pierce said, don't you think? He wanted the money to go toward research, educational, technical or scientific work in the general field of heating, ventilation and sanitation, for the increase of knowledge to the end that the general hygiene and comfort of human beings and their habitations may be advanced. Yummy!

So click through the site and learn what they do. The Foundation is located at Yale University, and they are currently doing research in the following areas:

- Affective sensory neuroscience
- Cellular neurophysiology
- Exercise and metabolic physiology
- Integrated environmental physiology
- Oral and cutaneous sensitivity
- Executive and motivational control
- Neural coding and multimodal integration of flavor
- Neurobiology of feeding
- Respiratory and sleep physiology
- Sensory information processing.

See any boilers or radiators in there? How about ventilation or sanitary systems? Comfort and hygiene?

At its start, the Pierce Foundation provided the funding for the Bureau of Research of the American Society of Heating and Ventilating Engineers. You'll recall the angry Irishman, Hugh J. Barron.

A.S.H.V.E became ASHRAE and somewhere along the way, the money got away from ASHRAE. It's out there doing what I suppose is very noble work, but I wonder what Mr. Pierce would have thought of all of this.

He was this kid from Maine who worked in a hardware store and fell in love with hydronic heating. He went on to build a tall building in New York City that looks like a coal fire. There's a tiny carousel across the street, closed now for winter. And there are also thousands of big buildings with cracked-open windows filled with uncomfortable people just nearby.

I think Mr. Pierce would have liked to see that money stay in the hydronic world but he died, and so, apparently, did his dream.

Think about that the next time you listen to someone cry the blues over how we don't have the money to do basic, unbiased research into the science of hydronic heating.

Because we once did.

But that money got mugged.

Hydronics taught me to visualize

Erin, I'm sure you remember that first year that Kelly spent at Notre Dame. Nothing like having a big sister at a big school, although you did great at Loyola Maryland as well.

South Bend, Indiana did have one thing that Baltimore didn't have, though. Remember how they didn't go on Daylight Saving Time? Most of the country would spring forward, but not the good people of South Bend. They'd stay put. And since the city was so close to Michigan, we could drive just a few miles and cross the time zone. It ran right down the middle of the road.

I remember having fun with all of you over that. We'd straddle the yellow line and tell each other what was going to happen an hour from now. You mentioned that it must be tough living on this side of the street and working on the other side. You mentioned how you'd be late for work every day, and I reminded you that you'd get an hour's overtime every night.

But time zones, like British thermal units and temperature scales, are just something someone made up and the rest of us agreed to go along with the plan. But playing with that yellow line sure was a fun mental exercise, wasn't it?

I was thinking about the time-zone lines the other day. In 1879, Sanford Fleming, who gave Canada its first postage stamp and cross-country railroad, suggested there be 24 standard time zones. He did this because he had missed a train while traveling in Ireland. The whole world was running on whatever time they felt like running on in those days. His idea was what gave us the lines. The rest of the world didn't fully get on board until 1929. Imagine that.

So these lines are on the globe and when they get closer to the North Pole and the South Pole, they, of course, get closer together. I wonder if time goes faster if you're traveling west to east up there near the North Pole. Or if you're running circles around the North Pole. Hmm.

And how about when you're standing right *on* the North Pole? What time is it then?

Hydronics taught me to see pictures in my mind's eye, so let's consider summer time at the North Pole. The sun never sets at that time of the year. So what do we see? I'm seeing the sun barely peeking up over the horizon. It never sets; it just moves around the horizon like the hand of a clock. At midnight it's directly in front of me. If I don't change the direction in which I'm facing, the sun will be directly behind me at noon. At three o'clock, I'll point toward the sun by lifting my right arm straight out from my side. At nine o'clock, I'll do the same with my left arm. Can you see it in your mind's eye? That's one of the keys to troubleshooting.

When I was first learning about hydronics, a guy I worked with, who was 15 years older than I was, told me to imagine myself as a marble moving through the pipes. He'd have me feeling the friction as I rolled along the inner surfaces of the pipes. He'd make me experiencing the crash of the marble as it entered a 90-degree elbow. He'd have me thinking about what I would do if I entered a tee. Which way would I go?

He was so good at making the movement of water visual. Even after all these years, if I'm trying to solve a problem with a hot-water system, I'll go back to being that marble. I'm red and blue. Which way would I go? And why?

That's visual thinking. It's key to troubleshooting hydronic systems.

Your mom and I were flying to Hawaii to do a seminar a few years ago (tough work, but someone's gotta do it!). We were in the plane for 12 hours, and I was getting bored so I thought I'd have some fun with your mom. She's crazy about me.

"Marianne," I said, "have you ever considered that there are only three possible ways to get to Hawaii?"

"What's your point?" she said.

"Can you name them?"

"Well, obviously you can fly there."

"Yes."

"And if you have the time, you can go by sea. That would be nice. If we had the time."

"It would be nice. What's the third way?"

She got stuck on that one. She went back to reading her book. Time passed. I waited. "Tell me," she said.

"Tell you what?"

"What's the third way we could get to Hawaii?"

"Think about it," she said.

"I can't stand you."

As I said, she's crazy about me.

"Well, think about it this way," I said an hour later. (She was reaching the boiling point. Long flight.) "When a problem faces most people, they'll approach it head-on. But a good troubleshooter will turn the question around and frame the problem it in a different way."

"Leave me alone."

"Ah, my little wahini, you're giving up too soon. Try this. Instead of thinking about *getting* to Hawaii, imagine that you're already there."

"And?"

"How could you have gotten there?" I asked.

"I could have been *born* there," she said.

And she smiled. See? Crazy about me!

And that's what good troubleshooters do. They imagine. They think visually. They ask the key question, What can cause that?

Hydronics taught me this, Erin. When I'm trying to figure out why the steam-heated building won't heat, I think like air because every steam system begins every cycle completely filled with air. And since air and steam won't mix, the steam has to push the air out the air vents. But often, people who don't know better replace the air vents with pipe plugs. So when I'm troubleshooting, I'll begin at the boiler, think like air, and ask myself, If I were air, could I get out? Then I leave the boiler room and wander, looking for the air vents.

That's visual thinking.

A contractor with a problem called me. "I fill up the boiler and the next day I have to fill it again. What's going on?"

"The system has a leak," I said.

"No, it doesn't," he said.

"Let's go over this again," I said. "You fill it up. It empties. You fill it again."

"Right," he said. "Again and again.

"That's a leak. When the water starts on the inside and then is no longer on the inside, it has to be on the outside. We call that a leak."

"I've looked all over. There are no leaks."

"Yes, there are. You just haven't seen them yet."

"You're no help to me," he said, and hung up.

Erin, there are people in this business who have problems. Someone else has solutions but the other person would rather have the problem I think this is because they like to say, "See? No one can solve this. Not even that guy who writes those books and magazine articles."

Often this business is more about people than it is about products.

Speaking of which, I once looked at a problem a rich guy in Manhattan was having with his steam radiators. His apartment (and what an apartment it was!) was cold. When I got there, I didn't see any radiators. "Where are your radiators," I asked.

"Oh, I had them covered," he said, pointing to the spaces beneath the wide windows.

"You had them covered with marble," I said.

"Yes, aren't the gorgeous?"

"They sure are," I said.

"So why don't I have any heat?"

"It's because you had all your radiators encased in marble," I said.

"I know. Do you like the look?"

"It's lovely."

"Why don't I have any heat?" he asked again.

"You had your radiators encased in marble," I said.

"I just *love* that look. The old radiators were so *ugly*. Why is it so *cold*?"

We went around like that a while longer. I finally had a chance to suggest he have holes drilled into the marble so the air in the room could come in contact with the hot surfaces of the entombed radiators.

"Are you out of your *mind*!" he shrieked. "Do you have any idea how much I paid to have that work done?"

"I'll bet it was a lot," I said. "But the air can't get at the hot metal."

"Why is it so *cold* in here?" he asked.

I suggested he think visually with me, but he wasn't in the mood. He was rich and thought the Laws of Physics didn't apply to him. I've met a lot of people like that over the years. They want what they want, and they don't care to listen, or to think visually.

They just want what they want. Now.

How to troubleshoot just about anything in life

1. Hold fast to what's undeniably true.

2. Ask what can cause that problem to occur.

3. Think visually.

4. Believe that something did indeed change.

5. Figure out what that is.

6. Consider the human factor because people will sometimes stand in your way.

7. Once you figure it out, be able to explain it all in a convincing way.

8. If they don't want to listen, smile, wish them well, and get on with your life.

Visualizing air

The first time I saw a Spirovent air separator in action was at a plumbing supply house in Brooklyn, New York. It was set up with see-through piping and I got to use a bicycle pump to inject air into the moving water. I stood there for a while, pumping away. The Spirovent caught the air and spit it out. It was fun, but then, I'm easily amused.

The salesman smiled at me and told me about microbubbles (a new term for me at the time), and how they would collide with, and adhere to, the inner workings of the Spirovent, and then leave by way of the vent. He also mentioned Henry's Law, which was something else I had never heard of, but I nodded with great respect nonetheless.

Didn't want to look dumb. A lot of people do that.

When I got home, I looked up Henry's Law in that old dictionary we used to have and learned that it has to do with the way a gas will dissolve in a liquid, depending on pressure and temperature. It turns out the more pressure you put on a liquid, the more gas it will hold in solution. Vice versa, of course. Oh, and the hotter water gets, the less air it will hold in solution (and vice versa). I sort of knew all of that by watching water boil and soda cans open, but I had never put a name to it. Now I knew.

And that got me thinking a lot about club soda. I had written my book, *Pumping Away*, and I needed a simple visual that would show what happens to dissolved gas when you lower the pressure on the water. Club soda fit the bill. I started taking a bottle of that fizzy stuff with me whenever I left home to do a seminar. Shaking a bottle of club soda and popping the top is a marvelous way of demonstrating Henry's Law to a group of contractors, and one they will long remember it. Well, at least the ones in the front row will remember.

I did this for years (still do) but I never gave much thought to who the Henry of Henry's Law was, so one day I decided to look into that. Here's what I learned.

Bill Henry's daddy, Tom, was a rich doctor who also owned an industrial chemical business in Manchester, England in the late 1700s. (Try putting those two professions together nowadays. You could probably make your own patients.) Tom Henry was the first guy to suggest that you could bleach clothing with chlorine. How about that? Isn't it good to know that Clorox and the proper location of hydronic air separators have their roots within the same family?

Anyway, Little Billy showed up just before the Christmas of 1774 and all went well until he reached the age of 10. That's when a beam fell from the ceiling, landed right on him, and left him with chronic pain for the rest of his life. Because of this, he wasn't able to play with the other kids, so stayed inside and hit the books. He hit them hard.

At 16, he began studying medicine, and at 21 he entered the University of Edinburgh in Scotland, but only stayed a year. He left the university to help his father with his medical practice and to work in the family business. He spent the next 10 years doing original research in chemistry, which plays a big part in this story. And then, because he didn't like to leave things undone, he returned to medical school at 31 and got his medical degree two years later. Oh, and he did his dissertation on, of all things, uric acid (a.k.a. pee), which I think is splendid because it ties Bill Henry even closer to the business of plumbing and heating.

Now we are all influenced by those who came before, and Bill Henry was no different. A generation earlier there had been a fellow in France by the name of Antoine Lavoisier. Heard of him? He was the guy who first said that matter can neither be created nor destroyed, and he also gave names to two things that are pretty important – those being oxygen and hydrogen. Lavoisier also came up with the first extensive list of elements, and helped create the metric system.

So there. What have you done today?

And you would think that the French would have appreciated all of this, but at the height of the French Revolution, someone accused Antoine Lavoisier of selling watered-down tobacco, so they chopped off his head.

Smoke 'em if you got 'em.

Bill Henry was fascinated by Lavoisier's work, and in 1801, while still working with his dad, he put together a book about it, and he did a fine job of explaining it all. He called the book, *Elements of Experimental Chemistry*, and this went through 11 editions over the next 30 years. He kept adding to it, and it was this work that introduced generations of chemists to the Frenchman's careful use of experimental measurement. Bill Henry was just 27 years old when wrote that book, and two years later he published the paper that established what we now call Henry's Law. Years and years after that, I'm in some plumbing supply house in Brooklyn and an air-separator salesman is bringing it to my attention.

Ain't life grand?

And how about this? Henry's Law came about because Bill Henry was sitting around wondering why our atmosphere, which is composed of all these different gases, each with its own density, doesn't separate into layers like oil and water. I've never wondered about that. Have you? I mean I've gone through six decades of life without once considering that. Gosh.

It was Bill Henry's initial thinking about our mixed-up atmosphere that lead to the theory of mixed gases, which we today credit mostly to Bill's pal, John Dalton.

I have to tell you about him. You've probably never heard of him. I hadn't. He's the guy who figured out that atoms make up everything. These two guys were hanging out together. One's figuring out atoms and the other's wondering why all the atmosphere doesn't look like a seven-layer cake. They're buddies.

John Dalton was brilliant but he was also clumsy and careless around the lab, and he had very little money for experimenting (he was a teacher). His buddy, Bill, had lots of money, though, and even more patience, so the two men worked together like salt and pepper.

They did most of their experiments with gases because gases are chemically simpler than other forms of matter, and when you're looking for atoms, this helps. Out of all this experimenting came Henry's Law.

Think about that the next time you see an air separator, or wonder why the air keeps coming out of that compression tank.

So John Dalton goes on to become famous for the atomic theory, which is very cool because suddenly, the world could identify and order elements. From this comes the Periodic Table of the Elements, something I know you had to study in high school. Ugh.

And it just occurred to me that John Dalton and Bill Henry are the guys who gave us H_2O. And can you think of a better hydronic connection than that?

And how's this for being wonderfully human? Although Bill Henry's experimenting helped John Dalton come up with atomic theory, Bill didn't want to back it. As he got older, he became crotchety and more reluctant to accept change. He didn't like it when his experiments pointed to something other than what he expected. He held onto his old beliefs, such as insisting that heat has mass (it doesn't).

In 1824, a series of unsuccessful surgeries on his hands took away his ability to manipulate instruments. He quit chemistry and turned his full attention to medicine, specifically to the spread of contagious diseases.

In 1831, a cholera epidemic hit the United Kingdom and it was horrible. Nowadays, we know that the way to prevent the spread of cholera is to wash our dirty clothing in real hot water and chlorine bleach, which Bill's father, Tom, had promoted years earlier, but they didn't try chlorine then. Rather, Bill came up with an inexpensive and simple device that used heat to disinfect clothing. It worked and it probably would have saved countless lives, but for some reason, Bill Henry decided that he didn't like the idea of the device, so he abandoned it. Thirty years later, Louis Pasteur told the world about the germ theory of disease, and we all began to pasteurize things with heat.

Thirty years later.

In 1836, chronically depressed and filled with the pain that been with him since that long-ago childhood accident, Bill Henry took his own life.

And after I learned all of this, I was never able to look at air separator or a compression tank in quite the same way as I had before.

Nothing ever gets built on its own.

And nothing ever happens until someone first imagines it.

And there's power in analogies

A contractor called to tell me that he was about my age and that he had been reading my stuff in the magazines for years. Then he said he had to ask me a question, but he was a bit embarrassed by it because he thought it was one of those things he probably should have learned by now. He didn't know who else to ask, so he came to me.

"Ask away," I said. "If you've got the right questions, I've got the right answers!"

"It's probably something you've been asked before," he said. "Here goes. Why can't I mix copper and cast iron radiators within the same zone?"

"Ah, that's one I can answer," I said. "The reason why you shouldn't mix them is because one gets hot faster than the other, and then cools off quicker as well. When you mix the two metals within the same zone, the thermostat gets confused because some of the radiators are staying hot longer than others."

With that said, I quickly shifted gears into an analogy because analogies are powerful teaching tools. I use them every day, with just about everyone that I meet.

"I went to a restaurant with the family the other night," I said to the contractor. "I ordered chicken fajitas. You ever try those?"

"Sure," he said.

"Yeah, I *love* those fajitas! They're much more than a meal; they're an adventure – food you can build with. You can hear them coming to the table from a hundred feet away. People get out of the way of the fajitas! Boy, I can still hear those fajitas sizzling on that red-hot, cast-iron plate. There was steam and smoke rising up off them and everyone around us stopped eating for a few minutes to just watch and take in the aroma. The waiter put that plateful of hot-as-hell right down in front of me. I could barely breathe from all the smoke and steam that was hitting me in the puss. And *guess* what the guy said to me."

"Don't touch the plate?"

"That's *exactly* what he said. But do you think I listened to him?"

"Nope," the contractor said.

"Of course, I didn't. He might as well have said, 'Don't put your tongue on that frozen flagpole, Dan.' Yep, as soon as he walked away from our table, I touched that plate. I just couldn't help myself. And you know what?"

"What?"

"It was *HOT*!"

"Were you surprised?" the contractor asked.

"Nah, just defiant. And believe it or not, that cast-iron plate was *still* hot when I was finished eating the fajitas. In fact, when we were getting up to leave, I reached down and gave that cast iron plate one more touch. Hot!"

"I know what you mean," the contractor said.

"You ever see them bring fajitas to your table on a copper plate?" I asked.

"Can't say as I have," he admitted.

"Ever think about why?"

"Maybe because a copper plate wouldn't get as hot?"

"I think it would *get* as hot," I said. "But I don't think it would *stay* as hot. Thing is, copper gives up heat about nine times faster than cast iron. And think about what's going on back there in the kitchen. The chef is fixing dozens of meals at the same time. The waiters are running back and forth between the tables, the kitchen, and the bar. They're doing their best to keep all the customers satisfied, but my guess is that my fajitas were probably sitting on some stainless steel shelf under a heat lamp for a few minutes before the waiter had a chance to carry them to my table. Since they used a cast-iron plate that had been in the oven, those fajitas were still sizzling when they got to me. But suppose they had used a copper plate?"

"You probably wouldn't get that sizzle," the contractor said.

"Probably not," I agreed. "Now, think about a big-cast iron radiator and a copper-baseboard convector. They're sitting right next to each other in the same zone. Let's say you've got 180-degree water flowing through both units. What has your experience taught you about which will get hot first?"

"The copper baseboard will get hot *much* quicker," he said.

"Right!" I said. "About nine times quicker. And which will cool off first?"

"The copper baseboard," he said again.

"Exactly! And once again, about nine times faster than the cast iron. But think about what happens once the cast iron finally *does* get hot. You tell me."

"It will stay hot for a longer time after the water stops flowing," he said.

"Just like the fajitas, right?"

"I got it!" he said.

"You know, my wife was making lasagna the other day," I said, swinging into another analogy. "You like lasagna?"

"Who doesn't?" he said.

"Anyway, she asked me to check on it, so I opened the oven and used a pot holder to slide the baking tray out a few inches. Then I lifted the aluminum foil from the top of the pan. I didn't use the pot holder for the aluminum foil, though. You know why?"

"Because aluminum gives up heat pretty fast," he said.

"That's right. And there's not that much mass to a single sheet of aluminum foil It can't hold the heat very well But when I had to push the steel baking rack back into the oven I used the pot holder again."

"I would hope so," he said.

"How come?"

"Because steel holds heat longer than aluminum," he replied.

"That's right. And the rack has more mass than the aluminum foil does. You starting to understand why you shouldn't mix all these different metals within the same zone?" I asked. "You can have a copper zone and a cast-iron zone in the same building, but you shouldn't mix the two together within the same zone because of the difference in mass, and the way different metals hold heat."

"It all makes sense now," he said. "Thanks for making it so easy to understand after all these years."

Now, Erin, you probably know about this business with different types of radiators. You have both steel radiators and cast-iron radiators in your house (those two metals heat and cool at about the same rate). I've come to believe that most folks in the hydronics business prefer stories to mathematical equations. I've listened to you make hundreds of them, so I know you know this. Analogies are word tools and there is not a technical thing in this world that cannot be explained through an analogy. Hydronics taught me that.

Consider how a circulator on a closed-loop hydronic system is just like the motor on a Ferris wheel. It's not lifting anything because the weight of the water going up is balanced by the weight of the water coming down. The circulator is just turning the big wheel of water.

And speaking of water, did you know that it moves heat 24 times faster than air can move it. Want a visual analogy? Blow up a party balloon and hold a match to it. It explodes instantly, right? That's because the air inside the balloon can't move the heat away from the balloon quickly enough.

Now fill the balloon with water and tie a knot. Hold the flame to it. The balloon won't explode. Carbon will form on its surface, but you can stand there all day with that flame and the balloon won't explode. And that's because water moves heat 24 times faster than air. Show it to little Bridget. She's the next generation after you.

And isn't that a fine way to compare a hydronic-heating system to a forced-air system?

Beyond word tools, other tools

Not far from where your twin, Colleen, used to live in Somerville, Massachusetts, there's a house that's for sale. I spotted it on Zillow. It's an old house, built in 1900 and not very elegant. It's a place anyone with a large family would want to own, or if you had the courage to rent to a bunch of tenants. You know the neighborhood. This place fits in well. It's ordinary. but it carries a price tag of nearly a million bucks, the only reason being that it's that close to Boston.

Daniel Stilson, who died from heart disease on August 21, 1899, lived in a house that was on that land before the current house arrived. He left a widow and two married daughters. For some reason, his widow had the house knocked down and this one built within months of his death. I don't know why she did that. Perhaps the old house held too many memories, or maybe she sold and moved in with one of her daughters. I wonder about that whenever I pass by. I'll never know for sure but it's worth thinking about because of Daniel Stilson.

He was 69 years old when he died. I was just reading the notice of his death in *The Metal Worker* magazine, which came out on September 2, 1899. He lived a good long life for his time. His grandfather was a captain in the American army during the American Revolution. Daniel Stilson was a machinist by trade, and he worked at the Charlestown Navy Yard, which we now call the Boston Navy Shipyard. It's one of the oldest shipbuilding facilities in the U.S.

The Civil War broke out and the Navy offered him a position as Acting Third Assistant Engineer on the R.B. Forbes, which was a fine place to learn. The ship went down in a gale during 1862 but all of the crew survived, and Daniel Stilson transferred to the U.S.S. Roanoke. That ship had begun its life as a wooden-hulled, steam frigate. The men in the shipyard turned it into an ironclad and sent it to war, but she was top-heavy and not a well-engineered ironclad. She rolled way too much and couldn't operate in shallow ports, so the Navy assigned her to harbor defense, which was what she was doing on March 8 and 9, 1862, as the Monitor and the Merrimack pounded each other. Daniel Stilson watched that battle through a porthole. Can you imagine what that was like?

Later that year, he resigned his position because of health issues, but once he recovered, he signed on as the Acting First Assistant Engineer on the U.S.S. Queen, which also saw action. He later sailed with David Farragut, who purportedly said, "Damn the torpedoes. Full speed ahead!" at the Battle of Mobile Bay.

Daniel Stilson saw much in his long life and I think about him whenever I pass through your sister's old town. How peaceful it must have seemed to him after the war, such a fine place to raise daughters. He was working as a machinist at the J.J. Walworth Manufacturing Co. by then. James Jones Walworth and his brother-in-law, Joseph Nason, had gone into business together in 1842 down in

New York City. They called the company Walworth and Nason and they were the first heating contractors. They more or less invented the radiator as we know it today. You'll recall Ara Marcus Daniels, who continues to be dead, and I spoke of him earlier in this telling.

Walworth and Nason later moved to Boston and got some good work going. They even installed the new steam-heating system in the White House, but then Mr. Nason decided to break the partnership and move back to New York. I read that he couldn't take the brutal Boston winters, and that makes me smile, considering that he was the first heating contractor and all. Mr. Walworth changed the name of the company to the J.J. Walworth Manufacturing Co. and went on to become a major manufacturer of valves. That company continues to do a grand business.

While working for Mr. Walworth, Daniel Stilson and his cousin, John Chapman, came up with the idea for a tool they called a pipe tong. It made the turning of gas pipes easier and it really caught on. They got a patent for it on October 31, 1865. All those years spent on ships were paying off.

Four years later, Daniel Stilson received another patent, this one for a tool that he had first whittled out of wood. He showed this tool to Levi Greene, who had been an engineer during the war on one of the ships where Daniel Stilson had been the fireman. They must have been delighted to find each other working at the same company after the war.

Mr. Greene showed the wooden prototype to Mr. Walworth, who told Daniel Stilson to go to the pipe room in the Devonshire Street shop and try it on a piece of 1-1/4" pipe. A half-hour later, Daniel Stilson returned with a broken piece of pipe and an intact wooden tool.

Mr. Walworth told him to go back to the factory and have the foreman make up 24 copies of the tool in metal and in different sizes. Daniel Stilson returned a few days later with these. Mr. Walworth then sent him to the Patent Office to protect himself. And isn't it amazing that the owner of a company would do that for someone in his employ?

Once the patent became final, Daniel Stilson offered to sell it outright to Mr. Walworth. He thought $2,500 was a fair price. His family was growing and he needed the money. He also didn't think any future royalties would add up to much more than that, but both Mr. Walworth and Mr. Greene urged him to keep the patent for himself and to accept royalties from the company. Can you imagine that happening today?

Daniel Stilson lowered his asking price to $1,500 for the full patent rights and still Mr. Walworth said he would not buy that patent. He instead urged Daniel Stilson to allow the company to have exclusive rights to make the tool and to take the royalties that were sure to come. Daniel Stilson reluctantly agreed, but then asked for a very high royalty. This made the tool too expensive for most of those in the trade, even though the contractors who had seen the tool yearned for it. Its durability and simplicity amazed them, but it was just too expensive.

Months passed and Daniel Stilson finally agreed to a lower royalty, one that brought the tool into the affordable range. It sold and sold and became one of the world's best-known and widely used inventions. More than $100,000 in royalties rolled in, and thanks to the royalties paid on the Stilson wrench, the most-common tool in any hydronic professional's toolbox, Daniel Stilson was able to raise those daughters in that house in Somerville.

He went on to file and receive 20 additional patents. He invented new types of fire extinguishers and sprinkler heads. He also held a number of important municipal positions in Somerville and was well-respected by all. If you stop by the Somerville Public Library you can see his name on the 1884 bronze plaque, along with the other members of the Building Committee. This was a good man.

The patent protection for the tool he had whittled from wood eventually ran out and many other companies began manufacturing the Stilson wrench. Walworth Co. continues to make and sell them. It's such a simple tool, but it built the hydronic industry.

There is a beauty in tools, Erin. My tools have been pens and paper, manual- and electric typewriters, word processors, computers, and podiums. I never trained as a mechanic but I've lived my life around mechanics. When you were very young and I was working for the manufacturers' representative, I wanted to get some hands-on experience, so I went to the larger, family-owned fuel-oil dealers and asked if I could work for a day or two as a helper to their best technician.

Most of the service managers I approached laughed and asked why I would want to do that. I explained that I needed to feel what they felt because I wanted to write about it. I wanted to clean boilers and work on steam pipes and rub sweat out of my eyes. They smiled and told me to report at 6 AM in old clothes. Don't wear sneakers.

I never told my boss I was doing this and I did it again and again across Long Island, New Jersey, New York City, and upstate-New York. Those guys gave me dirty jobs to do and they told me stories all day long. And they taught me about the tools.

I traveled with an oil-burner technician on Long Island for a very long couple of days. He had to produce, so he would clean any pin boiler we visited with a tree sprayer. He removed the top of the jacket and the insulation and then pumped up the tank and sprayed water and soot down into the combustion chamber. He'd then toss in a soot stick and let 'er rip. I asked him if that was the right way. He said it was *his* way, and he was Top Dog when it came to getting jobs done quickly. Those were his tools.

Another guy showed me how to check the stack temperature by spitting on the flue and seeing how it sizzled. It was like watching a short-order cook fry eggs. He checked the draft with the smoke from his Marlboro. See how quickly it rises? He could tell the temperature of the water in a pipe within a few degrees by grabbing the pipe in his calloused hand and holding it for a few seconds. Check him with a thermometer. Go ahead. His hands were his tools. Today we use electronic instruments to set up burners. He'd call us sissies.

I was seven years old when your grandpa moved us from Manhattan to Long Island. You'll remember I told you how he worked as the shipping clerk for a Manhattan plumbing-and-heating supply house. Well, he wanted a screened-in porch on the back of our house so he could sit outside during the summer and drink beers. He knew a million people in New York City, and he had more angles than a protractor factory, but he was a lousy carpenter. So he talked Mike the Russian into building the porch for him. The price was meat sandwiches and icy vodka. I'm sure there were other favors owed but that was between them.

Mike didn't own a car, so your grandpa and I drove into Brooklyn at sunrise on a summer Saturday to pick him up. He was waiting in front of his building with his tools.

These were a handsaw, a sharpening stone, a hatchet with a hammer head on the opposite side, his hands and his eyes. That's it, Erin.

He tossed the tools on the backseat with me, and your grandpa aimed the Mercury home. They laughed and smoked along the way and Mike commented in his Russian accent about the smell of Brooklyn. "Hey, Mike," your grandpa whispered, "the kid's in the back. He's not used to words like that." And Mike turned around and gave me a hard look that made me feel older. "Boy needs to *learn!*" he boomed. And that was the last your grandpa had to say on that subject. I've heard much worse since.

Mike built the whole screen porch in a day. He could have shaved with that hatchet. I watched him work for hours. He looked at pieces of wood and corners and angles and then he mitered the wood with a few strokes of the hatchet and with ridiculous speed and confidence. The wood acted as if it had been waiting for him. His level was his eye; his ruler was his hands. His handsaw ripped through wood like it was snow. I had never seen anyone work like this. He was meant to live in an evergreen forest, not in a city.

Years later, I read about the Church of the Transfiguration of the Savior that Russians had built on the Island of Kizhi in 1714. Google an image of it. You'll be amazed. It looks like a massive wooden wedding case and it contains not a single nail. It's mitered and fitted and held together by gravity. I thought of Mike the Russian when I learned of that church because old men can hold us long after they're dead.

Years later, we were on one of our summer vacations in Cape May, New Jersey. You and your sisters were still at the beach with your mother. I was back on the porch, reading a book. At one point I looked up and noticed the way the wood beneath the porch roof came together. It was absolutely perfect. It was also in a spot that people wouldn't notice unless they were sitting in this seat and looking up. The person who did that work cared about it.

I reached for a pen and paper and wrote these words:

A hundred years from now, they will gaze upon my work and marvel at my skills but never know my name. And that will be good enough for me.

When we got home from vacation, I had that saying printed on tee shirts. We sold a lot of them, so smile if you ever think of that unknown carpenter. He helped put you and your sisters through college.

There's a beauty in tools, Erin, and in the people who use them.

But back to Mike the Carpenter. Three years passed. Our family grew, and Mike's screened-in porch morphed into a bedroom. Your grandpa and grandma wanted a second bath, so he and I drove to Brooklyn again, but this time we returned with an old Jewish plumber named Moe, who had a rattling laugh I can still hear.

I watched Moe put soil pipe together with molten lead. I had never seen this done before. He jabbered on about how he had learned this and that and he was funny. And then he got to the horizontal pouring and that's something I'll never forget. How difficult that is to do, but he did it every day. That lead was primal stuff, Erin, and it was beautiful to watch. It was a liquid tool. No one knew then how dangerous the lead was. It was just beautiful.

I mentioned that your grandpa was a shipping clerk. That was a big job at the time because this country was booming in the '50s. Building started up again after the war and copper and steel were available and very valuable. Grandpa ran more than two dozen trucks out of that supply house on East 79th Street. His drivers were his tools and they were his friends. Many of them came to our house to visit.

One of these men was Billy Escowitz, a former Golden Gloves boxer and a guy who had been to war. He looked like he was made of concrete and used auto parts. Billy had hands like oak-tree roots. He wore bib overalls and always carried two pairs of pliers in the middle pocket, close to his heart. It was the sort of thing that could catch a kid's eye.

One day, I was at some bar with your grandpa and I started thinking about Billy and why he always had those two pairs of pliers so close at hand. I mean he was a truck driver. What did a truck driver need with two pairs of pliers?

I remember Grandpa smiling. He sipped his beer and said, "That was how Billy took care of business." Then he told me of the robberies that were happening after the war, and how street toughs would wait for a truck to stop at a traffic light. They'd approach from both sides and pull open the doors. Then they'd yank out the driver and kick him to the curb. Take his truck.

"Did they try that with Billy?" I asked.

"A few times," my father said.

"How'd that work out?"

"Well, you remember his fists, right? How huge they were?" I nodded. "When those guys yanked open the doors of Billy's truck, he would brace himself and in each of those big fists he held a pair of pliers. And then he'd go to work.

"Nobody ever took what was Billy's. *Nobody.*"

To this day, I cannot pick up a pair of pliers without thinking about that that man. There are many like him in this business. There always have been.

And there have always been the tools.

Hydronics grabbed me early

My earliest memories are of living on Cherokee Place in Manhattan. It's a small street, on the concrete bank of the East River. I was four years old, and I remember this so well because John Jay Park is right across the street from the apartment building where we lived.

In that park, one summer day, your Uncle Ed, my big brother, had me stand up in a red wagon, which he then pulled out from under me. I remember the visit to New York Hospital, and I can still see the scar on my noggin when my hair is short enough.

I still love him, though.

I learned much later the significance of this building in which we lived. Mrs. William K. Vanderbilt had this place built as model tenements in 1911. She named it, appropriately, The East River Homes. It was actually four big buildings, all drawing heat and power from one central plant, which was underneath the central courtyard.

The buildings housed 385 families, in apartments that had from two- to five rooms, and a bath. The rent for two-rooms and a bath was $3.20 a week. Four rooms and a bath went for $5.30. They get a bit more for those apartments these days.

I remember this place so well because it had windows that went practically from floor to ceiling, and our apartment faced east. I never went to kindergarten but started first grade at five years old, and I can remember your grandma getting me dressed in a shirt and tie for my first day at Saint Monica's on East 78th Street. She was so beautiful in that morning light.

And this is how different those times were, Erin. John Jay Park, across the street, had rock-hard monkey bars, industrial-grade steel swings on thick steel chains, tall steel slides that got griddle-hot in the summer and presented road-rash concrete at the bottom to each screaming kid. Oh, and tailbone-busting, finger-munching see-saws with a wicked uppercut, of course.

We were supposed to practice common sense.

All of that was normal in 1954. Your uncle and I would hurt each other while your grandma sat with her lady friends, talking and smoking. She'd often call me over and say, "Run up the corner and get me the *Daily News*, the *Daily Mirror*, and a pack of Luckies."

Now, running up the corner involved crossing York Avenue, which was thick with city traffic, and keep in mind I was either four or five years old at the time, but the guy in the candy store would give me exactly what I asked for. Just like that.

Today, she'd probably be in jail.

But back to 1911. Mrs. Vanderbilt had principally built The East River Homes for families who had a member afflicted with tuberculosis. I'm reading an article about the mechanical system in these buildings. It's from *The Heating and Ventilating Magazine*, which appeared in 1911. This is the part that really caught my eye:

Of the two systems of heating (steam and hot water), the central system of forced-hot-water circulation offered the following advantages:

(a) Economy of operation, averaging approximately between 15% and 20% less than a central steam-heating plant. This is largely accountable for by the fact that a better control of the heating in the apartments is obtainable to meet the varying temperature conditions, the greatest economy of this type of system being attainable during the milder weather periods, when only a slight modulated heat is necessary. This, of course, became a decidedly important factor, when considering that the class of tenants occupying these apartments are in poor health and, therefore, the requisite heat to keep the apartments warm at all times is demanded.

(b) Hot water has the decided advantage over steam by permitting better heat control at the individual radiators.

(c) With the overhead system of hot-water heating, no air valves giving off their obnoxious odors, thereby vitiating the air in the rooms, have to be contended with, which air valves in the case of steam heating have to be located in the individual rooms.

(d) With forced hot-water circulation, the piping can be materially reduced and run irrespective of grade and level.

(e) No water hammer or air-pocketed radiators have to be contended with.

(f) Absolutely positive circulation by means of circulating pumps

(g) No excessive back pressure, which represents a considerable amount of power wasted in the average combination power- and heating plant.

Richard Ruppel, the article's author, then notes that steam had the advantage of being 18% less expensive than hot-water heat to install, but the other advantages of hot water won out, especially considering the poor health of many of the tubercular tenants.

The hot-water radiators would have to be larger than the steam radiators, of course, and they would need about 25% more radiation to meet the building's needs on the coldest days. And had they designed the system without circulating pumps, and tried to run the four buildings individually on gravity circulation alone, they would have needed nearly 50% more radiation than they would have used if they had chosen to use direct steam.

And then Mr. Ruppel writes, "It might be interesting to know that, due to the extreme close clearances to which all of these rooms had to be designed, in order to meet the tenement-house laws of the city, even the increased space of the radiators was considered important enough at one time almost to give up the idea of hot-water heating, if it had not been for the very important factor of sanitation. These figures showed that by increasing the radiation by 50% for a given room, the increased radiation space went as high as 34% in some instances per radiator, depending on the design and style compared.

"I have purposely gone into detail with regard to the above, in order that it might be shown conclusively at the start why this type of system was adopted in preference to steam heating for the conditions imposed."

That should give you a sense of how unusual this building was for 1911, a time when most big buildings were getting steam heat.

The buildings drew their heat mainly from the exhaust steam that was coming from the lighting plant. The exhaust steam went into a condenser and transferred its heat through a heat exchanger into the circulating hot water.

They used big, horizontal-split-case, De Laval circulators, which had turbine drives. These ran off the exhaust steam as well. Those big boys could deliver 1,500 gpm at 80 feet of head when all of the exhaust steam was available.

So your uncle and I were kids in this place for a few years. He was knocking me around and I was just happy to be going to school, and living so close to such a dangerous park. We didn't consider that our apartment was perhaps the first really big hydronic- heating job in New York City, and probably the whole country. Kids don't think of stuff like that.

Mrs. Vanderbilt built it for the poor souls who suffered from tuberculosis. The engineers chose hydronics for sanitary reasons. None of us knew that when we lived there.

I also didn't know that I would grow and have a long career in the hydronics industry, and a daughter that would join me in the business. I didn't know that I would be father to such strong women and raise them all on stories of this business.

You chose this industry, and will own this business long after I'm gone. That delights me. And life's tapestry, being as wondrous as it is, wove your big sister, Meghan, into the United States Agency for International Development, where she travels the world, working with foreign governments to battle tuberculosis in their own lands, so that it does not get on an airplane and get off in an American city. We're supposed to be done with that horrible disease here. She and the late Mrs. Vanderbilt have much in common.

Such wonderful threads run through the tapestries of all of our lives, and they ebb and flow between the living and the dead. I know that you know this. Keep finding the time to stop and marvel at it all. We both know that it's worth it.

Lake Ronkonkoma

How's that for a Native American name? Sort of rolls off your tongue, doesn't it? To get your Uncle Ed and me out of the city and into the country for a while, your grandpa would drive the sixty or so miles from Manhattan to Lake Ronkonkoma, which used to be quite lovely. Private beaches ringed the lake, many with pavilions that stretched out over the water on pilings. Tall slides that had hand pumps at the top stretched out into the deeper water. We'd climb, pump to take the brutal summer heat off the steel, slide and scream our way into the lake. We'd be out there on our own and your grandpa and grandma would be drinking beer and watching us from a wooden picnic table up on the pavilion.

Each summer, we would spend a week at Quick's Motel, an old-school place across the street from the lake. Mrs. Quick kept goats and a dog named Flea. One day, your grandpa went out for a drive, and when he returned, he told us that he had just bought a plot of land with the shell of a bungalow on it for $2,500. He had to put $25 down to hold it. He was now a homeowner, which was his American dream. And he was going to finish that bungalow for us. It would be our summer place. Your uncle and I danced the Dance of Joy.

Now, this is how your grandpa finished that tiny house. He was working for that plumbing-and-heating supply house in New York City back then. The place was on East 79th Street, directly across the street from our apartment building. There's a high-priced condo there now. He was the shipping clerk, and in those years after World War II, there was all that building going on. Your grandpa ran a couple dozen trucks that made deliveries all over the city and out onto Long Island. He told each of his drivers that when they made a delivery, they should ask the foreman if they could please have one 2 X 4 and one brick. "No one will ever refuse if you ask for a little," he said to me. "And a little adds up to a lot after awhile."

On Friday, one truck always made a run "Out East" to deliver to the tract housing that was sprouting like weeds all over Long Island. Your grandpa would load his free wood and bricks onto that truck and his driver would dump that load on his lot. He finished that house and built even more before he was done. That house is still there.

At first, the place had no indoor plumbing or running water. He dug a hole and built an outhouse. He had a shallow well dug and connected a hand pump to that. He built an eight-foot high frame out of his free wood, mounted a steel drum on top of the frame, painted it black, and screwed a shower head into its bottom. He told us that this is how he and the other soldiers had showered in the Philippines. Each morning, he would pump buckets of water, climb the ladder, and dump the water into the steel drum. By evening, that water was almost too hot to bear.

This was my first exposure to solar thermal. I was four years old.

That same summer, Hurricane Carol visited Long Island and dropped a huge oak tree on the bungalow. I remember us driving out there to see the damage. It was like being inside a tree house. I loved it. Your grandpa and the neighbors got together and cut up the tree. They didn't have any power tools. Did it all by hand. They saved the wood and burned it during the summers to come. There was some beer involved in that, of course, and I remember helping him bury all the steel cans in the morning.

He added a pump to the well in 1956 and piped cold water into the house. No more hand-pumping for him, and with the new water heater, our days of solar-thermal showers were over.

He got some Slant/Fin baseboard and a bronze-body circulator from the supply house, and ran a heating loop from the water heater. This did a nice job of keeping the place cozy during the fall and spring.

It dawns on me now that he was setting us all up of a dose of Legionnaires' disease with that open system he had built. The domestic water that ran through the baseboard stagnated all summer long, but no one knew of legionella bacteria back then, though, and we somehow survived.

In 1957, he decided to get us out of Manhattan. The Long Island Expressway was working its way out onto Long Island, and each weekend, your grandpa and grandma would pile us into the car to go look at houses. We kept moving eastward from exit to exit until we got to the town of Hicksville, where they could afford to buy a house. He had sold the bungalow in Lake Ronkonkoma to get the down payment on the Hicksville house.

Hicksville was a funny name for a town. Valentine Hicks had founded it, along with the Long Island Railroad. It wasn't really "hicky," although the roads were made of tar, covered with pebbles. There were no sidewalks or curbs. During the summers, we'd pry the tar from the road in front of our house with a stick and smear it onto our PF Flyers. Then we'd go walk inside the house. Your grandma did not approve.

And here's a good one for you, to keep down the dust, the town would send a truck rattling through the neighborhood every week to dribble oil onto all the streets. What today would be an environmental disaster, was then simply road maintenance. We also tracked that into the house.

Oh, and asbestos was still the Miracle Mineral. And mercury was in our toys. Lead as well. Who knew?

The Hicksville house had a basement and that's where the boiler was. A loop of copper wrapped around the basement ceiling and branches feed the upstairs steel convectors through diverter tees.

I became acquainted with the Bell & Gossett's Series 100 circulator at seven years old. During my rep days I would sell a lot of those circulators, but the summer of my seventh year had me sticking pencils into the spinning spring coupler. I loved the sound that made. It sounded like the Topps baseball cards I would clothespin in front of my bicycle spokes. RRRRRRRR!

We had oil heat and I also loved (but didn't understand) the boiler's barometric damper. I thought it was a cool place to drop your grandpa's tools. I also loved to pop the relief valve. It made such a cool sound.

I'm glad you never did any of that stuff.

The other thing about growing up in Hicksville (besides going to school with Billy Joel) was that everyone we knew had hydronic heat. I don't think I ever went into a house with a furnace. It was boilers all the way, and mainly steel convectors up in the rooms. Baseboard followed as people renovated their houses and added zones.

Levittown was right next door, as was Westbury, and these towns were loaded with radiant heat. Most of the houses were on concrete slabs and these had their boilers in their kitchens, hidden under an appliance cover. Soft copper tubing, buried in the concrete provided the warm floors.

Before I met your mother, I had a high-school sweetheart, who lived in a Levitt house. I spent many winter hours on that warm floor with her, watching Hullabaloo and Dark Shadows on the black-and-white TV. This was my introduction to radiant heating, and it was, let's just say, pleasant.

Hydronics taught me about the world

I had to get off Long Island and away from New York City to gain a true sense of where hydronics stands in the world. I had a lot of adventures along the way and met some very interesting people.

Once I crossed the Hudson River and headed west I began to realize that America runs on furnaces and not boilers. Before World War II, it ran mainly on hydronics. I looked at the U.S. Census and learned that during those days, half the buildings in this country had boilers. The rest heated with stoves, or fireplaces, or furnaces, and most of those were gravity furnaces. Forced-air came later.

During the war years, there was no heating industry to speak of. Every company involved in making heating equipment prior to the war switched their production to make equipment for the war.

Dwight Eisenhower served as president from 1953 until 1961 and this was the start of the Cold War. There were few highways in the U.S. after the war, and Eisenhower pushed to have the Interstate Highway Act passed into law, and when it did pass, 41,000 miles of highway began to crisscross the nation. The hidden purpose of these roads was to give Americans easier access out of the cities, should war break out with the Soviet Union. I remember well the days of ducking under my school desk during atomic-bomb drills.

The byproduct of the new highway system was the development of the suburbs, and the cookie-cutter houses that made up suburbia. Furnaces heated most of these new homes because a furnace will always be cheaper than a boiler. This had nothing to do with air-conditioning at the time. Few people had air-conditioning in the '50s.

Speaking of Interstate highways, did you know that even Hawaii has them? Yep, there's H-1, H-2, H-3, and H-201. All official Interstates, but don't try to drive to California on them.

As I traveled, things just got more and more curious.

Sweden

In December 1990, I found myself in a hotel in Stockholm, Sweden, and that's when I first saw snow-melted sidewalks and noticed the way the Europeans run their pipes. It was ridiculously cold outside and there was a panel radiator with a thermostatic radiator valve under my hotel room's window. The TRV was locked at about 65-degrees, so I used my Swiss Army knife to recalibrate it. It's good to know how to do stuff like that.

The small-diameter steel pipes running to and from that radiator hugged the corner where the wall met the floor and I thought this was really strange, being a New Yorker and all. We're not used to seeing pipes. We seem to be ashamed of them.

The next day, I asked a Swedish engineer about this bold showing of their pipes, and he told me that they install the pipes inside the room so that they won't freeze, and also so that the heating professional can get at them, should there be a problem.

"You put your pipes in the walls, don't you?" he asked. I nodded. "You must have problems with freezing when it gets very cold," he said.

I explained that fixing frozen pipes is an entire industry in our country, and that many people depend on this for their livelihood. It's an American tradition.

He thought that was pretty funny. And come to think of it, so do I.

"But with the pipes buried inside the walls," he said, "how do you know where they are?"

"Well, they're easy to find," I explained. "All you have to do is hang a picture on the wall. The nail will find the pipe every time."

He thought that was hilarious.

"It's true," I said.

He doubled over laughing. Couldn't catch his breath.

"Seriously!"

This is how we make friends in foreign lands

Oh, and there are absolutely no furnaces in all of Sweden.

Germany

Speaking of making friends, the first time I went to Germany I met an engineer at the big ISH tradeshow in Frankfurt.

"Your accent," he said. "You are an American?"

"I am," I said.

"You sound like you are from New York."

"Guilty," I said.

"You people are pigs."

Say hello to my new friend.

"Why do you say that?" I asked.

"I've been to New York. You people heat buildings with steam! That is Nineteenth Century technology!"

"Yes, I know," I said, "but we have many old buildings."

"Pfff," he pfffed. "You don't know what old is! I have underwear older than your buildings! You should get rid of the steam!"

"Hey, we can't just get rid of it."

"You can if you have the will," he shouted. "We got rid of *ours*!"

"Well, actually," I said, "*we* got rid of yours. Remember?" I made the falling-bombs gesture with my 10 fingers.

"Ya, that's true," he said. "But still."

This, too, is how we make friends in foreign lands. Just keep talking until you find agreement.

There's this picture-postcard square in Frankfurt, Germany. It looks medieval, but thanks to the aforementioned Allies, it dates only to the 1950s. It's a recreation of what was there before Herr Hitler showed up. They call this place Dom-Römer, and it's within walking distance of ISH, the enormous plumbing-and-heating show Frankfurt puts on every odd year. I went to all of them between 1991 and 2015, usually with my buddy, Bob Boltz. We'd do the aisles of ISH until we're numb and then we'd look at each other, shrug and head out into the streets of downtown Frankfurt.

It makes for a nice break from the show, wandering through the streets of Frankfurt. There are thousands of people there and they walk fast and straight like New Yorkers. There's so much to see.

Bob and I reach the picturesque square and head for that tiny bar over there on the corner. We walk in and sit on the same two stools. There are only eight stools in the place and our two are always available. Nice.

Ella, the barmaid, hasn't changed. She has been there since before we arrived in 1991, and she is still there today. She says hello to us in German and we say hello to her in English and she raises an eyebrow and we say, "Bier." She nods and begins to build them. It takes her a good 10 minutes to do this. It's a slow pour and there's no hurry in this place.

She puts a little paper ring around the stem of each glass and places them on round cardboard coasters in front of us, and she looks at us as though we had just gotten up to go to the john two years ago instead of home to America. "How have you been?" I say and she smiles and nods, answers in German, which we do not speak. It's been two years. This place is timeless.

We stayed in a hotel just outside the city that year. It's the same place we stayed back in 2001. It used to be a slaughterhouse. There are carved animal heads above the main doorway. When you walk through the courtyard and down the hallways of this hotel the lights turn on and off automatically as you pass them. You're always walking in a pool of light, like an actor on stage. The lights follow you and give you just enough guidance to find your way to your room. There's some serious energy conservation going on there.

And when you get to your room and reach for the light switch you find that nothing happens when you flip it. You try it a few times and then wander back through the small pools of light to the front desk to ask what the heck is going on. How come the lights in your room don't work? The person behind the desk will smile at you in an efficient German way and explain that you have to put your card key in the slot in the wall just inside the door in order to make the lights work. And the heat. There's a panel radiator over there by the window. It has a thermostatic radiator valve on it and you can adjust it to suit yourself. But that valve also has an electrical component that's tied into the card-key slot by the door. If you're going out, there's no reason for the heat to be on, is there? And certainly there's no reason for the lights to be on. Or the TV. Or anything else. You're not in the room, and this is Europe.

And I'm thinking like an American who might be staying at the Holiday Inn in Moose Snot, Maine. Or the Ramada in Cow Flop, Iowa. I'm thinking, hey, I'm paying for this room and if want to leave the TV on so that it sounds like someone's in there when I'm out having dinner at Bob's Big Boy, that's my right as a good American. Isn't it? And if I want to keep every light in the place blazing and the heat pump set on high (for all the good that does) and the hot water running in the shower so as to add humidity to the place, well, that's okay, too. I paid for this room.

In Frankfurt, they just smile at you and tell you to stick your card key in the wall slot if you'd like electricity. They sort of force you to be a responsible person. It's quite un-American.

We spent some time in Heidelberg during our 2001 trip. We had a busload of people with us, most of them first-timers to Europe. That's why we took them to Heidelberg. Because it's a fairytale city with a castle on the hill and the oldest university in Europe down below. And there's this beautiful winding river. And bier.

While riding the bus back to Frankfurt that day I noticed that we stayed in the middle lane of the autobahn and that there were only trucks in the right lane, and nothing but maniacs in the left lane. I asked our English-speaking guide why we were staying in the middle lane, and why the speed of the bus never varied. I found this all very un-American.

She explained that trucks were allowed to go only as fast as they were currently going and that they had to stay to the right. And that even though our bus was allowed to go a bit faster than the trucks, we had to stay in the middle lane. The left lane has no speed limit, other than $E=MC^2$, and is reserved for people who want to die *right now*.

"And what keeps the buses and trucks from cheating?" I asked, as any good American would.

"The cameras on the bridges," she said, pointing to one as we passed beneath it. "They're automatic and on every overpass. They check your speed and snap your photo if you go too fast. They send you the ticket in the mail."

Europe.

I spent some time on a job in the suburbs of Frankfurt. I was with a boiler manufacturer. This particular job was at a medical facility just south of the city. The job had two boilers, one lead and the other lag. They used both on very cold days. There were four-way valves on the boilers and each had a Brial circulator, which we don't see in America. That was it – two circulators for the whole building. Each main circuit had a Btu meter because there were two tenants in this building and each would pay for the Btu they used each month. The boilers fired natural gas. Each was good for 92,000 Btuh, and they were in a room on the top of the building. There was no domestic hot water load on these boilers. They had point-of-use water heaters for what little domestic hot water the place needed. The job had panel radiators and thermostatic radiator valves.

The system had a reset controller over there on the wall. This sensed what was happening outside and operated both boilers. There were also reset controllers on each boiler and that seemed strange to me. That made for three independent reset controllers on one job, all doing the same thing. It looked like the Department of Redundancy Department had engineered this system, so I questioned it. Figured I'd learn something new.

But here comes the best part. I was there with the contractor, whom I was told spoke no English. The building owner was also there and they told me that he also spoke no English. Then there was the guy from the factory, who was driving me around. He spoke very good English. If I wanted to ask the contractor or the owner a question, I was told to direct my question to the factory guy, who would then translate for me and get me the answer.

"How come there are three separate reset controllers on this system?" I asked the factory guy. "Seems to me that you could get the job done with just one. I wonder why this guy bought three. Seems like a waste of some serious money."

And that's when the owner's eyes went as wide as cue balls. "I knew it," he shouted in very good English. "You cheated me!" He shook his fist at the contractor. "You're a thief and this man just proved it!" He pointed toward me and I was delighted that I could suddenly cause Germans to speak in tongues.

The contractor, who looked a lot like Sergeant Schultz in the old *Hogan's Heroes* show, shouted back at the building owner, "He knows *nothing*! *Nothing*! He's from *America*!"

Ah, Frankfurt.

On another trip to Frankfurt, again with Bob Boltz and a couple of other friends, I found myself in a suburb of the big city. We were in the office of this big design/build firm. We were trying to get some insight into how the Europeans design their hydronic heating systems. The fellow who was lecturing us that day did so in German, but we had a translator with us, and he was a huge help.

This was the day that I learned that the main difference between them and us is that they focus on pressure differential, while we focus on big flow. They run little pipes from the boiler to manifolds, to which they then connect their panel radiators. The radiators all have thermostatic radiator valves. They run continuous circulation between the boiler and the manifolds, and they let the TRVs modulate the flow between the manifolds and the panel radiators. They also install differential-pressure regulators between all their supply and return lines so that the TRVs can throttle without backing the circulator up on its curve. That solves the problem of banging control valves and velocity noise, both of which are also American traditions. This was before we had smart pumps with ECM motors.

During a break, I wandered over to one of the panel radiators that were under the window of this large conference room. The radiator had a thermostatic radiator valve, of course (German law required them for rooms larger than eight square meters), and the supply and return pipes looked like they were going right through the wooden baseboard molding and into the wall. I thought that was strange, especially since the building was old and the walls were made of concrete, so I asked about it.

"Why do the pipes go into the wall?"

Our translator turned to our host and repeated my question. Our host looked confused. I pointed and gestured. He started laughing. Then he explained, through our translator. "The pipes do not go into the walls," he said. "That *is* the pipe." And he pointed at what I had thought was wooden base molding. It wasn't wood molding. It was a steel pipe.

"*That's* the pipe?" I said. "That square thing?"

Translator, back to our host. Host nods.

"Why is the pipe square?" I asked.

Translator back to him, and then back to me.

"The pipe is square because the corner is square."

"Oh," I said.

"Square pipe fits in square corner," he further explained to Big Stupid. "Round pipe. Square corner. Not so good."

"Oh."

Turns out, this square pipe ran around the perimeter of the office building, feeding panel radiator after panel radiator, much like we would do with a diverter-tee system here in America. One of my traveling buddies looked at this and chuckled. "They must have some sort of diverter tee in there," he says. "Otherwise, water won't flow from the square pipe into the radiator." I nodded. "Ask him," he said.

So I did.

Now, our host didn't understand the concept of a diverter tee, so I grabbed a pen and paper and drew what I thought was a pretty good sketch of a one-pipe, diverter-tee system. Our host looked at it, mumbled something nasty in German and scowled at me.

"Hey, Dan," my buddy said, "that was a really stupid question."

Turns out, I was showing our energy-conscious host an American system that is designed to waste electricity by having cumulative fixed resistance built right into it from the get-go. Diverter-tee systems lead to piggy-pump selection. Bigger is always better, right? You know, another American tradition?

But I soon learned that the pressure drop through a panel radiator is so slight that the water favors it over staying in the square pipe. And that's why it works without diverter tees. Who knew?

Well, they did, but still.

Then Bob Boltz whispers, "You know what, Dan? This job can't possibly work because the water from the first panel radiator is cooling the supply to the next, and so on. Just look at it. They can't run supply water hotter than about 155-degrees in this country. It's the law. So how the heck are they going to heat all these offices, especially the ones at the end of the loop?"

"I don't know," I whispered.

"*Ask* him," Bob whispered back.

"*You* ask him," I said.

"But he already knows you're stupid," Bob said. "Why should I get involved in this? Just ask him."

So I did. And that's when our host took us to the basement and showed us this most wonderful hydronic bouquet, made up of a circulator, a four-way valve, a switching relay, and a timer. It begins by circulating water clockwise through the loop of square pipe feeding the panel radiators. After a half-hour, the timer shuts off the circulator and the relay reverses the position of the four-way valve. Then the circulator restarts, but now it's moving the water in the opposite direction around the big loop. The supply water goes this way, and that way, and this way, and that way. And did you ever see a Lassie go this way and that?

Meanwhile, everyone upstairs is cozy.

You could have fit a softball in my mouth.

We've since used that piping arrangement a bunch of times on the Wall at HeatingHelp.com. Some guy will pop in and proudly proclaim that he just did his first radiant job.

He buried a thousand feet of 3/8" PEX tubing in concrete, and now he wants to know what size circulator he should use.

One of the Wallies will ask, "How many circuits did you use with that thousand feet?"

Our new friend will say, "Circuits?"

We will then explain that to pump water through a thousand feet of skinny, buried-in-concrete PEX he can either stop by his local firehouse and see if they can help out with one of their big pumper trucks, or he can use the four-way valve, timer, relay, and circulator trick to get out of the hole he dug for himself.

It usually works.

But we weren't done on that day in Germany. When we got back upstairs, Bob's eyes lit up. He mentioned that every other half-hour, water will be flowing *backwards* through the TRVs on the panel radiators. "This job can't work," he whispered. "A TRV will sound like a machine gun if you put it in backwards, and that's what this guy is doing every other half-hour. Tell him it can't work."

"*You* tell him!" I said.

"But you're on such a roll," Bob said.

So I mentioned how the job can't work to our host, and he explained how differential-pressure regulators keep TRVs from hammering, and then he shook his head sadly, and called me bad names in German.

Square pipes. Reversed flow. Who knew?

Learning every day.

Oh, and in Germany, they also have this guy they call the chimney sweep. He has the power of the police and he will show up at random times to check the efficiency of your boiler. If it passes, the chimney sweep will affix a sticker to the boiler, which gives you the right to use it for the next six months. If it fails, however, he will red-tag it. You now have two weeks to have your boiler replaced. If you decided to ignore this directive, the chimney sweep has the legal right to remove your boiler from your home when he returns to check.

Try doing that in central-Pennsylvania.

And there are no furnaces in Germany, nor is there any steam heat. It's against the law to have steam heat.

It's also against the law to have a single-speed circulator. Everything has to run on an ECM motor over there.

Can you legislate behavior toward the environment?

Yep.

Iceland

Bob and I were getting some fresh air out in front of our hotel in Reykjavik. It was March; it was snowing, and Bob and I were on our way back to New York from Germany. We had spent days there, roaming the streets, riding the trains, talking to people, and looking at the buildings. We also went to the big ISH show again, but we balanced what we heard at the show against what we saw in the cities, and heard at our tiny bar in Frankfurt. It's important to do that with ISH because that beast of a show has the power to blind you. The show is about what's possible. Outside the show is about what is.

A guy was smoking near us in front of the hotel and he laughed at something one of us had said, so we said hello and learned that he was from Boston. He told us that he was there with his wife, who worked for Icelandair, which prompted me to say, "She must be beautiful."

"Nah, she's American," he said.

Boston. Gotta love it.

Each time we flew back from Germany to New York City, we soared over Iceland. It has always called up to me and I've yearned for its stark beauty. You can tell, even from 38,000 feet, that this place is special. I'd tell my friends that we absolutely had to stop there the next time. I finally won them over by researching all the geothermal magic the Icelanders were performing. I told them we could get to see all of that. I explained that Iceland is doing things with heating that no one else in the world is doing, and I finally wore them down. We were there.

In 1973, OPEC decided to shut off the oil faucet, and we had to wait on long lines to get gasoline. The price of fuel spiked and the heating industry changed forever.

And, oh, we were going to do magnificent things in America! We were going to change our ways, and there was such hope and invention, but then, being Americans, we fell back into our old habits as soon as the price of fuel fell a bit. We accept high prices, as long as they're not rising. We get used to them, and we pay. We send our money to countries that want to kill us, and we're perfectly okay with that. It's just the way we are.

The folks in Iceland are different. In 1974, they decided to get off fossil fuels in a hurry, and they put together a plan. They drilled holes in the ground and brought up this super-hot water that lies not very far below the surface. They could drill down just 600 feet and hit water that's twice the boiling point. They could do this because Iceland is made of lava and magma and snow, and it's expanding by about an inch a year. The tectonic plates are moving away from each other, not toward each other, and that's the secret to their success. They have constant earthquakes, but it's not the Japanese sort that knocks down buildings. They have the sort of earthquakes that keep the pot stirred, always pulling the plates apart and leaving spaces into which the water from the glaciers and the sea can seep. It takes about 200 years for surface water to reach down through the porous lava to where the magma lives. When it gets there, it turns into high-pressure brine, which becomes steam that can turn huge turbines. These massive machines make enough electricity to power 80 percent of the country.

The steam screams from the high-pressure turbines, into the low-pressure turbines, and then on into the heat exchangers that make domestic hot water, and house-heating water for most of the country. The wastewater then flows through pipes under the parking lots and sidewalks to melt the snow. Some of that waste also flows onto the black lava and forms the Blue Lagoon, which sits next to the power plant and is one of the most beautiful outdoor spas in the world. They gather up the minerals from the wastewater and turn these into expensive cosmetics. It's freezing, snowing and the Icelanders are swimming in the hot water and drinking booze.

And when they're done with all that, they pump the rest of the waste water, which is nearly all of it, back into the ground, where it turns back into high-pressure brine and comes screaming up again into the high-pressure turbines. It's a circle of engineering and power that's both primal and somehow mythological. This is the earth giving itself to the people.

I asked our guide how long an installation such as this could sustain itself. I don't mean the equipment, which will need replacing, but the earth beneath the high-pressure, geothermal plant. How long can this cycle of take and give back continue before it runs out? "We estimate a hundred-thousand years for this location," he said.

I had to think about that for a good long time.

I wish you could have been there with me, Erin. As you drive around and look at this starkly gorgeous landscape, you'll notice these brightly painted tanks up on a hill over there, or level with the homes over here. They look like American oil- or gasoline tanks, but they're not. They contain hot water that flows naturally from the earth. It comes right out of the ground and flows to people's faucets.

You do have to be very careful when showering in Iceland, though. The domestic hot water temperature is nearly 180 degrees and OSHA is nowhere to be seen. As it was with John Jay Park in 1954, you're supposed to practice common sense.

I was in a bar with friends (go figure), and chatting with the bartender about all of this. He drew a glass of cold water from the tap and had me taste it. It was as pure as anything I've ever tasted. It comes from a high aquifer. Then he drew a glass of hot water, which comes from a few hundred feet below the cold-water aquifer. He told me to taste it once it cooled. I did and then made a face. It tasted of sulfur. "We don't drink that," he said.

"But you give it to me?" I said.

"You asked," he shrugged. And now I know, and I'll never forget it, and that's better than any textbook.

That same hot water flows through heat exchangers in people's homes. The homes have no chimneys, which you notice from the plane as you're landing. The hot water flows to the radiators, and also to the snowmelt systems under the walkways and driveways. I asked how much all of this costs and our guide told us he pays about $130 a month for the electricity, heating, and snow melting in his modest home. Imagine that.

There are few trees in Iceland. During the 14th Century, the people cut the trees and used them for firewood. Once the trees were gone, the relentless wind roared in and blew the topsoil out to sea. They didn't know this would happen, but by the time they figured it out, it was too late. Some things are too precious to waste, but we often don't realize that until they're gone.

This is good to keep in mind as we rush to turn our Southern forests into woodchips to send to Europe. We've become the biggest exporter of woodchips in the world.

That scares the crap out of me.

When we walked the streets of Germany with Bob, we talked about the quality of their windows. German law doesn't allow you to have lousy windows. Lousy windows waste fuel and Germans know how to write laws.

Wander around Iceland's capital city of Reykjavik and you'll see windows such as those we have in America – some good, but most are old and drafty, like what we had in the '50s. It doesn't matter as much there in Iceland because the heat is abundant, seemingly forever, and ridiculously cheap.

An Icelander asked me if I had heard that they have no army and I said, yes, I had heard that. "It's not true," he said. "We do have an army. It's called Salvation." And he clapped me on the shoulder and let loose the most wonderful laugh.

"Also, did you know," he leaned in and whispered, "that our island is expanding one inch per year?"

"Yes, I heard that, too," I said.

He looked over his shoulder to make sure no one was listening, and then he whispered, "This is our secret plan to take over the world!. Shhhh."

We both laughed until it hurt.

Somewhere between here and there is this magical place called Iceland, where the people share everything and laugh most of the time. You can walk up to the simple home of the Mayor of Reykjavik and knock on the door. He will answer and might even invite you in.

Go there someday. See what they're doing with energy. Listen to their stories and take in the beauty of the place. It has the power to change you.

Denmark

Denmark is lovely and its people are gorgeous. I was there twice with Bob Boltz on two trips. We were visiting with the good folks at Danfoss on one trip, Grundfos on another, and we drove all over the country.

Before the first OPEC oil embargo of '73, Denmark was 100 percent dependent on foreign oil. They realized that this is a very dangerous place to be, so they set out to become energy-independent, a condition they have just about achieved.

If you throw a stick in Denmark, you're probably going to hit either a wind turbine or a solar panel. And if you're in Copenhagen, you'll be getting your heat and hot water from garbage. Denmark burns all their garbage in huge, very-efficient boilers and transfers the heat into their district-hot-water system, where it flows to 98% of the buildings in the city. They also import garbage from other European countries for burning. Garbage is golden in Denmark.

To cut down on carbon emissions, they encourage people not to drive. They do this by adding a 220% sales tax to new cars, a 200% sales tax to used cars, and a 180% sales tax to motorcycles. They also slowly eliminated most of the parking spaces in Copenhagen. You can drive there if you'd like, but you won't be able to get out of your car once there. Oh, and at more than $8.00 per gallon, they have the highest gas prices of any country in the world. So there.

Can you legislate behavior toward the environment?

Yep.

Because of all of that, most Danes ride bicycles. And they ride them in all weather. I was there when it was snowing and people were peddling along the bike roads that parallel the motor-vehicle roads. And when we visited the Grundfos and Danfoss factories, we saw huge bicycle-parking garages.

Bikes are everywhere in this beautiful country. People park them on the side of the road, unlocked, and get onto the bus. They also leave them unlocked in the broad plaza areas around the train stations. Being a New Yorker, I asked a local if there was a concern about people stealing other people's bicycles.

"Oh, yes, that happens," she said.

"And what do you do then?"

She shrugged and smiled. "Just take someone else's."

A nation of stolen bicycles, and no one is getting upset. Nice.

I check into my hotel and notice that nothing in the room works. I can't turn on the lights, or the TV. The radiator is cold. Then I remember the thing with the room card-key and I look for the slot by the door. I insert the key, and now everything works.

So un-American.

I think again of the American Holiday Inns, or the Sheratons, Hyatts, Marriotts, and every other U.S. hotel, where the person checking me in always asks how many keys I would like. I'm standing there all alone and the person is asking me how many keys I would like.

"May I have twelve?" I say.

She smiles and gives them to me.

In Denmark, as in the rest of energy-conscious Europe, when it comes to hotel keys, it's one and you're done.

And the escalators don't run if no one is on them. Why would they?

So much to learn, Erin.

On our first visit, Bob Boltz and I were in a restaurant. Something had been nagging at me during the few days we had been in the country, traveling around. When our waitress brought our food it dawned on me that there was not one fat person in this whole country. Probably because of the bicycles.

I looked around the restaurant to confirm this.

The waitress smiled at me as she put down my plate.

"Is there anything else I can do?" she asked.

"Yes," I said. "I have a question for you."

"Yes?" (sweet smile).

"Where are all the fat people?"

Still smiling. "In America," she said.

Yep.

(Speaking of bicycles)

Believe it or not, they played a significant role in plumbing-and-heating history. I have a photo from a yellowed trade magazine that's more than 100 years old. It's of a plumber's shop in a Midwestern city, and the people in the photo look proud as they pose for the camera. It must have been such a big deal to have your photo taken for a magazine back when photography was still relatively new. The older men in the photo wear derbies, and I've learned that this means they are the Masters. The younger men in the photo, the apprentices, are all wearing beanies. Nice way to separate them, but I can't imagine doing that today.

Nearly all of the people in the photo are staring straight into the camera's lens. One of the Masters is chewing the stump of a cigar. He has his big hand on a tall, cast-iron radiator. It's a beauty, and probably still in service in some old building.

Radiators last a long time in America.

On the right-hand side of the photo, there is a tall apprentice. He looks to be in his late-teens, and he is not staring at the camera. He's turned a full 90 degrees to his right, and he's looking downward. We follow his gaze and he appears to be looking at a large, cast-iron radiator. Or so I thought.

As time went by, and as I learned more about our industry, I came to realize that the apprentice in the photo wasn't looking at the radiator. He was looking at the bicycle that rested against it.

He's wearing a long-sleeved white shirt, long trousers, a dark vest and a bowtie. He has that beanie on his head, and his hands on his belt. He's learning forward slightly, and he's smiling a bit. He looks like he wants to jump on that bicycle. It was a new invention, and it was taking the heating trade by storm. It was how a strong young man could stand out.

There's another old magazine in my office. They published this one on July 17, 1897, and on one of the pages, there are three advertisements. One is for the beautifully ornate Gem radiator from the Corry Radiator Company of Corry, Pennsylvania. The company lasted only two years before U.S. Radiator bought them. I'll bet there are still Corry radiators in service. They're gorgeous.

Next to the Corry ad is an ad for, "Your friend. . . the Kenwood Bicycle – a wheel you can depend upon." That's what they called bicycles in those days. They called them, "wheels." I learn from the ad that for lightness, swiftness and strength, the Kenwood is unsurpassed. It was a very popular brand back then, and Kenwood showed their wheels at the Eastern National Cycle Exposition during the winter of 1898. This show took up two floors at New York City's Grand Central Palace, which was, after Madison Square Garden, the largest exhibition space around. There were more than 200 exhibitors at that show. Bicycles were the latest thing, and Kenwood and other manufacturers had they eyes on the trades.

Just below the Kenwood Bicycle and the Corry Radiator ads, I see another ad. This one is for the Octa-Brass Union, manufactured by the Kelly & Jones Company of Greensburg, PA. The ad explains, "These unions are heavy and well-made, and on account of their octagonal shape can be made upon pipe quickly with a wrench, avoiding the use of tongs."

I'll bet that must have made Daniel Stilson smile. And isn't it wonderful that there was a time in America when a simple union, a fitting that can be made upon a pipe with a wrench, something now considered a boring commodity, was once worthy of its own ad in a national magazine. A new fitting that can be made upon a pipe with a wrench. Gosh.

Everything that we today take for granted was once new and exciting to someone. There really are no boring products, Erin. There are only people who can't, or won't, see the beauty of invention in each product.

And each product that we touch has presented a threat to someone at some time or other. This is from *The Metal Worker* magazine. The date is August 5, 1899.

"It is apparent that the bicycle is held in different esteem by plumbers in different parts of the country, and the effort is being continued to prevent its use in some sections, while some men will use it in preference to the streetcars for reaching work. A master plumber in an Eastern city of 30,000 inhabitants, which has a large outlying suburban population, keeps five wheels for hire and the use of his men. It is a frequent occurrence that he has no wheels to hire, owing to his men having them all in use, going from one job to another. The men prefer riding to waiting at stations for trains, and are conscientious enough to want to do a fair day's work even when it is jobbing to be done in a half dozen different country houses a few miles apart, where the train service would not be convenient. An entirely different view is taken in Los Angeles, California, where the Herald says:

" 'One of the causes of frequent bickering is the bicycle. The Plumbers' Union has a rule, which is rigidly enforced, prohibiting the members from utilizing the bike in connection with their work. The rule is regarded as necessary to protect the men. When the bicycle came into popular use, the plumbers found that some of their number would go spinning around town on their wheels for the benefit of the bosses. The result was that the plumber without a bike soon found himself at a disadvantage. One of them explained the matter in this wise: 'Suppose two

*men were sent out on a job and both had practically the
same kind and the same amount of work to do. They would
both leave the shop at the same time, but the fellow with
the wheel would reach the place where the work was to
be done before his brother plumber would. If some tool
or piece of material had been forgotten, the man with the
wheel would go spinning to the shop, while the other fellow
would have to walk or take a streetcar. The man with the
wheel could make better time on a job in consequence,
and the boss would be liable to find him a more desirable
man, notwithstanding that it was no fault of the other man.
In fact, the man without the wheel might be the fastest
and best workman. We want this rule against the bicycle
enforced in all the shops.' "*

Threatened by a bicycle. Isn't that fascinating?

But I'll bet the guys on the wheels where skinnier than
the fat guys waiting for the streetcars.

The Danes would approve.

France

I wish you could have been with me on this trip, Erin.
Your mom and I had a ball.

Wilo, the German pump manufacturer, invited me to fly
to Paris to try to explain hydronics, American-style, to the
folks who run most of the huge European boiler companies.
I told them about the good systems and the not-so-good
systems, and I told them about the steam heat that is still in
so many of our older cities, and probably will be for many
more years because, as you know, we don't change easily
in America. I told them about how, in the luxury apartment

buildings of Manhattan, there are often people on staff who ride the service elevators all winter long and knock on doors. These people enter multi-million-dollar digs and then proceed to open and close the radiator valves for people who have way too much money. I explained that we call these people on staff, two-legged zone valves. My new European friends liked that.

And it's understandable. I mean those old steam radiators are often encased in exotic wood that you just can't buy anymore, and the pipes are buried like dead bodies inside marble soffits, and have been for a hundred years or more. Those pipes are tough to get at.

And fuel is still relatively cheap here compared to what it costs in Europe. I told them that, and I told them that most Americans don't care if they waste a bit of energy, as long as they're comfortable. And besides, in most of our steam-heated buildings, the heat is included in the rent. Close the windows, or open the windows; you'll still pay the same rent. So leave it open a few inches, or a foot. Fresh air is good for you. And besides, if you close the window you'll probably suffocate because the radiators are as big as footlockers.

My audience thought all of this was delightful in a primitive sort of way – that we use 19th-Century technology to heat many of our buildings. They looked at the photos in my PowerPoint presentation as if they were something recently picked from a nose. They looked at each other. They looked at me. They shook their heads. Some giggled.

I explained that we have no heating police in America, no Chimney Sweeps, and that this has a lot to do with the way we live. We're free to waste as much as we like. We're Americans!

I tried to lead them in a chorus of U.S.A.! U.S.A! but they weren't going for it.

What can you do?

I told them that there are two basic types of installers in America. First, we have the Boutiques. These are the people who sit and salivate over the prospect of the next container ship from Europe and what it might contain. I explained that Boutiques will try anything new, and that they are wonderful prospects for every European manufacturer, no matter what that manufacturer makes. Systems can't possibly be too complicated for Boutiques. They dream in calculus, measure in metric, and speak in gibberish.

Which can be a problem, since the only people who understand Boutiques are other Boutiques, and when Boutiques speak to each other, they're almost always arguing over who has the larger brain. No customer has ever understood a Boutique, and that's why more American stuff gets sold in America than European stuff. Boutiques don't like to sell American stuff. It's too, well, American. Denny Adelman, an American who used to write for the trade journals before moving permanently to France in the early-90s, once commented that most American boilers can be found in the generic-foods aisles of most American supermarkets.

Gosh, that guy had a way with words. He was a Boutique I could almost understand.

And that brings me to Grandpas. Grandpas sell the American stuff, and the older that stuff is, the longer it has been around, the better. A Grandpa won't try anything new and he'll always ask you for stuff that you haven't stocked for 20 years. Grandpas are just now getting used to copper tubing. They think plastic is for communists. They like single thermostats with mercury tubes and they like these to start and stop big pumps on long loops of big pipe that run out to huge radiators. The bigger the better. They like boilers that maintain 190° F. water 365 days a year. They drool over tankless coils and they love getting paid in cash. They write their proposals on the backs of their business cards because they know that too much detail just confuses people.

By the time a Grandpa tries something new, it's no longer new, but, oh, can they talk! Grandpas, like most consumers, have opinions about everything, and this is why the two get along so well. Both agree that things ain't what they used to be, and that nobody makes anything good anymore. And both groups believe that a boiler should last at least eighty years, maybe ninety.

I explained to my new European friends how American consumers will get the idea of efficiency in their heads when the price of fuel is rising, and they'll call the Boutiques to learn more about that because Boutiques usually advertise (Grandpas don't have to advertise). The Boutique will stop by, talk to the consumer in white noise, and then give a price that will make the consumer's ears bleed. The consumer will hurry that price over to the Grandpa, who will explain to the consumer that the Boutique is a no-good thief and a socialist, and that none of that stuff from Europe works. How come? It's from Europe. Buy American!

My audience was enthralled.

I showed photos of one Grandpa's exposed wiring that looked like a bowl of linguine with clam sauce. I also showed the precision work of Boutiques, who level every wire in the house. "See?" I said to my new friends. "In America, we go both ways." They looked at each other.

I showed them boilers that had once burned coal, and had since been converted to burn oil, and now natural gas. Same boiler, and it was the size of a minivan and had no jacket. "We like to conserve natural resources," I explained. "Here, we are conserving a ton of cast-iron." They gagged on their coffee.

"I live in a place called the Isle of Long," I told them. "It's a small country off the east coast of New York. We have our own language. Rosetta Stone has a five-level program for it." They smiled and nodded. Some had visited this peculiar country. "On the Isle of Long, and in many other parts of North America, there are people who heat with fuel oil. Fuel oil dealers deliver the oil with trucks and hoses. I know you have such companies in Europe." They nodded. "Well, here's the difference between our fuel oil dealers and your fuel oil dealers," I said. "In many parts of America, if you heat with oil, you don't have to pay for service or parts. All you have to do is threaten to buy your oil from the competitor, and your current fuel oil dealer will give you at least five years of free service and parts. He will come to your house any time of the day or night, and any day of the year, and breathe new life into your antique heating equipment. It doesn't matter how old the equipment is, or whether it's walking or limping. He will keep it running. There is never a reason to buy anything new in America if you have a fuel-oil service contract." My new friends choked on their French pastries. "This, too, is how we conserve heating equipment," I said. "It's all very green. Moldy, actually."

Oh, and in that Manhattan apartment building with the two-legged zone valves? I told them about how I had visited an apartment that had just sold for $16.5 million. The new owner had the place gutted right down to the concrete and was redoing it to his taste. The old place was move-in quality, but some people are funny that way. They want what they want. I told about this and one of my new friends said, "Surely the new owner is having a modern heating system installed." He still didn't get it.

I explained that they were replacing the old boiler with a new one. "That's why I was there," I said. "They wanted an opinion on the old steam system."

"And what sort of boiler will they be putting in now?" he asked.

"Same thing," I said. "Steam." (more gagging).

"And the radiators? Will someone still have to open and close the valves for the wealthy tenant when he is too hot and too cold?"

"Oh, sure. That's all part of the service this building offers. Pretty swanky, don't you think?"

Gag, gag, gag.

Labyrinth

A year or so before we made that trip to Paris, your mom and I were in France with a couple of Canadian friends, Bill Lowe and Steve Thomson. At the time, both guys were working for Wilo, the German pump manufacturer, and both have gone on to do other mighty fine things since. There's a lot of moving around in the hydronics industry, but few leave it completely.

Bill had left us to go on to one of the Wilo factories, so your mom, Steve and I were traveling together. We were in France and decided to visit the Chartres Cathedral, mostly because I was begging them to go. Chartres is one of the world's most beautiful cathedrals, and in its nave there is a labyrinth that dates to the year 1200 or so.

I've walked labyrinths in San Francisco and at my old school, Hofstra University. Chartres was the model for both. Normally, the labyrinth at Chartres is covered with chairs, but we were lucky enough to be there on a summer Friday, the one day of the week when they move the chairs and allow visitors to walk the path.

The labyrinth is about 40 feet in diameter, and the path to the center winds back and forth, back and forth. Walking it is a spiritual experience. The rhythm of my steps, moving forward, turning, moving forward, turning put me into a peaceful trance. Other people were doing the same and when we met, we embraced for a moment before moving on. None of us knew each other. The brief embrace recognized that we both had led individual lives that had brought us to this moment in this holy place, and at the exact same instant. It seemed natural to hug, and to smile. And then to move on.

The labyrinth isn't a maze. The path leads only to the center of the circle. The walk inward signifies your past life. The center symbolizes now. You pause there a few moments and breathe deeply. Perhaps say a quiet prayer, and then you follow the same path outward. This represents your future. It takes maybe a half-hour to do it properly. It's incredibly peaceful.

Well, not all the time.

When I got to the center, I stood there with my eyes closed and prayed.

And that's when the 30 or so Asian tourists arrived. Their guide, flag in hand, rushed them all to the center of the labyrinth, nearly knocking down the people who were walking, praying, and hugging. The tourists gathered around me, snapping photos of the cathedral and jabbering away as the guide pointed to this and that.

Your mom and I shrugged, gave up and left.

So much for spiritualism.

The labyrinth is a nice metaphor of the hydronics industry, though, which in itself is a journey. We're guided along the way as we enter, some by good mentors, some by experiences hard won. We reach a point in the center of our career where it consumes us, and we linger there for a time. Then strange people come barging in when we're trying to get things done. They knock us around. We do our best to get out of their way. And then, older and hopefully wiser, we begin to work out way out of the labyrinth, moving back and forth, frequently changing directions, stopping along the way to appreciate the beauty of it all, and to hug a stranger or a friend who is on the same path.

To have lived our whole lives just to arrive at this one place together. What a wonder that is!

And all the while, I of course am thinking about the marble rolling through the pipe.

Ireland

Remember when your big sister, Kelly, was on that University of Notre Dame-sponsored service project, teaching second grade in that very poor Irish village just outside of Dublin and your mom and I went to visit her?

None of the people living in any of the public housing (which was adjacent to the school) had central heat. I asked Kelly if the people burned turf, romantic that I am. She shook her head and explained that the Irish didn't do that near the cities anymore because of air-pollution rules. They burned, instead, coal, but of the smokeless variety.

Some improvement.

We stayed with her for a few days, and on one of those days, we hired Dermot Buckley, an excellent driver and chatty tour guide, to take us up into the majesty of the Wicklow Mountains. As we worked our way up the tiny roads, Dermot pointed out heather, which is so beautiful that it hurts your eyes, and near the heather he showed us the black earth, which is the turf that the Irish once used as their primary fuel.

The turf was cut away in great deep rows, and as we drove slowly by I thought of the generations that labored in those bogs, cutting and stacking and setting it aside to dry. And the more I travel and read and learn of this life, the more I marvel at how far we've come. And at the same time, I think about what we've lost along the way. Some of that loss is the result of the fine work that we do.

A bit of your heritage, Erin. The Irish made fires that never went out. Did you know that? The fire in the hearth was for cooking and for warmth, and it smoldered for hundreds of years in some cases. Think of it. Generations tended that endless fire.

Dermot Buckley dropped the three of us off at a little pub in a town near ancient Glendaloch. He spoke softly to the owner, who nodded and then greeted us with a smile and a gesture toward a dark-wood table just next to the fire. There was a beautiful aroma in the air and I asked the owner what it was. "The turf," he said, pointing to the fire, and that's when I saw it for the very first time. It was lovely and peaceful. We ate fine stew and drank Guinness stout, and we watched the turf burn.

When the famine visited Ireland and many of the people, filled with despair, decided to leave, those who remained held American funerals for them because leaving was as good as being dead to those who remained. Few returned. And as a family left, the father of that family would take a shovel to the family's fire, which had burned continuously in that hearth for perhaps hundreds of years, and he would carry a bit of that fire to a neighbor's house where he would place it among their embers. It was the departing family's way of balancing the American funeral. Keep this until we return to our beloved home. The fire was life. It was the family's past, present, and future.

During the bad times, the Irish would say to each other, "There will be many warm shovels this year," and when I think of that expression I get very quiet in my soul. And I thought of this as I sipped the good Guinness and stared into the turf fire in the little pub near Glendaloch.

From time to time in the old days the shanachie would arrive in a village. He was the professional storyteller. He roamed the land and carried with him the history of the people. A family would welcome him in, and after they shared a meal, they would sit by the hearth that held the fire that never went out, and the shanachie would tell tales that would make the old remember, and the young dream. The fire strung them together, the young and the old, the living and the dead, like the beads of a rosary.

Your great-grandfather came to New York City from Kilkenny in Ireland, and he got a Tammany Hall job working in one of the public baths. He kept the fire going in their big boiler. That was his job, and it was a good one. I never knew Jim Holohan because he died when your grandpa was still a boy. Grandpa, also gone now, remembered him as being somewhat crazy, and I have a photo of him on my desk. I look at him each day while I'm working and I wish I could ask him about the coal in the old boilers, and about the turf in the old country, and about the warm shovels.

Your grandma and grandpa grew up in tenements in Manhattan, where the only heat was from a stove in the kitchen. Your grandpa told me that the family would sit around that stove for warmth in the bitter New York winters, and that this is where he learned many of the stories that he told me as I grew.

I was the first generation of Holohans to experience central heating as a normal thing from birth. We treat it now as if it has been around for a long time, but it hasn't. It's changed the way we live, though. There was no need for me to huddle around a stove with my mother and father and my brothers when I was a boy. We were warm in all the rooms of our apartment, and later in our house in Hicksville. We huddled, instead, around the television set. The TV was the new shanachie, and the family members didn't talk to each other as much anymore. We knew more of the world because of the TV, of course, but we also knew less of each other. I'm not sure that was a good trade.

I married your mother and we bought our house with hot water heat. We now had zones, and as you and your sisters arrived and grew, we also had an electronic shanachie in each of your bedrooms. Central heating had us seeing less of each other, and we had to work harder to find time to be together, and to share stories of the day. The fire, which had once been life and history, is now inside a box in the boiler, and we think of it only when it's not there. And when it's not, we call for service.

We lost the fire along the way, and with it, we lost a part of ourselves. It no longer draws the family together. And there are no more warm shovels when a family moves.

They just move.

And this is why we I built that fire pit in the backyard. You and I make a living talking and writing about this wonder called central heating, but something is missing. I think in our hearts we long for the turf fire, for the talk that goes with it, for the companionship, for the stories, and for the life that the fire represents. It's primal.

And I think, especially of late, that we long for its simplicity.

Russia

A few years ago, Fred stopped by for a chat. Somehow, the talk turned to steam. Fred was working for Consolidated Edison in New York City at the time. As you know, Con Ed provides the electricity and steam for New

York City. "A lot of people say that Con Ed has the largest district heating system in the world," Fred said, "but I hear there's a bigger one in Russia."

"I'm pretty sure that's a district hot water system over there," I said.

"You sure?"

"One way to find out," I said, walked into nine by 12. I posted the question on the Wall at HeatingHelp.com at 11:33 AM and got an answer from Jim Sokolovic at 11:37. Jim said that he had co-workers in Russia and that he would ask them. What specifically did I want to know? I told him that I wanted to know if it was steam, hot water or a combination of both. He got back to me at 11:55 with this:

"Dan, the heating plant is a single boiler, usually oil-fired, and they keep it in a garage-type structure. It supplies hot water through a continuous circulation system underground. Cast-iron radiators are in the buildings, which the government owns. There are no thermostats in the buildings, but the rooms never get warm enough, anyway. It's chilly over there."

Christian Egli then posted a terrific article that had appeared in the Moscow Times on August 7, 2003. Here's a bit of that:

"It's summer, and your hot water is turned off again.

"But the shutoff that often bewilders foreigners unfamiliar with the peculiarities of Moscow life might not always be an annual tradition: Engineers say a solution is in sight.

"However, it might take 200 years before your neighborhood has hot water all year round.

"Moscow Heating Network, the subsidiary of Mosenergo in charge of the main pipes that ship steamy-hot water from electric power plants to neighborhood heat-exchange points, sees the city's savior in a new pipe that is resistant to rust -- the main culprit that forces it to turn off hot water for repairs every summer.

"The pipes are protected by a special water- and heat-proof coating that is several centimeters thick and filled with rust-fighting polyurethane foam," said Viktor Tarasov, deputy chief engineer at Moscow Heating Network, or Teploseti. The pipes also are equipped with detectors that alert engineers about the need for small repairs before any major damage occurs.

"All this means that the new pipes can remain in service for 25 to 30 years without any major repairs, thus allowing hot water to be kept on all the time," Tarasov said.

"Just about every neighborhood takes its turn without hot water for three weeks every summer as engineers repair a vast and aging pipeline system that stretches for thousands of kilometers under -- and sometimes over -- the ground.

"The problem is that Moscow's heating and hot-water supply systems have a level of technology dating back to somewhere in the 1930s," Tarasov said in a recent interview.

"In most cases, city dwellers get their heating and hot water through a complicated system in which extra-hot water -- heated up to 130 degrees Celsius (266 F) in the peak of the winter -- is pumped through the main pipes to the neighborhood heat-exchange points. There, through special heat-exchange equipment, household water is warmed up -- but not mixed with -- the water from the power plants, and the cooled-off water is returned to the plants. Some of the longest main pipes stretch 20 kilometers from the power plants to the neighborhood heat-exchange points, or nearly halfway across the city," Tarasov said.

"This relatively unique heating and hot-water system was adopted primarily due to the city's vast size and the area's cold climate," Tarasov said. "And since electricity is produced anyway, the hot steam is effectively a byproduct that is a free source of heat," he said. "It would have been silly to waste it."

So Fred had his answer, but the folks on the Wall weren't through yet. Clif Heeney added this:

"Dan, I live in Tallinn, Estonia. Estonia was formerly a part of the USSR, so I believe that the heating systems that we have here are probably basically the same system as in Russia today. We have district heating serving probably half the city, which has 435,000 people. As far as I know the boilers are all fired with oil and only make hot water, which is then piped into the district that that particular plant serves. There is a power-generating plant on the outskirts of the city, which, of course, uses steam to operate the generator. I believe that they then use the steam through a heat exchanger to make hot water for the district heating in that particular area of Tallinn.

"Each building has a meter and pays for the amount of hot water that the people use. Some of the apartment buildings that have been renovated have also placed individual meters in each apartment so that the bill can be divided evenly. Where there are no individual meters, the apartment owners pay a percentage of the total bill, based upon the size in square meters of their apartment.

"The temperature of the hot water produced by the district-heating plants is based upon the outside-air temperature. So just imagine a giant-sized, outdoor-air reset.

"Sorry that I can't answer your question about Russia right now, though. My wife's favorite aunt lives in Moscow; we'll send her an email tomorrow and see what she can find out for you."

Two days later we heard from Clif again.

"My wife, Tuuli, called her favorite aunt, Evi, in Moscow today. Evi and her husband, Sergei, believe that almost all, if not all, of the district heating in Moscow is with water. They have heard of a few older buildings, and some of the new ones being heated with steam, but they don't think that is being done with a district-heating system. More than likely the individual building has its own steam boiler dedicated for the use of that building. They weren't able to verify that, though.

"They also believe that most, if not all, district heating in Russia would be with water, not steam. They have traveled somewhat and they have only seen hot water being used in district heating set-ups.

"We asked them if they knew of anyone who works in that utility and unfortunately they don't. They are going to ask around, though, and try to find someone who either works in one of the district-heating plants, or who has a friend who does. I'll let you know what they find out.

"I was born and raised in Vernal, Utah. I have lived in Estonia for about six years and have been married to my wife, who is an Estonian, for 5-1/2 years. We have two children. Our daughter, Nancy, who turned two years old today, and David, who is eight months old."

Small world isn't it? Later that day, Eric Petersen wrote, "Central heating is a feature of some housing developments in Finland. A friend of mine bought a new house in the Helsinki area and the whole development is heated by a central system that provides hot water. I remember walking to his house from the bus stop and seeing where they were laying the heating-distribution pipes deep in the ground for a different set of houses. The control mechanism was TRVs, but I don't know how they charged for usage. I do know that these types of houses are very well made, insulated, and comfortable all through the winter. Actually winters near Helsinki are not that much colder than Chicago.

"One other thing, my friend views American housing developments (especially apartment complexes with hot-air heating) as somewhat barbaric in that it seems wasteful for everyone to have a separate heating appliance in their unit. Wasteful and noisy (hot air that is)."

A few hours later, Clif Heeney was back to say. "Just got off the telephone with our Finnish friends who live in Vantaa, a suburb of Helsinki. Their apartment building is heated by district heating, as most are in Helsinki. They are not charged by how much hot heating water that they use, but rather a flat rate, based upon the square meters of their flat. It is built into their monthly maintenance fee. Each apartment or flat is owned by an individual, and they all pay a monthly maintenance fee, I think it's similar to what a condo owner would pay in the U.S.. No steam is used in their systems."

So that answers Fred.

When you're looking to learn, it sure is good to have friends in exotic places.

Iran

Well, Erin, you know I've never traveled to Iran, but I do seem to have a reputation there. I learned this in 2000, when I got an email from the editor of an engineering magazine published in Iran. He introduced himself and told me that I was the most widely known and highly respected technical writer in the entire Iranian heating industry. He asked if I would provide him with my books, which he would then reproduce and distribute to his readers.

I was gobsmacked.

I wrote back and asked him how this could be. I certainly had never sent any of my writings to anyone in Iran. He answered that they had been getting my stuff off the Internet and republishing it for years, and would I please send him my books.

I wrote again, explaining that all of my writing was copyrighted and could not be republished without my written permission. He very respectfully answered that folks in Iran didn't follow American copyright laws, so that wasn't an issue, and would I please send the books.

I sat and fumed over that for a while, but then realized that, because of the wonder of the Internet, the only thing I could do to stop this guy from doing what he was doing would be to stop writing altogether, which wasn't a pleasant option. And besides, he was really polite and seemed like a nice guy, so I figured I'd go along with him and maybe learn a bit about that ancient land and its people, beyond what I was seeing on the TV.

I told him that I couldn't send him the books, but would love to see a copy of the magazine that had made me the most widely known and highly respected technical writer in the entire Iranian heating industry. He sent me several issues.

They were in Persian, of course, but he had marked the pages with my articles. I could recognize my name and nothing else, other than the advertisements for various hydronic products. It was clearly an engineering magazine, sort of like the ASHRAE Journal.

I wrote back and thanked him for sharing. He asked if I would be willing to have my photo taken, holding their magazine. "Our readers would be delighted to see that!" he wrote. I said sure, and your mom took a photo of me out in the backyard. I held up the Iranian magazine and smiled like a highly respected technical writer should.

He wrote back to tell me that I was holding the magazine backwards, and would I please turn it around and try again.

Right, Persian goes the other way. Got it.

So I did that and sent it and he was very pleased.

Next, he wrote to ask me if I would agree to an interview. He would send me a list of questions about hydronics in the U.S. and I would answer. I said sure and did all of that. He sent me that issue, along with photos of me. I was having a ball.

Since then, I've emailed with lots of Iranian contractors and helped them figure out job problems. They send lots of photos and I marvel at how they manage to get done what they get done, especially in their current economic- and political situation.

I've gotten to know these workingmen over the years. They face the same challenges on jobs as we do, and they don't talk politics. They just want to do good work, get paid on time, and raise their kids in peace.

I'll share this note with you. It's from a friend. He's a hydronics professional who just happened to be born and raised in Tehran, and who just wants to work hard, make a living wage, and take care of his family. It's about the work. No politics. Listen:

"With regard to the project, which I have sent its drawing, I shall say that this project suspends by its owner. The story starts when I sent all estimated invoices (installation and purchasing expenses) to landlady. She first accepted, owing to the fact that she has known my crew and I for nearly a decade and we have done couple of heating projects for her and her brother. Our installations were satisfying.

"Unfortunately, at the eleven hour, her project manager and architect decided to show their fidelity to her by causing problems for us. They first provided all materials that we need for the job. Also, we introduced an honest company that accepted their checks and delivered all those materials. But, when they encountered the installation fees they started questioning me profusely. We had three business meeting to negotiate about the installation fee. They just strove to cut down the fees by half, and I found that their intention had been to copy our drawing and give to another installer to do the job.

"At the last business meeting they were five engineers who bombarded me with too many sarcastic questions to dishearten me. As you know better, God stands with right . I outspokenly defeated them by technical answers and referred them to reliable standards. Also, I accused them of playing trick on me. So, I left the meeting without reaching any agreement.

"The landlord is on a business mission. We have been waiting to see what will happen as soon as she comes back. Fortunately, I did not share this drawing with them because I felt that I could not put my trust in them from the beginning of this project.

"In the end, I told them two English quotes which embarrassed them noticeably. The first one, 'An honest enemy is always better than a friend who lies to you. Pay less attention to what people say, and pay much attention to what they do because their reactions always show the truth.'

"The second quote was, 'Honesty is an expensive gift. Never expect it from cheap people'. Furthermore, they asked me why I spoke to them bilingually, and I told them honorably that I am learning this industry in English language and I could not translate those unforgettable lessons and information into Persian, and this is not my problem.

"I am so sorry for the long story. But when I share it with you I feel comfortable."

I will never judge people, especially working people, by the regime under which they live simply because that is where they were born. No one gets to choose their parents or their place of birth.

Count your blessings.

Hydronics gave me lots of advice

Erin, you were just a dream to me when I took my first job in the industry. It was with an air-conditioning/refrigeration supply house, but I'm still counting it because the people on that side of the business are just as wacky as the people on the hydronics side.

Want to know what got me there? It was your grandfather. He had taken that job at the plumbing-and-heating supply house when he got back from fighting in the Pacific war. The supply house offered a lot of overtime, and that was important because, as growing boys, your Uncle Ed and I ate a lot.

Your grandpa counseled me to get into the heating business because, "Everybody needs heat, especially in the winter. It's the next best thing to Civil Service."

The closest I could get was air conditioning and refrigeration (it gets hot every summer!). My job was to drive a delivery truck and work behind the counter in one of their smaller branches, which was about 30 miles further east on Long Island in a town called Brentwood. I was 20 years old and still living at home. I had to give your grandma half of my take-home pay, which still seemed like a great deal.

I'd drive the two miles from our house to the local branch of the supply house, hustle to load the box truck with what the smaller branch needed that day, drive it out to Brentwood, unload it, and wait for someone to tell me what to do next.

So here's the first bit of advice I got when I stared in this business.

I'm young and strong and eager, loading the truck on Day One, hustling and trying to look good. Working up a real sweat. Gotta get out to Brentwood!

Three guys walked over to me. They looked like they had worked there since I was playing in John Jay Park. The biggest of the three grabbed me by the arm, and in a friendly, but very firm, whisper hissed, "Slow down, kid. Slow *down*. You got all day." And then he gave me a little slap on the cheek. The smile was gone.

I slowed to a normal pace.

He gestured downward with two hands the size of shovels.

I slowed down some more.

He nodded.

I now understood this place.

My boss, the head counterman, was 30 years old. This is when I first met the contractors. They'd come to the counter and send me scurrying down the aisles for things I knew nothing about. They'd tell me stories about stuff that happened to them as they worked out there in the real world. The stories were mostly wacky, and they *swore* they were true.

When I drove the truck, I'd get to see some of these stories unfold in real life.

One day, my boss sent me on a delivery to the local State mental hospital. This place was as big as an Army base and I had no idea where I was going once I got on the grounds, so I stopped and asked a guy near an old brick building for directions. He told me to wait right there. He went inside and returned in a few minutes with two burly-looking men. They climbed into the back of the truck and unloaded the whole works onto the middle of the road – all the while giggling like crazy.

Which, I later learned, they were. But crazy is pretty close to normal when you come right down to it, isn't it?

I met your mother just after I started that job. My 30-year-old boss invited us to dinner at his apartment on a Sunday afternoon. We met his wife and their two little kids. Over a cold beer, my boss told me how much he and his wife wanted to get out of that apartment and into a house, but they weren't sure they'd ever be able to afford it because this industry just doesn't pay people well enough. He mentioned that he and his wife had saved for a *month* to buy the steaks that we were about to eat. "We bought the *best* steaks, Dan. We ordered them special from the butcher, just for you and Marianne." Sweet, right?

He called me on the phone early one hot summer morning. I was working the counter.

"I won't be in today," he said. "Too dangerous. *Much* too dangerous!"

"Why?" I asked him, truly bewildered.

"HIGH WINDS ON THE LONG ISLAND EXPRESSWAY!" he shouted into the phone. "NOT SAFE! NOT SAFE!" And then he hung up.

The air was perfectly still that day. And so was I.

He never came back to work, and I never found out what had happened to him. He just vanished.

I was making $90 a week at that job. Your grandpa, who was working for the manufacturer's rep at that point, needed an assistant to shuffle papers. He offered me the job. It paid $100 a week.

So for ten bucks, I left the world of air-conditioning and refrigeration and became a Wethead.

Inside guy vs. outside guy

So your grandpa sits me at a desk and gives me office supplies, a coffee cup, and an ashtray. It's August 17, 1970 and I'm wearing a tie. I'm not allowed to talk to customers on the phone, which is a good thing because I don't have anything worthwhile to say. I am a young Bob Cratchit, shuffling papers. Your grandpa is Scrooge.

I realize that he has to be Scrooge because we are the first father/son team ever hired at this company. He tells me that I was not an easy hire because there was a concern about nepotism. He might treat me with kid gloves.

No worries there, he treats me like a fresh recruit in basic training.

I was commuting the few miles to work and back with him day after day. We even went home for lunch to save on food money. Your grandma would make us sandwiches, usually bologna on white bread. We would scarf them down and then catch a few minutes of *Search for Tomorrow* with her. She had been following that soap opera like a disciple since she carried me in her womb. She really cared about what might happen to Joanne and Stew. She loved stories.

Back at the office, I was living a recurring Search for Today as I tried to figure out what was going on in this business. We were manufacturers' representatives. We sold heating products and plumbing products, and my father and I (sort of) guided the NIBCO portion of that business. I learned that NIBCO was an acronym for the Northern Indiana Brass Company. I had never been to Indiana but I knew what they made because your grandpa had taught me how to solder when I was a boy. I also had a Plumbing merit badge from Boy Scout Troup 91, which I earned at 12 years old, and which still sits here on my desk.

We didn't stock NIBCO's products. The factory shipped all the fittings and valves directly to the wholesalers. Our job was to accept orders from the wholesalers, write those orders by hand, mail them to the factory, and then open the factory's mail each day and record what they had shipped and when.

So I had this mindless job of reading one list of items and transferring that list onto another page. I'd make mistakes. Your grandpa would land on me like a falling oak tree.

One day I wandered out to the warehouse where the company kept a very small supply of copper fittings, which the outside salesmen used for samples. I picked up a half-inch copper elbow and carried it back to my desk. I liked the way it blinked brown and shiny in the florescent light. I found myself playing absentmindedly with that copper elbow. I stuck my pinkie through it and felt its smoothness. I remember wondering how they got it to be that smooth. I had never been to a factory. I could only wonder.

In the days that followed, and mostly out of boredom, I began to think more and more about that simple copper elbow. I picked it up and held it to my nose. Copper has a particular odor that's unlike anything else. It reminded me of the taste I'd get in my mouth when I ran hard on autumn days during touch football games. That simple copper elbow reminded me of friends who had moved away years before.

As the days went by I started to think about where the copper came from. I imagined a mine in Chile or some other exotic place I would probably never get to visit. Chile was in the news a lot back then and I read that they had copper. I thought of the men who went down into the earth and clawed the copper from the rocks. I imagined their skin to be as brown as the copper itself. I wondered what their lives were like, if they had wives and children, and if their children would someday work in the mines, too.

I began to think about the ore and how the copper got from the mines to the smelters and then (in what form?) to the factory in Elkhart, Indiana. I thought of the ships that must carry the ore northward, and the men who piloted those ships. I wondered if they got bored staring at the sea and their instruments day after day. I thought of these things as I made my check marks on the customers' orders: One hundred number 607 copper elbows shipped, size, half-inch. Two hundred number 611 copper-by-copper tees, size, three-quarter inch. I checked them all, and wondered if this was how my life was to be.

When the copper got to Elkhart it had to be unloaded and someone must be doing that hard work right now I imagined. I tried to picture what those men looked like. How big were their arms? Did they stop on their way home and drink beer and complain about the boss while their wives waited for them with crying children. I figured these men had much in common with the men who mined the copper. I tried to imagine them meeting in some roadhouse on a gray Midwestern afternoon. Would they recognize each other?

I thought about the machines at the factory that were powerful enough to bash copper into the shape of an elbow, or a tee, or a threaded union. How much force would it take to do that? And what would it sound like? And who invented and built that machine? And what did it weigh? And who figured all of this out on paper?

I closed my eyes and tried to imagine what it must be like to go to work in that factory day after day after day, knowing you would probably be doing this for the rest of your life. I imagined what it might feel like to be a former, small-town football hero who has now grown a potbelly. He does this work every day in the Heartland of America. The crowds no longer cheer. He has only the pounding of the machinery, and that pounding must be relentless.

And then I thought of the constant buzzing of the semi's wheels as it races along Interstate 80 on its way to New York City with the copper fittings. The driver stares as far as his headlights will allow through a bug-splattered windshield. He smokes an unfiltered cigarette, and a country song plays softly on the radio. The driver stubs out the butt, and then lights another as the miles fly out from under his heavy truck. He thinks about his wife, who is as far away as next week.

And in New York City, a young man drives a forklift onto the back of another truck and unloads the fittings into his boss's warehouse. He has a date that night with a girl he will someday marry. He's not thinking about the copper, only about the girl.

The fittings sit on the wholesaler's shelf for a while and quietly gather dust. One day a heating contractor picks up a heavy cardboard box filled with fittings and a half-dozen other items and tosses it all into the back of his old van. He goes from job to job, making repairs and installing new equipment, and on one Tuesday morning, he reaches into the box and comes out with a simple copper elbow. He cleans the inside of the fitting with a stiff wire brush, swabs some flux over it, and slips it onto the end of a bright copper tube. He never stops to think of how precise that fit is. He never considers what has gone into the mating of fitting and tube. People working all over the world have played a part in this precision, but none of them give much thought to this mating. They just go to work every day and do their repetitive tasks. Just like me. We will never meet.

The contractor touches a spark to the end of his torch and watches the fire pop to life. He holds the flame to the base of the fitting and waits. The gas, which once slept deep in the earth, kisses the copper in a way that is as old as creation.

When he has finished his work, the contractor lets water surge through the tubing and around that simple copper elbow. He packs up his tools and walks out to his truck. He's going to take his young son to a basketball game that night.

That evening, a homeowner sits and reads his newspaper in his warm living room. His wife watches television and his children do their homework. The man casually flips past a small article about trouble in a copper mine somewhere in a country that is too far away to concern him. He wets his fingertip and flips the page.

Those were the thoughts brought on by boredom. The years of flipping through those pages and tracking the moving of those copper fittings across American were like years in a monastery. There was much time to think.

And then I'd get smacked upside my head by your grandpa. It was the nepotism thing. If I was looking too dreamy, he'd use the skills he'd honed as an Army sergeant during his war. I'd come to attention.

And the, each day, as we drove home, I would go dark. I didn't want to talk. I just wanted to smolder. Why I had I agreed to take this job? Why?

And then he'd say, "Well, son, how's that son-of-a-bitch boss treating you?" And he'd reach over with his meaty fist and lay a good one on my thigh, just above my knee. And I'd curse and then laugh, and limp a bit when I got out of the car. And we'd be okay again. Just father and son again. Until the morning.

I miss him terribly.

Reps gain and lose lines. It's just the way it is, and there came a point where NIBCO decided to go another way. The company made your grandpa the service manager and warehouse manager, and they moved me into the heating side of the business.

I talked to customers now, mainly the wholesalers, who called to place orders, but there were also the contractors, who called in with their problems. I was reading a lot at this point. I've never taken an engineering course, but there was a library of old books spread throughout the place and I picked them up, one at a time and read them whenever I could.

We had a switchboard out in the lobby, and Maggie, an elderly woman who wore long shirts and high collars, pulled cords and plugged outside into inside all day long. It seems so very old-fashioned when I think about it now, but it wasn't that long ago - just the early '70s. I was answering about 80 calls a day, and so were the two other guys who worked what they called "inside sales." We weren't really salesmen, though; we were order takers. There's a big difference.

The phone would ring. I'd answer, make notes, hang up and try to do what I was supposed to do with that customer's request. But then the phone would ring again. So I'd answer again. And that was our day. Call after call, like waves crashing on a beach.

The outside salesmen would stop by and come in with their nice suits and their questions. We mostly hated these guys because they dressed better than we did and they had company cars and expense accounts. They went to lunch with customers and drank lots of booze, which was okay because that's how business got done in those days. They'd have questions for us, but the phones kept ringing and the pressure kept mounting.

And here's the thing I remember: We inside guys thought of the customers as adversaries. The guy who was calling was keeping us from doing something we were supposed to do for the guy who had called before this guy called. It was an ocean filled with demands and we longed for a day when customers would just stop calling. We could get so much done if it wasn't for these customers.

And, not-so-secretly, we longed for the day when we might also be outside salesmen, so we could slide into quiet company cars, go drink booze with customers, bring back big orders, and get huge raises at year's end.

And sure enough, the day arrived when I graduated from inside sales to outside sales and I could not have been happier. They gave me a brand-new Chevy, a credit card for gasoline, another credit card for phone calls. They also gave me an expense account and a company credit card so I could buy good food and booze for customers. And best of all, I could now get away from that wave after wave of annoying phone calls from customers.

I was an outside guy now.

So put on my new suit and got into the car, and then I sat there for awhile, trying to figure out what to do next. The phone wasn't ringing. There were no outside salesmen telling me what they needed me to do for them. It was just me, my suit, my briefcase filled with office supplies, my catalogs, my brand-new Chevy, and my Hagstrom atlases spilling over with the roads of Long Island, New York City, and Westchester County.

The phone wasn't ringing. No one was telling me what to do.

I had to plan my own day.

So I drove to a contractor who had an office nearby and knocked on his door. He was busy and couldn't see me.

No problem. I drove to a fuel-oil dealer who did a lot of service and bought a lot of parts from a local wholesaler. He was also too busy to see me.

I went to the wholesaler and watched lots of inside guys talking on phones, taking care of customers. The counter men were running around. No one had time to see me.

I went back to our office. My boss asked what I was doing there. "No one in here is going to give you an order, Dan," he said. "Get back out on the road."

So I got back into my car and sat there, trying to figure it out.

And that's the difference between Inside Sales and Outside Sales. Once outside, I realized the customer was not an adversary, looking to take up all of my time. The customer was the reason we were in business, and more important, he was not mine. I had to find him, convince him I was worth seeing, and then try to earn his business. I got it, but I couldn't make it happen. I fumbled with it for months but got nowhere.

My boss realized I wasn't ready and pulled me back inside. I was fortunate because he could have fired me. He didn't and that gave me a few years to change the way I saw the world and the people who bought what we were selling. I now understood the difference between an order taker and a salesman, and I knew why those outside guys made more money than I was making. They were the ones who were making the phones ring.

I wasn't.

And nothing happens unless somebody sell something.

They gave me another shot at the outside world a few years later. This time, it stuck.

Life-changing Advice

Erin, advice sometimes comes unsolicited, and other times it comes after you've asked for it (if you're lucky). I have been very lucky with some of the advice I received over the years. And I was especially lucky that the most important advice came when I was young. This advice changed my life.

Never say no.

I went on my first big-deal, manufacturers-rep business trip in 1978, which had me all agog. We were attending a convention in Atlantic City, NJ and the first casino had just opened. I felt like one of the big kids.

I was having dinner with a bunch of people from the companies we represented, and sitting next to me was the president of one of those big companies. We were a few drinks into the dinner and I asked him what advice he would give a person my age.

"Never say no," he said without hesitating. "If you say no to your boss or to your customers, they'll go find someone who will say yes."

That seemed simple enough but I was young and quite dumb at the time so I asked my second question: "But what if I don't know how to make yes happen?"

"Just say yes and then go find what you have to do to get it done."

"Oh."

Position the sharing of knowledge.

"Is there anything else I should know?" I asked.

I remember again how he didn't pause before answering. It was as if he had been waiting for someone to ask this. "Yes," he said. "If you have knowledge that can help your career, and holding back that knowledge for a while won't hurt your company, then keep it to yourself until a time arrives when sharing it will do the most good for you. Always position the sharing of knowledge. Don't just give it away freely. It has value. Make the most of it."

This was coming from the guy who was president of a company we represented. Gosh.

I've been thinking about that advice for all these years. I've considered it so many times as I've watched people wrangle their careers. I've watched people take the ideas of others and run with them. I've listened to people who lost control of their good ideas complain about the raw deal they got, and how this or that stinker got ahead of them by using their ideas. I've seen people go to their graves carrying that anger with them.

It seems to me that if a company creates a culture where everyone is rewarded when the company prospers then the advice the company president gave me in Atlantic City wouldn't be sound advice. But he was a professional executive, a guy who had sat in many leather chairs over the years. He had moved around a lot, and always toward a better position for himself.

I think he knew that internal competition is the fuel that feeds the engine of most companies. He was being honest, and holding back that knowledge from me wasn't going to affect his career one way or the other, so that's why he said what he said.

And I've been thinking about that every day since then.

You'll be 36 anyway.

I was 30 years old and in this business for a decade. Your sisters, Kelly and Meghan were keeping us busy, and you and Colleen were on your way. Your mother hadn't had a paying job since Kelly arrived, and I was working like a sled dog at three jobs. I thought that if I could go to college and get a degree in something (it turned out to be Sociology, which is the best degree there is for this business) then I would be able to do better for all of us. But it would take me six years of nights, weekends, and summers to get that that degree, and it would be tough work since I still had to pull that sled during the day.

I mentioned this to the wife of a friend who was about 15 years older than I was at the time. "If I go back to school part-time, I won't graduate until I'm thirty-six years old," I whined.

"So?" she said, "In six years you're going be thirty-six anyway, with or without a degree. Your choice."

"Oh."

Decide.

A remarkable woman named Alice Kessler-Harris was my professor in a history course I took during those six years. She had us read a series of books, divided into brilliant pairs. Each pair examined an historical event from totally opposite perspectives. For instance, consider two books about the career of Lyndon Johnson. One is wildly supportive of the former president; the other is brutally critical. Both books are scholarly and absolutely convincing, and the reader comes away quite confused. Week after week, Professor Kessler-Harris explained how the victors write the history and that truth is as malleable as taffy. It all depends on one's perspective. I got it.

My term paper was about the Cuban Missile Crisis. I spent weeks in the library, researching and documenting. I wrote logically and methodically, presenting the case from all sides. I turned it in, expecting an A.

The paper came back to me with no grade but there was a short note written in blood-red ink at the top margin. It read, "NO DICE! See me."

"I made my case from all perspectives," I told Professor Kessler-Harris. "What's wrong?"

"You didn't *decide*," she said.

"About what?" I sputtered.

"About the *truth*," she said.

"But truth is as malleable as taffy! That's been the focus of this whole course. That's what you taught us. I believed you. That's what I've learned from reading all those books that come at issues from opposite poles."

"But what is *your* truth, Dan?" she said. "What do *you* think? What have *you* decided after doing your research? A good citizen must be well-educated, but a good citizen much also decide. You haven't."

She gave me the weekend to rethink and rewrite. I worked like a maniac. I made decisions and I supported them well enough to get an A on the paper.

You stuck on something. Don't know what to do?

Decide.

Take a chance.

Two years after I graduated, I took a hard look at my job. I had been with the rep for 18 years. I liked it there and I was making a decent salary. I had company-paid insurance and a company car but I also had you and your sisters, and you were all growing like corn. It dawned on me that in 2000 you would all be in college at the same time. I would have two freshmen, a sophomore and a senior (and that's how it turned out). How was I to afford that?

I went to my boss with this dilemma and asked if there was any possibility that I might someday buy into the company so I could do right by my children, as he had done right by his children. He explained that I would always have a good job there but I could never own a piece of the rock because there was family involved. I asked him what he would do if he was me, and just like that company president in Atlantic City, he didn't hesitate. "I'd quit," he said.

"And do what?" I asked.

"That's for you to decide, Dan," he said. "But I can tell you this for certain. *Nothing* is ever going to happen for you unless *you're* willing to take a chance."

I decided, said YES, and arranged a time to leave that was right for both the company and me (I gave six-months notice). We stayed friends.

Nothing happens for you unless *you're* willing to take a chance.

So true.

My first seminar, and Ray's advice

And speaking of taking a chance, years before I left to go out on my own, I decided to do a seminar for the contractors. My dream was to do a bunch of seminars, but starting with one is a good place to begin, so I got permission, reserved our conference room, which held about 30 large people, and made a mailing to the local contractors.

We decided to charge $25 for this magnificent seminar because if you give training away for free most contractors will think it's not worth anything. The mailing was so incredible that we sold out the class in a couple of days. My boss was delighted.

So now I had to go do it. I set up the room with the overhead projector and the blackboard. I even got fresh chalk. I scheduled the seminar to start at 9 AM and conclude with cheers at 5 PM. I did this without realizing what a very long time eight hours is, even if we stopped for lunch and coffee breaks. I was a world-class idiot.

Anyway, I began at exactly 9 AM because I believe that being prompt is a virtue. I had all my notes and overhead slides in place, right there on the desk in front of me. The blackboard was over there and the new chalk was in the tray. So far, so good. I would speak for the entire day.

Okay, hang on.

Here we go!

At precisely 10:15 AM (I remember this because I glanced at my watch) I realized that I had shared with the contractors absolutely *everything* that I knew about steam heating. My head was empty. The only thing left was my foolish grin.

"Are there any questions?" I asked, hoping the group would have answerable questions that I could stretch toward five o'clock, which seemed as far away as Australia.

And that's when I met Ray Combs.

Ray was sitting in the back row. He was much older than me and very dry behind his ears. He raised his hand and said, "Dan, would you please explain the difference between a condensate pump and a boiler-feed pump?"

"A condensate pump and a boiler-feed pump," I said, never having heard of either device before that moment. "A condensate pump and a boiler-feed pump?"

"Yes." Ray said, "A condensate pump and a boiler-feed pump."

"You want to know the difference, right?"

"Yes," he said. "The difference."

"Well," I said, "one pumps condensate. You can tell that by its name. And the other feeds a boiler. It's a boiler-feed pump so it feeds. A boiler. Right? One pumps. The other feeds."

"You don't know the difference, do you?" Ray said. "You never heard of either of those common components of a steam-heating system, have you? You don't know what the hell I'm talking about, do you?"

He waited for me to answer.

"And you really don't know what the hell you're talking about either, do you?" he said.

Now here comes the scary part. Ray shook his head, sighed, got up, and walked to the front of the room, held out his hand for the chalk, which I handed him. "Take a seat in the back, kid, and I'll explain the difference to these people. That's what they paid for. And don't get up here again until you know what you're talking about."

That was Ray's advice.

I scurried back to his former seat, sat down and tried to disappear. Ray taught the rest of the class off the cuff, and he did a great job. I now knew what a condensate pump was, and what a boiler-feed pump was, and the difference between the two, and how to size them under just about any condition imaginable.

My boss came in to watch for a while. He looked at me and at Ray and I tried to get smaller. At one point, I disappeared entirely. But before I did, I promised myself that this would never happen to me again.

Ray Combs taught me a fine lesson that day and I was lucky to learn it at an early age. I should *never* open my mouth in front of a group unless I know what I'm talking about.

And I should understand how very long eight hours is.

I studied hard after that, mostly out of pure terror, and I think I got better. Years later, Ray returned to one of my seminars. When he walked in, I felt nauseous. He sat quietly through the whole day, never asking a question. At the end, he came up to me and said, "That's better, kid." And then he just walked away.

Ray had a brutal brand of kindness, one that did not suffer fools. He knew that anyone teaching has a responsibility to the audience, and that anyone speaking or writing from a position of authority has a responsibility to the listener and to the reader. I think that every young person who thinks he knows it all should have a guy like Ray Combs land on him like a Mosler safe, and the earlier in life that this occurs, the better.

More years went by and I was in business for myself and speaking at a big trade show at the Hynes Center in downtown-Boston. The subject was steam heating, of course, and I had about 500 contractors in the audience. On my way in, I spotted my old boss, who was now retired and living in Boston. I hadn't seen him in more than 10 years. We made a date to have dinner that evening. I left him in the back of the room with my contractor buddy, Al Levi.

Before I began the seminar, I drew the group's attention to my old boss, sitting there in the back with Al. I told of how he had raised me in the business, and how he had believed in me at a time when I needed that most. I didn't tell the story of that first steam seminar and how he had watched Ray deliver the seminar I was supposed to be doing. The group gave my old boss a round of applause and he beamed.

After the applause died down, Al said, "So how do you like the way he turned out?"

With a twinkle in his eye, my old boss said, "He turned out just fine. But the birthing was difficult."

He's gone now, and so is Ray, but I'm going to keep trying to please both of those guys. I owe them. They delivered very tough, but also very good, advice, and at just the right time for me.

Thanks, gentlemen.

Uncle Tony's advice

Erin, you never saw my Uncle Tony that much, but you might remember him as a sweet old guy. He was your grandma's little brother and always great to me when I was a boy, and as a kid in this business.

I didn't think it would be appropriate to bring a dozen Dunkin' Donuts when I went to pay my respects to Uncle Tony at his wake, so I let it slide. The fact that he was dead was the only reason I could get away with that lack-of-donuts indiscretion, but it still felt odd.

The first time I called on Uncle Tony at the Long Island supply house where he worked for a good long time I was a young rep with a significant amount of moisture behind my ears. I was astonishingly stupid in those days, which is why I walked in without the donuts. Uncle Tony greeted me with a hearty, "*Danny!* How *are* you, kid? How's my sister?" He even gave me a hug.

Then he leaned around me, both sides. He stepped back, looked at the top of my head and then my feet and everything in between, and then again at my hands. "Where are the donuts?" he asked.

"I'm supposed to bring donuts?" I said.

Uncle Tony looked from me to Mel, the other counterman. Mel glanced at me, shook his head sadly, and walked away down an aisle. Then Uncle Tony looked at the contractors who were waiting at the counter. They all looked at me like I was something just whipped from a shoe. They shook their heads. Idiot.

And here's what happened next: Uncle Tony, who had the agility of a squirrel in those days, came around the counter like the place was on fire. He never stopped moving. He just grabbed my arm as he went by with this meaty hand that felt like a four-foot wrench. He swept me out the front door and onto the sidewalk.

"*Never* come in here without the donuts," he said.

"You're kidding," I sputtered

"HEY!" he snapped, pointing a rock-hard finger at my mouth, which did the right thing by closing immediately. "*DONUTS*," he snarled. Then he went back inside. I stood on the sidewalk, a hydronics orphan.

And then I went looking for a Dunkin' Donuts.

That first sales call on Uncle Tony actually went better than it might have, but that was only because he was my mother's little brother. And he loved me. In the years that followed, I'd creep into that place, one soft step at a time, and always armed with two-dozen donuts.

I was in there one day when a contractor stopped by to ask Uncle Tony for some advice. The guy was going on and on about this problem job, and about how many times he had tried to get it right, but it just wasn't working like it should. This was during the days before we had an Internet. When a contractor got into trouble on a job, the only true place he could go for answers, if he didn't have a relative also in the business, was to his wholesaler. The wholesaler knew everything.

Uncle Tony stood there listening to this guy. He was as quiet and still as cast-iron pipe. Every now and then he'd give a twitch of a nod. The more Uncle Tony listened, the more the contractor talked. Finally, Uncle Tony held out the palm of his right hand like a cop stopping traffic. "Is this going to take much longer?" he asked.

"Wadda ya mean?" the contractor asked.

"The *story*. Is it going to take much *longer*?"

"Yeah, a little bit longer," the contractor said.

"Minutes, hours, or days?"

"I don't know yet," the contractor said.

"Okay, then hang on," Uncle Tony said. He reached under the counter and came up with a fuzzy blanket and a Teddy Bear that some kid had left in the place years ago when the kid's parents were in there looking at sinks. Uncle Tony climbed up onto the counter, stretched out, nuzzled the Teddy bear, pulled the blanket up around his chin, and said to the contractor, "Please. Go on." And then he stuck his thumb in his mouth and started to suck.

The contractor stood there with eyes as big as manhole covers.

And that's what I was thinking about when I was kneeling at his coffin. I was thinking about what a wonderfully wacky business this is, where grown men could do stuff like that and be loved for it.

Your grandpa and Uncle Tony used to work together at the Manhattan supply house. Go to that neighborhood now and you won't believe there used to be such a place on that swanky, Upper-Eastside block. Uncle Tony moved way out onto Long Island and took a job at the place I've been telling you about.

John Hassett, the man who owned Uncle Tony's supply house was an old fellow who looked like he was made from the spare parts of a half-dozen Muppets. He was worth about a zillion dollars but he didn't spend a penny of his fortune on clothes or hygiene. From time to time, he'd need things that he didn't carry at his Long Island supply house, so he'd get in his car, which was as weary as he was, and he'd drive to Manhattan, to your grandpa's place.

"Nobody knew who he was," your grandpa would say. "He looked like a landfill. He'd stand at the counter and the guys would wait on everybody except him. They didn't know who he was. He'd just stand there, as patient as death. But whenever I'd spot him, I'd leave my office and go wait on him. I'd call him Mister Hassett, get all his stuff together, carry it out to his old beater and put it in the trunk, and the back seat, and the front seat. Or wherever else it fit. I'd chat a bit with him, show him the respect he deserved, tell him to please give my best to Tony and Mel. I always came away with a tip that was bigger than my weekly paycheck."

Your grandpa told me to learn this lesson: In this business, *never* judge people by the way they look.

Good advice.

I'm calling on Uncle Tony another time and this contractor is asking him questions about a job where he had been replacing part after part, but he still doesn't know what 's wrong, proving once again that *everyone* gets to work on heating systems in this country.

Time goes by and Uncle Tony is once again being deathly quiet and occasionally twitching his head up and down. I'm waiting for the blanket and the teddy bear to appear, and sure enough, up comes the palm to stop the guy's words.

"You, my friend, are today's winner!" Uncle Tony says. "You can stop right there."

"Wadda ya mean?" the contractor says.

"Here," Uncle Tony says, handing the guy a toy sheriff's badge. "You may wear this for the rest of the day. But be sure to bring it back tomorrow."

The guy looks at the badge, which has a piece of masking tape over its front. On the masking tape, written with a thick, black, felt-tipped marker, are the letters D and F.

The guy looks at the badge and then pins it on his shirt. He gives Uncle Tony a goofy smile and says, "What does D.F. stand for?"

"Think about it," Uncle Tony says.

The guy thinks for a good long moment and then says, "Oh." And then he cracks up laughing.

We all laughed. Uncle Tony helped the guy, of course. He gave him the advice he needed and the right parts, just as he had done with the Teddy-bear guy. That was the thing about Uncle Tony and those times. There was a lot of ball-busting and skin seemed to be much thicker then. I think that had to do with there not being an Internet. Contractors had fewer places to go back then, and their wholesalers were the technical centers of their universe, the place where you went for advice.

Back then.

And as much as I cherish those memories, I'm not sure Uncle Tony could get away with all of that stuff if he were working today. That's sad in a way, but it's also the nature of our business. Times change and so does the technology. People retire. They grow old and sometimes lose their memories, as Uncle Tony did, but what's nice is that they leave others behind to remember them.

I remember him well, and I hope you will, too, through these stories, Erin.

I really should have brought the donuts to his wake, though.

Hydronics taught me the power of story

I had my first exposure to the Hydronics Institute when it was still the Institute of Boiler and Radiation Manufacturers and I was working for the rep. My boss tasked me with passing out these cardboard counter-cards to the local wholesalers to spread the word that the I=B=R school was coming to town. I'd get permission to shove some stuff out of the way on the counters, open the easel back, place the card in a good spot, and hope for the best.

This was at a time when only NASA and universities had computers. The rest of us had thick binders, filled with tables and charts, and that's what the two-day I=B=R class was all about. And they filled quickly because hardly anyone was doing any generic teaching in those days. If you wanted things straight-up, and without a manufacturer's sales pitch, this seemed to be the place to be.

Having done so well with my pass-out-the-counter-cards duty, they asked me to be a proctor at a class in Rockville Centre, Long Island. I learned a lot that day, and much of it influenced the direction of my career.

We began on time. Each student had his or her thick binder, note paper and pencils. The instructor, an older gent named Ozzie, told everyone to open to the first page in the binder. Everyone did as told. Ozzie next placed a clear plastic slide of that page on the deck of his overhead projector. And then he read what was on the page.

People listened.

"Please turn the page," Ozzie said. The students did so. He read this page.

"Please turn the page." More reading.

And so it went, hour after hour.

He was speaking to people who were used to being in trucks, and attics, and basements. They were used to moving. Few, if any, had gone to college. Few were fans of mathematics. Many, I believe, were dyslexic. I watched closely as the hours slogged by. Some students didn't come back after lunch. Others didn't show up the next day. Many dozed off. Ozzie kept reading. He had blessed information, delivered poorly.

Those two days hit me so hard. I remember them so clearly. At the end of that class, I decided that if I ever got the chance to speak to, or write to, these people, I would do it all through story, and not through numbers. I would try to bring concepts screaming to life, and to make this stuff both real and fun for them.

And, Erin, my memories of this class are not at all negative. I owe my career largely to what I saw during those two days, and what I realized as a proctor for the I=B=R school: Contractors who do the work learn differently from engineers who design the systems. I've have tried my best ever since to bridge the two groups.

I've watched many speakers since then. Bell & Gossett's Gil Carlson, who smoked constantly while lecturing to engineers, and always sat at his overhead projector with his head down, was fascinating to watch. His bosses at B&G had sent him to a class to learn how to speak more effectively, sort of a hydronics charm school.

The instructor there told Gil that he needed to make eye contact and to smile more at his audience, so this is what he did. About every five minutes, Gil would pause in his talk and push himself up into a crouching position. He'd take the butt out of his mouth, smile like a clown in the circus, and beam that smile left, right, left across the room, like some crazy hydronic searchlight. It was quite startling. The engineers in the audience would look at each other and then back at Gil, who by now, was again seated and talking.

Five minutes later, he'd do it again.

And again.

That was his style. He was doing what his coaches had advised him to do. Good job, Gil!

Hoffman Specialty had a guy names Joe Flash (and isn't that just the best name ever for a teacher?). We called him Jumpin' Joe Flash because he thought he was a gas, gas, gas.

He taught Hoffman's steam-heating class, and I learned a lot from him, too, but he was a man of the '50's, and he thought that no seminar should start or end, and no coffee break should begin or conclude without him first telling the filthiest joke you can possibly imagine. And Jumpin' Joe Flash had plenty of them.

Just us boys here, right? I cringed at each one. I'm still cringing after all these years. Ouch.

But that was his style.

There were many others, and each had his or her own style. When I was going to college at night, I had a professor who would say, "If you will" at the end of every other sentence. "The meaning of this, if you will..." and on and on. It was so distracting that the people in the class actually ran a pool to see how many times she would say those words. At the start of each class, each of us put in a buck. Two people kept count. Whoever guessed closest to the actual amount of if-you-wills, won the pot. We did this for an entire semester and she never found out. It was the only way we could keep from screaming.

Her style.

All of which got me thinking about how we learn best. Consider the film industry and the TV industry. Think about printed books, electronic books, audio books and magazines. And social media, of course. How many hours a day do we spend staring at screens?

And do you know why we do this?

We all crave stories, Erin.

I fell in love with your grandpa's stories when I was a boy, and the contractors' stories in the years that followed. One was better than the next, and I used many of these stories when I was doing my seminars.

One stands out. I was doing a seminar in a city I can no longer remember. A guy came up to me during a break and told me a story. It was such a good story, so funny in parts, and it made the point I had been trying to make so well that I thanked him and embraced it.

A week later, I was in a different city with the same seminar. When I got to the part where I had to make that point, I used the guy's story instead of the one I had been telling. They absolutely loved it! I smiled, quietly thanked the guy who had told it to me, and moved on.

So now this story was going to be a permanent part of my seminar, and since I have a fine imagination, I stared to change it a bit. I did a little nip here, a little tuck there. That's okay because I'm a writer and a teacher, and stories are word tools.

Years passed and the story truly became my own. I had added fur and feathers to it. I had put wheels and wings on it and painted it a hundred colors. It got better with age and the people who were coming to my seminars were learning from it and never forgetting what they had learned. That's the power of a great story. It teaches.

Even more years passed and one day I found myself back in the same city where the guy told me the original story. I had met so many people in the intervening years, and this guy had blended into all of them, like smoke in the wind.

I got to the point in my seminar where I launched into the story and noticed this guy sitting up front. He was giving me the strangest look. I continued with the story, which was now *my* story, and he started to squirm a bit in his chair.

And that's when I made the connection. He was *the guy*.

Crap.

But I had already jumped out of the plane and there was no going back, so I just continued to the end and called a coffee break (always have a great story, and not a filthy joke, just before a coffee break).

The guy scurries up to me and introduces himself. He tells me that he had taken my seminar years before. I smiled and said, "Welcome back!"

"You know that story you just told?" he said.

"Yes," I gulped.

"Well, you're not going to believe this, but a similar thing once happened to me!" And then he launched into the original story, which I listened to with even more appreciation.

I kept the rest of that story-morphing business to myself.

Erin, this is one of those cases where, if someone says to you, "You can't make this stuff up," you should just smile and say, "Why, *sure* you can!"

We writers call that poetic license.

Or borrowing.

Or research.

Oh, and this story I just told you. It's absolutely true of course.

Of *course* it is!

How to get good ideas

Years ago, when I was working for the rep, I had the job of writing a monthly newsletter for contractors. My name wasn't on the thing and I wrote in the third-person, corporate "We" voice, as in, "We were on a job with a contactor the other day when we ran into this interesting challenge." I was storytelling and I never thought I'd run out of things to say, but after a few months, I hit rock bottom.

I remember the day it happened. I just got to the point where I thought I had written everything I could possibly say about troubleshooting, strange problems, bizarre incidents, mechanical mayhem, history, you name it. I was empty and I was in a panic because my boss still expected that newsletter to go out once a month to about 5,000 people. I didn't know where to turn.

That's when James Webb Young came into my life. Mr. Young had been a copywriter for J. Walter Thompson, the big advertising agency, when he wrote a famous ad called, The Curve of a Woman's Arm. It was 1919 and the ad was for a product called Odorono. And I think that's a delightful name for underarm deodorant, which was something brand-new at the time. A tough sell, but he did it.

Mr. Young went on to teach business history and advertising at the University of Chicago, and out of that came his little book, *A Technique for Producing Ideas*, which I came across while wandering through my local library, looking for inspiration. I took the book home and read it in an hour. That was the last time I ever suffered from writer's block, and it's the last time I was unable to come up with ideas (some have been better than others). Reading that little book opened doors for me because it made me think differently, and see the world differently. It taught me how to connect bits of thoughts into good ideas. I continue to use his technique every day.

Here's a shorter version of what he wrote in five simple steps:

1. Gather raw material constantly This first step requires you to open your eyes and really pay attention to the world around you. Notice the way other businesses get your attention. Take note of things that please you and things that annoy you. Look for problems because within every problem there is a new business. Notice things.

For instance, I don't like waiting on lines. I was in a Holiday Inn the other day and they had this special line for Priority Club members. I like that because it saves me time. I also liked it when we went to Disneyworld and found that we didn't have to wait on line if we took advantage of their no-wait system. I think that's absolutely brilliant.

I also love the EZ-Pass method of paying tolls. I just zip through while others have to wait. And I can now pay for parking at the airports with my EZ-Pass. I can see a time not long from now when we won't be carrying cash.

Look at problems and then look for solutions in other areas that are not apparent at first.

Gather raw material constantly on things you like and don't like. Do this everywhere you go, and take notes, lest you forget. I carry index cards and a pen with me wherever I go. I'm constantly noticing things and jotting them down.

2. Combine old elements in new ways. Consider chewable vitamins. How about baby thermometers in the shape of pacifiers? Or disposable diapers. I wish I had come up with just one of those ideas. Cruise control. Outdoor reset. Flexible plastic tubing. All simple combinations of old elements. New ways of thinking about things lead to new products. Cell phones evolved from car phones, which evolve from house phones and radios.

I've often wondered why Kodak didn't invent the digital camera. It was probably because the idea of a digital camera threatened their film processing business. Missing that one put them out of business.

Why didn't the U.S. Postal Service invent FedEx? When you're involved in a routine and doing okay business the same way from day to day, you seldom stop to combine old elements into something new. You get stuck in a rut and often miss the possibilities of looking at ordinary things in new ways.

3. Go do something else for a while. Once you spend some time playing the "What if?" game with yourself, put it all out of your mind and go do something else for a while. Just let that stew of good stuff simmer in the back of your brain. You're cooking ideas and that takes time.

Mr. Young didn't mention rhythm in his little book, but I've found that while I'm doing something else for a while, and waiting for my good idea to marinate, it pays to do something rhythmic. I'll take a walk, or I'll sit in a chair and rock. I don't know why it is, but the rhythm of repetitive motion puts me into a creative frame of mind. I've spoken to others about this and they've told me that they like to bounce a ball, go for a run, swing a golf club, or swim laps while they're waiting for ideas to arrive. Try it; you'll see what I mean.

4. Wait for the idea to come. This is the hardest part, but be patient and just wait. Do other things in the meantime. Your idea will come. It may take a day or it may take a week. It may come in the middle of the night (always keep pen and paper near your bed), but it *will* come. Promise.

5. Take the idea to friends for their review. Once you get the idea, think it through for a while and then take it to some friends and ask for their opinion. They'll see your idea in slightly different ways and they'll make suggestions that you can either accept or reject. Most of the time my friends make my ideas better than I was able to make them.

It's a simple technique but a very powerful one. Give it a try and you'll see what I mean. It was Mr. Young's gift to me many years ago, and now it's my gift to you.

Clustering

It was at this same time that I discovered Gabriele Rico's book, *Writing the Natural Way*. She taught me how to write by first putting together a cluster diagram. This is a non-linear way of dumping all your thoughts on paper. You relax and focus on a topic, and then quickly write *everything* that comes into your mind, regardless of how silly it may seem. Don't stop until you feel empty. The cluster diagram will look like a big bunch of grapes (hence the name).

Most of my writing is for the magazines, or for HeatingHelp.com, and that means it has to fit into a frame. Magazine articles are usually between 1,200 and 1,500 words, because that's how the magazines sell their ads. An advertiser might pay a premium to appear on the page opposite one of my columns. The length of the column assures that it will jump onto the next page, taking the reader with it, and that page will have spaces for advertisers, as will the facing page.

That means that when I sit to write, I have to know how to get in, move forward toward my main point, glancing left and right along the way and commenting, and get out just in time. That doesn't happen on its own. I need a roadmap, which, to a writer, is a good outline.

You learned how to make an outline in grade school, but the problem with the traditional outline is that it is linear. One point follows the next, in a list that is rigid. Gabriele Rico's method of clustering takes that rigid outline and twists it into a non-linear form, and that allows my mind to wander like a bee in a field of wildflowers. I come up with connections (like Step 2. in Mr. Young's formula) that I would probably miss if I was locked into a traditional, linear outline.

This isn't the place to go deeper into how all of this works, but if you're looking for new ideas, and better ways to express those ideas, I urge you to Google Gabriele Rico and read her book.

Talking on paper

In 1972, when I was two years into my time with the manufacturers' rep, and just married to your mother, I discovered Rudolph Flesch and his brand-new book, *Say What You Mean*. The message in that book was that, to be effective, a writer should talk on paper. I took that to heart and stared to write as though I was speaking to just one person, and that person was right there with me. It's you!

Can you feel that?

What was reinforcing this at the time were the public-speaking courses I was taking. I had just finished the Dale Carnegie Course, which changed my life. I was very shy before that course. The teacher asked each of us to stand up, say our name, and tell where we worked. I was terrified and barely able to do that. There were about 20 people in the class and everyone was looking at me. I gulped, stood, mumbled a few words, and quickly sat down.

Twelve weeks later, they couldn't sit me down.

If you're looking to speak and write better, Dale Carnegie is a great place to start.

I followed this with a course in New York City at the American Management Association. It lasted a week and we all had to get up and speak each day. The difference here, though, was that they videotaped us. And this was at a time when videotape was new. It was amazing to see myself on TV. I was doing things I didn't realize and the group picked me to pieces. It made me a better storyteller, and a better presenter.

After that, I joined a local chapter of Toastmasters and spent a few years at their meetings, getting up and speaking to groups of people every week. We were all in the same boat. We helped each other and I got better. It was great preparation for what was to come.

All the while this is going on, I'm working for the manufacturers' rep. I told you earlier about what happened the first time I thought I could do a full-day seminar. Ray Combs came down on me like a Mosler safe, and I learned my lesson about knowing my subject inside and out before I got up in front of a group. And I learned about how to fill the time assigned. Eight hours is a very long time when you're speaking.

Time had gone by and I was now writing *The Problem Solver* newsletter. We sent this for free to about 5,000 contractors in the New York City/Metropolitan area each month. I had gotten the inspiration for *The Problem Solver* from a man I had never met. His name was Ed Tidd and he worked for Bell & Gossett and was gone before I arrived. He left a series of field reports, each printed on green paper and three-hole punched. He called them, Tidd-Bits, and each one was about the length of a magazine column. B&G sent them to their reps. The reports went into a binder and served as great reading because Ed Tidd talked on paper. I could see the job in my mind's eye. I could smell the sweat and experience the triumph of figuring out what was wrong. I wanted to write like that.

So when my boss gave me the chance to write *The Problem Solver* newsletter, I gave him a smile you couldn't remove with a jackhammer.

We didn't have a mailing list so I went to the libraries in and around New York City and hand-copied 5,000 names and addresses out of the various Yellow Pages. My hand still hurts from that. We had the names stamped onto metal plates, which stood back-to-back in long drawers. We'd feed the drawers into a machine that printed the names and addresses on envelopes. Today, that machine seems very steam-punk, but it was the latest and greatest that year.

When I put together my next steam seminar (Post-Ray Combs) I decided to speak it like I was writing. It was going to be all stories and lots of fun. I had had a lot more field experience by then and I wove all of that into the seminar. I was enjoying the tough-guy poetry of Robert Service at the time and decided to try my hand at writing some of my own, which I would then use to open the new steam seminar.

It went like this (and this is a true story. Really!)

Dangerous Dan and the Hole in the Ground

I'll tell you a tale that will keep you spellbound,

Of Dangerous Dan and the Hole in the Ground.

It started out simply on a day just like this,

At a steam seminar I wanted no one to miss,

Especially Pete, who was a plumber by day,

And who wanted to come but his boss said, "No way!"

But I wanted him there for this was Pete's dream.

You see, the plumber by day was a student of steam.

And at night he would sit 'til the first crack of dawn,

With the books and the drawings of a Day Long Gone.

And he studied the steam and the work of Dead Men,

Who had come years before and who weren't there then

To teach him the art he so wanted to know,

So when he heard of this class, well, he just had to go.

So I took up his fight and I spoke to Pete's boss.

I said, "Look at this day as a gain, not a loss.

"How valuable Pete will be after that day!"

And Pete's boss relented, and he said "Okay."

"But have him back Friday or you'll take the heat.

"I've a steam job to do, and for that, I need Pete."

"He's the only one here who can or ever would

Tackle the steam. The others are no good.

Sure they know hot-water, leaky pipes and clogged drains,

But for them, steam has always been too much of a strain.

So I promised sincerely that I'd have Pete back there,

But what I didn't count on was Pete's glassy stare.

Like a small kid at Christmas Pete was at our place,

And I should have known then by the look on his face,

That the very next morning, not giving a whit,

Pete would call up his boss and just simply quit.

"I'm striking out on my own!" Pete said with a scream,

"Now that I know all there is about steam!"

And as he hung up the phone the boss started to gag,

Because he was left there holding the proverbial bag.

So my phone rang that morning at nine.

"I'd kill you, you bum, if I just had the time!"

"But I don't!" said the boss. "I've a steam job to do,

"And no one to do it, thanks to you. Thanks to YOU!"

So I offered to help. Oh yes, there on the job.

"I'll bring my books. You send your mob.

"So what if you men don't know what to do.

"With my books and their tools, somehow we'll get through."

And as I hung up the phone I choked back a sob.

For up until then, I'd never been on a job.

But what was there to it? Why, I had this old book!

Hey, I'll just go down there and take a good look.

But when I got to the job I stared, thunderstruck,

For there on the back of this blue pick-up truck,

And straining the tires down into the mud,

And hissing, and bellowing, and crying for blood,

Sat the meanest and heaviest shape known to man.

"What's *that*?" I asked. "Why, that's the boiler, Dan."

In all of my days I'd never seen such a sight,

And I blinked with my eyes to make sure they saw right.

'Twas a boiler for sure, but I was soon to find,

It was bigger than the one on page ninety-nine.

I'd flipped past that one many times with great ease,

But this beast would soon have me down on my knees.

Yes, we struggled an hour with that son-of-a-gun,

And just when I thought that the battle was won,

The man with the tools asked the kid with the book,

"Where do you want it?" So I took a good look.

And then in my very-most-confident voice,

I said, "Over there is the logical choice."

So we struggled and grunted for ten minutes more,

'Til the beast settled heavily down onto the floor.

And we sat back exhausted. And we all took a break.

As I thought of the decisions I'd soon have to make.

On supplies and returns, and the Hartford Loop, too.

And I opened my book so I'd know what to do.

And I walked to the boiler. And I laid my book down,

When just then my ears heard this crumbling sound.

"Twas the book that had done it. The very last straw!

And that boiler went CRASHING right down through the floor.

Down in the hole the three of us fell,

The boiler, and me, and my textbook as well.

It seems a washing machine, piped into the ground

Had undermined the floor and made it unsound,

And try as I might for the rest of that day,

I could find nothing in my book that would say

What to when a job takes an unfortunate hitch,

So I decided to "pit" that son-of-a-bitch.

"Look here," I said, in a confident voice.

"*This*, after all, is the logical choice.

"With the waterline difference of an inch or two,

"The boiler *belongs* in a pit. It's true!"

And the men gathered 'round me, and they stared at my book,

And each had his turn to take a good look.

And they all started nodding and they laughed with delight,

For the saw by the book that the hook-up was right!

And once they got over their initial alarm,

They piped in that boiler, and it worked like a charm.

And Dangerous Dan was a hero that day.

And the boss called me up, 'cause he wanted to say

That experience *shows*, and this *really* proves it

For he *never* would have thought of digging that pit.

Well, I learned me a lesson from my day in the hole,

A lesson that went to the depths of my soul.

There comes a point in your life where you put the books down,

And you learn all the rest from a hole in the ground.

And it worked. The contractors loved it because most of them had been to seminars that were dry, dull and terribly boring. I began with that epic poem and they didn't know what was going to come next. I followed with story after story and the seminar was a hit.

Word got out and we caught the attention of *Supply House Times* magazine. They sent a reporter to see the seminar and she wrote a story about us, with a nice sidebar about Dangerous Dan, along with some funny photos of me flailing my arms as I preached the glories of steam heating. The magazine also declared us the Manufacturers' Rep of the Year.

My boss smiled. I had (almost) made up for the Ray Combs fiasco.

There's a lot to be said for talking on paper and telling stories.

Ten years or so went by and I became a monthly columnist for *Supply House Times*. Back then, I never dreamed that that would ever happen.

Life is filled with more twists than a fusilli factory, Erin.

The importance of reading widely

You know I read a lot. I read magazines, newspapers, technical books, non-fiction and fiction. Those books take me places I'll never get to visit, and that includes the past. There's so much we can learn about this business from the past, and I find the best lessons come from stories.

Each year, I set out to read at least 100 good books. This is my hobby and also a big part of my job. Writers have to stand in a pounding surf of words and absorb the stories.

In 2011, I decided to read all the books that have ever won the Pulitzer Prize for Fiction. There were 85 of them at the time. They begin in 1918. Some years, such as 2011, had no winner. I decided to read the list from both ends, aiming for the center, which was 1964, a year in which there was no winner. Each book is wonderful in its own way. Some are page-turners; others are head-scratchers. While fighting my way thorough one of William Faulkner's tomes (he won the Pulitzer twice), I came across a sentence that went on for five and a half pages. I went immediately from that sentence to the liquor cabinet.

But I digress.

What I really want to tell you about, though, is the way that heating appears in just about all of the old novels, and almost as a character. The stove, the fireplace, the boiler, the radiators – they all move with the plot and affect the lives of the people in the stories. The novels keep circling back to things mechanical, to how it all worked or didn't, and the crying need for warmth.

The newer novels are mainly about angst (and sex, of course), and if they mention heating at all, they get it wrong. We come across, for instance, whirring pumps that circulate steam through the pipes. This usually gets me talking aloud to the pages. Are there no technical editors at these current publishing companies? Couldn't this brilliant novelist have called his local heating contractor and hired him for an afternoon to answer some basic questions? Or just ask at HeatingHelp.com?

But stuff like that seems to be important only to those of us in this business. Most modern readers don't sweat the technical details of heating and what it takes to stay warm. Only the writers of the earlier novels cared about that.

And there's a lesson there.

Joseph Pulitzer wanted the prize for fiction to go to books that dealt with American life, which is what makes them so delicious for me. Each novel or book of short stories freezes American life at a point in time. We find people living in cities, trying to get the fires going in boilers. We learn about coal and all that it involved. We also learn about what it takes to make a good fire in the fireplaces, and who had to do that each day. We come across troubled and starving families living in prairie homes, and sleeping together to keep warm. This idea of warmth, which we take for granted, was as essential to them as smart phones are to us. We joke that we can't live without our smart phones, but those Americans were serious when they said they couldn't live without the fire. Warmth was life.

So I begin with the 1918 Pulitzer Prize for Fiction winner (*His Family*, by Ernest Poole), and also with the 2011 winner (*A Visit from the Goon Squad*, by Jennifer Eagan). Then I take the next two, one from each end; read these and then pick up the next two. And so on. I immerse myself in these people's lives month after month. Taken together, it's like watching a time-lapse film of America, played from both ends and at the same time.

As the months went by, I learned that we, as an industry, have done a very good job. Most Americans are comfortable now and they take what we do for granted. If the writers mention us at all these days the comment often involves a butt crack. There's very little respect for the heating trade.

Read any of these older novels, though, and you'll marvel at the way the writer treats this profession. Central heating and ventilation were brand-new then. Read these older books and you'll quake at what happens when neither heating nor ventilation is right. You'll begin to see winter as they did so many years ago. For them, winter was a perennial brute, something for which you must carefully prepare. If not, it will steal your children. The frigid cold is a living character in these older books but not so anymore because we have done our jobs well.

In 1918, the person who could bring steam- or hot-water heat to your home was nearly a magician. This was a person who could change lives for the better – who could save lives. But generations slid by as the Pulitzer Committee awarded the prizes. The people in the HVAC business learned from each other. The equipment got better and then it became automatic. We got so good as a profession that we disappeared. People take us for granted now. Winter is artificial now. It's something that's outside and easily avoided. Thermostats watch us move around rooms and learn our habits. They tell efficient boilers and furnaces when to start and stop and this happens without Americans thinking about any of it.

They think of us only when things break and then it is with resentment. We don't come quickly enough because this is a Twitter world now. We charge too much because, after all, when we are through making repairs, they will only have what they had before we showed up, and nothing more. And when you take something such as warmth for granted, you assign it little value. We perceive warmth as a *right* these days. It has lost its urgency.

And all because we do what we do so well. Our professional competency has devalued us. And this is why there is a crying need for story right now.

Warmth is *not* a right. It must be worked for and earned. What would American life be like without us? Suppose we stopped doing what we do so invisibly from day to day? Read those earlier novels and the later ones. Read your way toward the center. Read and think, or don't read and just take my word for it. The important thing is to tell people the story. Begin like this: Once upon a time, winter was inside as well as outside. We came along and changed that. And in doing so, we changed American lives for the better. What we do is important. We save lives. And we are essential.

How's that for a novel thought?

Hydronicheating

I'm almost always finding a connection to heating. On July 20, 1998, Modern Library put out a call to readers, asking them to vote on what they thought were the 100 best novels written in the English language during the 20th Century. Modern Library closed the voting three months later, after nearly a quarter-million people had voted. I can't resist lists like that one, and it was a fine journey.

Number 77 on that list is James Joyce's basically incomprehensible, 628-page tome, *Finnegan's Wake*. Pick it up sometime if you're looking to improve your powers of concentration while becoming even more confused than you already are.

It's worth the effort, though. There's not much plot in there (if any), but he does have a character named Dan Holohan on page 147, which I found delightful (he was doing something nasty).

The rest appears to be gibberish, but if you read slowly and concentrate, you'll begin to get it – sort of. For instance, at one point, he writes, "Money. Pleasend."

Please send.

Geddit?

I was thinking about that and the rest of the dog's breakfast of phrasing and enigma that is *Finnegan's Wake*, when I spotted the unusual word, hydronicheating, during a Google search. It occurred to me that if you remove the space between hydronic and heating you get a brand new word with a whole new meaning, one that applies to some folks who ply the trade of heating with water. I think Mr. Joyce would be proud.

Here are a few examples of hydronicheating:

Guessing at the size I had a guy call me the other day to ask if I thought a certain size boiler would be okay for a certain size building. I asked him if he had done a heat-loss calculation on the building because that's the only way to know for sure with a hot-water boiler. If it was a steam system he would measure all the radiators. He said that he hadn't figured the heat loss so, curious, I asked him why not. "It takes too long," he said. "And I'm really not sure how to do it. And I don't like math." So he called and wanted me to tell him it was going to be okay. That's hydronicheating.

Skipping the air separator James Joyce could bend and twist the English language like a champ, but an installer would be practicing hydronicheating if he tried to bend the laws of physics when it comes to removing air from the system. William Henry's Law declares that gases dissolve in liquids in proportion to pressure and temperature, meaning that the hotter the water gets, the quicker the dissolved gases will leave it. And since gases are lighter than water, they will rise to the top of the system, where they will probably block the flow of water and screw up the system balance. Air separators catch the air at a point where the water is hottest and that's good. Skipping the air separator is cheating. Every job needs one.

Skipping the plates Radiant tubing works best under a wood floor if the tubing is snug within metal plates that will move the heat by conduction from the water to the wood. Lots of smart people have studied the difference between having plates and not having plates, and the plates win every time because they let you lower the water temperature, and that's certainly good for the client. Leaving them out is hydronicheating.

Leaving it dirty I introduced you to one of my favorite Dead Men, Ara Marcus Daniels, earlier. We talked about the history of radiators. In 1928, he penned these words, "Uncleaned boilers may be the cause of seemingly faulty heating systems. No installation is complete or finished until the boiler has been thoroughly cleaned."

Now there's some great advice that's even more important today. Just imagine how dirty that system is after all these years. But many contractors do their best to avoid cleaning the insides of both steam- and hot-water systems after they work on them. Avoiding cleaning is cheating and also a fine way to mess up your reputation when the dirt-related problems show up.

Leaving out the valves Service valves add to the cost of the job, sure, but an installer who takes the time to explain the benefit of these simple devices to clients will always look smarter than the other guy. What homeowner wants to pay for the time it takes (and the mess it makes) if a service tech has to drain the whole system to change a part? Everyone wins when the right valves are in the right places. Installers should tell their story well and do the right thing. That's good hydronic *heating*.

Thinking short-term And speaking of service, I shudder at how many times I've been on a job where the original installer didn't think of the serviceperson to come, and how much trouble that poor soul was going to have trying to get at that component that's blocked by his misplaced pipe. I once looked at a gas pipe that actually touched the back end of a circulator. The contractor I was with had to drain the system and remove the whole circulator to change its broken coupler. Hydronicheating at its worst.

Not knowing The guy was changing the boiler on an old steam system. He called to tell me that the homeowner said his system needed a vaporstat and not a pressuretrol The guy asked me if that was true. I asked him what sort of steam system it was. He said he didn't know but would go back and look. He called a while later and told me the system had a Trane return trap. I told him he was working on a vapor system and that the homeowner was right. It needed a vaporstat. The guy said he would reinstall the one that was on the old boiler because he didn't want to buy a new one, and then asked me if the old one would work. I asked him if it was broken and he said he didn't know. When the homeowner knows more about the system than you do, that's hydronicheating.

Enigmas and puzzles After finishing *Finnegan's Wake*, James Joyce commented, "I put in so many enigmas and puzzles that it will keep the professors busy for centuries arguing over what I meant, and that's the only way of insuring one's immortality."

That's a fine way for a great writer to think, but if an installer fills the job with enigmas and puzzles, if he builds a dog's breakfast of piping that few can understand, he won't be immortal. He'll be immoral.

So here's hoping professionals take pride in *every* job. Here's hoping they learn the right way and don't cheat. And here's hoping they do it all day long, or as Mr. Joyce wrote, "From gold dawn glory to glow worm gleam."

And isn't that a gorgeous bouquet of words?

Oh, one more thought about Mr. Joyce. The first sentence (actually *part* of a sentence) in *Finnegan's Wake* reads:

riverrun, past Eve and Adam's, from swerve of shore to bend of bays, brings us by a commodious vicas of recirculation back to Howth Castle and Environs.

The *last* sentence in the book is actually the beginning fragment of the first sentence in the book. It reads:

A way a lone, a last a love a long the

This invites the reader to start all over again, which I am not about to do. Once was more than enough, for me.

But please savor these few words. Read them aloud and read them again, and feel the water and the recirculation and the bends and swerves and the beautiful motion and rhythm of the water as it flows by the Garden of Eden and into the city of Dublin in a time long gone.

A way a lone a last a love a long the riverrun, past Eve and Adam's, from swerve of shore to bend of bays, brings us by a commodious vicas of recirculation back to Howth Castle and Environs.

The world is *charged* with meaning, Erin.

Regarding puke

After I got involved in the heating side of the rep business, my boss sent me to Bell & Gossett's Little Red Schoolhouse in Morton Grove, Illinois. I was looking forward to the class, which went on for several days.

Bob DeWyze taught the classes at that school for 40 years and he was good at it, but those classes were mainly for engineers, and I was not an engineer. I don't get along well with math, but the Little Red Schoolhouse had a lot of hands-on equipment and that helped me a lot. I went back and took a few more of the classes as the years went by.

When your mom and I started this little company in 1989, I was writing for a magazine called *Fuel Oil and Oil Heat*, and a year later, I began my freelance writing career for *Plumbing & Mechanical* and *Supply House Times*. I was attracting a large contractor audience, mainly because I was talking on paper and telling stories. This got the attention of the management at Bell & Gossett and they hired me to write a program that I called, *Zoning Made Easy*. It was a booklet, overhead slides, and some pocket-size cards that held a lot of easy-to-use sizing information. The idea was that the reps around the country could present the program to the contractors and leave them with some very solid information, all of which I had put together with installers, and not engineers, in mind.

I used a lot of stories, analogies and simple drawings, things an installer would like. I submitted the program to B&G, and they asked me to fly to Chicago and meet with the folks at the Little Red Schoolhouse to discuss it.

There were four of us in the conference room that day. Bob DeWyze, Gil Sommer, one of the B&G engineers, and Jack Waterfield, the marketing manager who had hired me. Jack said he loved what I had written for them. He thought that it was going to be as successfully nationally as *The Problem Solver* newsletter had been for us locally in the NY/Metro area.

I sat there smiling, thinking that all was well, but then Jack had to leave the room for a few minutes to take an important phone call. That left me alone with Mr. DeWyze and Mr. Sommer.

As soon as the door closed, Mr. Sommer turned to me and said, "I have to tell you that when I read your stuff it offends my engineering sensibilities. It makes me want to puke. I hate it."

And then Mr. DeWyze said, "Kid, we're going to do all that we can to see that this never sees the light of day, and that you never get hired by us again."

Jack came back into the room and those two guys were all smiles.

I never found out what happened after I had left, but *Zoning Made Easy* had a good long run, made money for Bell & Gossett, and I think, changed the way contractors had been thinking about them at the time. I had worked for their rep for 19 years and I owed them that much.

To this day, contractors mention that program to me. Have I ever seen it? I should check it out. Whoever wrote that writes just like you.

I smiled.

Not everyone is an engineer, Erin.

Hydronics taught me about being a rep

Reps are, almost without exception, malleable. Their unbridled optimism allows them to always see the best in the lines they represent. Their unbridled pessimism, on the other hand, allows them to always see the certain forthcoming demise of the competition.

Reps are as changeable as chameleons and just as colorful.

The people who run the rep agencies are entrepreneurs. They live on the edge. A rep's agreement with a manufacturer runs for 30 days and is infinitely renewable – or cancelable. Either side may drop the other, and at any time, and for any reason, although it's usually the manufacturer who dumps the rep. This is especially true for that class of rep that does the missionary work in our industry. A manufacturer will come out with a new product, or introduce a foreign product to America. The big, well-established reps don't want these lines because there's too much work involved in getting them off the ground. You have to make cold calls on contractors, and plead with engineers for specifications. You have to make mailings, both print and electronic, and you have to stand for long hours at trade shows and at wholesalers' counters. You have to think better than most and you have to work your butt off.

And as soon as the line takes off, the manufacturer will, almost without exception, pull the line from the missionary rep and give it to one of the big, well-established reps. The manufacturer, at that point, is interested in distribution.

The missionary rep will curse, shrug, and then take on a new line and do the same thing all over again. These are the eternal optimists of our industry. You cannot keep these people down. They glow.

And then there are the soldiers. These are the salespeople who work for the reps, regardless of size. They move around a lot, these people. If a salesperson is good, the competing rep will make them an offer they can't refuse. These are the folks who come calling on contractors with one product this month and a brand-new product next month. Which is the best product? The current one, of course. Pay no attention to what they told you last month.

These folks are slimy, but they're also lovable and you forgive them because you understand that this is the way the business works.

The people who answer the phones at the rep agencies are particularly misunderstood. You know I did this for a bunch of years. I remember the day when my boss dropped a McDonnell & Miller catalog on my desk on a Friday afternoon. "We now represent this line," he said. "Take their catalog home over the weekend and learn it."

I felt like I was about 12 years old at the time. I had never seen a steam boiler. The McDonnell & Miller catalog was filled with pictures of products that were not attached to steam boilers – not that I would have recognized the boiler had they shown one. I did my best with the pictures, specifications, and what seemed like 12,000 part numbers that Saturday and Sunday. When I returned to my desk on Monday morning the first call of the day was from Morris of Psycho Supply in Brooklyn, New York. He wanted to know which McDonnell & Miller control he should use for a 5,000-year-old boiler that had a hole the size of Rhode Island and just had to make it through this one more winter. When I didn't answer instantly, Morris called me dirty names and hung up, but not before saying that he was now going to call the competitor.

Which is one reason why you should go hug a rep.

There are manufacturers from the Heartland who couldn't possibly deal with Morris from Psycho Supply. Morris thinks "pop" is something you do to a contractor's nose when he doesn't pay his bills on time. For the same reason, I'd like to see a New England manufacturer try to set up shop in Montana without a good rep. A New England manufacturer thinks "jerky" is something you call a contractor when he doesn't read the installation-and-operation instructions.

I'd like to see any manufacturer from any part of the world try to deal with those knuckleheads in California without a good rep that knows how to address important issues such as Circulator Consciousness and Radiant Karma. No, we *need* local reps. They understand the products, more or less, but more important, they understand the local contractor. A good rep can be a contractor's best friend. He will stand up for his rights and help him fight his battles when there's a product problem. He will get results, even if it means it may cost him the line in the long run. Or his job.

Hug these folks. Appreciate them because without them contractors would be dealing with Dilbert at the end of an 800 number.

Young Turks start rep agencies because they think they can do better than their bosses. Sometimes they can. The Young Turks are the salespeople in the field who know the products and the contractors, but more often than not, don't know the first thing about running a business. Two or more

Turks get together and decide they're going to try to take the line away from their bosses. I have seen this work only once. Usually, the manufacturer calls the bosses within five minutes of the call from the Young Turks, who then find themselves unemployed.

The Young Turks who manage to make it into the business generally become the missionary reps. Out of frustration, they take on the new, unknown lines that no one else wants. These lines are usually great ones, and the Young Turks work their butts off telling the world about them. The Turks will lose these lines, of course, as soon as the contractors start buying. Such is the way of the world, but theirs is the spirit that drives our industry forward. They *never* give up.

Bill, the old-school rep

I used to work with Bill Muller. I was the new kid and he had his wheels down, ready to retire.

During the heating season Bill usually wore a brown suit, a long, brown topcoat, and this 1940s fedora, which he cocked over one eye, like Sinatra. He smoked a pipe that he lit in the morning and put out at night. If you didn't like it, tough.

He had a smile that could fill an auditorium and a laugh that could rattle the windows. He was a big, tough, thick-headed salesman, and he set out to teach me a thing or two.

Bill called on the wholesalers of Brooklyn, New York, of which there were once many. He would sometimes see 15 or more wholesalers during a single day because

Brooklyn has more people than some western states, and all those people need heating.

Bill would set out on a Monday morning to see the same people he had seen on a similar Monday morning, say, two weeks ago. He was like a dray horse in this way. If you ever wanted to blow him up, I could have told you exactly where to put the bomb and how to set the timer. Bill would walk into a wholesaler's counter area like an arriving dignitary. He would greet everyone in the place by name. He'd smile at the head counterman and say, "Is Sam, (or Abe, or Joe or Morris, or Lenny, or whomever), ready to see me?" and from the office that person would suddenly appear. He would rush to shake Bill's hand and then lead him to the back, where together they would look over the shelves and make a list of what the wholesaler would need to get through the next two weeks.

I was working the phones at the time. My job was to answer when it rang, take orders (and general abuse) from wholesalers, follow up on backorders, and do the best I could with my meager knowledge to solve the myriad problems of the New York/Metro-area heating contractors. I'd take about 80 calls a day and this is how I learned.

One day Bill showed up at the office and glared down at we three telephone jockeys. He filled the doorway with that big topcoat and fedora, and he was not happy.

"If Moe from Insanity Supply (names changed here to protect the ridiculous) should call, and he *will*, you are *not*, under *any* circumstances, to accept his order. You tell him that I will see him again in two weeks on Thursday afternoon. At our usual time. The time he did *not* respect *this* week."

Moe called. I told him that I was not allowed to take his order. Yes, I knew he needed the inventory, but there was nothing I could do. Sorry. He would have to wait for Bill to return to his place two weeks hence. "But I'm running out of stuff!" Moe yelled. "Will you have Bill call me? *Please*?"

Bill called in for his messages. "Moe wants you to call him," I reported.

"Let him sweat," Bill sneered. "And if that son of a bitch calls again you just tell him that he had his chance to place a stock order *yesterday* with Bill Muller. As usual. I was there, as I am *every* other Thursday afternoon at three o'clock, but he stayed on the telephone. He looked up and saw me. He *knew* I was waiting. Me! Bill Muller! We have a standing appointment for Thursdays at three. He *knows* that. I waited ten minutes and I walked out. Now he'll have to wait for *me*."

Moe called again and I gave him the bad news. To my astonishment, he was contrite. He begged me to intercede on his behalf with Bill, to offer his *most* humble apologies, and to say that he will *never* let this happen again.

Bill called. I relayed Moe's message. He said he would consider it.

The next day, he accepted Moe's groveling apology over the telephone and I was then allowed to accept Moe's order for about 1,000 one-pipe steam air vents, along with dozens of other hydronic specialties. It was a really big order.

And that's a true story, Erin. That's the way I grew up in this industry. We had manufacturers and we had manufacturers' reps. The manufacturers sold to the reps who stocked the products. The reps sold to the wholesalers, who also stocked the products. The wholesalers then sold to the contractors, who installed the stuff for the building owners, and the whole world was quite orderly. In fact, this system of distribution was so ingrained in everyone's mind that Bill, this old curmudgeon of a rep, could act like Don Corleone and get away with it. The wholesalers *needed* the stuff. The rep had it. No one else had it. If the wholesalers wanted it, they had to get it from the rep. It was all pretty simple. And wholesalers didn't switch brands in those days. That would have been disloyal.

Imagine that.

It was a different world then, and you know what? It just occurred to me that I am beginning to sound like an old curmudgeon myself by just telling you about this.

Thing is, I can't *imagine* a rep doing this to a wholesaler these days. Can you? The wholesaler would tell the rep to go pound salt. He'd have new products on his shelves before lunchtime. Times have changed.

On the day that Bill stomped into our little office and commanded us not to take an order from Moe I remember having this boxy mechanical calculator on my desk. It was as large as a microwave oven and as noisy as an unbalanced washing machine. The accounting department was just beginning to consider looking into a computer, and for the bookkeeping functions only. The computer they finally purchased was as big as a coffin and about as useful. We kept the inventory on index cards in a big steel bin, and handwrote everything.

The mid-'90s arrived, and one day a bunch of contractors from all over the country e-mailed me notes about this guy who was selling hydronic- and electric-radiant heating products directly to consumers. Here's what he had to say on his Web site:

"We are a distributor, not a manufacturer. This means that we can talk with you, the customer directly. We will listen to you, design the system for you and SELL THE PRODUCTS DIRECTLY TO YOU!!! We will not pass you off to some wholesaler who doesn't want to deal with you, or to some contractor when you want to install the product yourself."

One contractor wrote to say, "This is the sort of crap I now have to deal with. It is time to pick sides."

The guy on the Internet named the hydronic radiant manufacturer whose equipment he was offering to ship anywhere a UPS truck travels. They were a major player. I picked up the telephone and called a fellow I know at the manufacturer's place. He said that the guys on the Internet were indeed buying their products, but only through a wholesaler. He's an old-timer and he wanted to make sure I understood that fine point. We talked some more. Yes, he knew these guys were shipping stuff all over the country. Yes, he knew they were assisting the do-it-yourselfers by way of e-mail and bypassing the contractors completely. But he had no control over any of that. "It's a brave new world," he said.

While I was listening, I kept thinking about Bill, who, by the way, handed in his lunch pail a long time ago. What would he have thought of all of this? I can imagine how he would have reacted if one of our manufacturers sold to a distributor in another state who then showed up in Brooklyn trying to bypass Bill's wholesalers and contractors. Bill would have put his lit pipe out on the guy's head and kicked his butt at least three sewers.

After I got off the phone with the manufacturer, I took a ride over to The Home Depot. I wandered around and listened to the advice people were getting on all sorts of plumbing-and-heating products. Some of the advice was a bit wacky, but you get what you pay for in this brave new world.

I started thinking about the Internet guy. He was bound to happen back then (and now). What he was doing should not have come as a surprise. The contractor who wrote to say that it's time to pick sides was right, though. He was going to have to compete with the guy on the Internet now. He was going to have to go out there into the field and sell himself like never before. He'd have to add value to the products that any do-it-yourselfer can pick up at The Home Depot, or receive from the UPS guy.

But you know what? It's all turning out okay. We're a malleable industry and we adapt, create and overcome.

But you have to figure Bill's spinning in his coffin.

Carl's crap

Half of our rep business operated in Northern-New Jersey. I was riding with Carl Sigl, an old-school salesman who saw the world as Bill saw the world east of the Hudson. Grundfos was out with their small, water-lubricated circulator at the time, as was Taco with their 007 circulator. Some wholesalers were giving these new circulators a try. They were half the price of the Bell &

Gossett's Series 100 circulator and seemed like a good idea. Small circulators that didn't need oil. Sounded pretty good.

The funny thing was that many of the wholesalers who tried the smaller circulators kept them hidden under a tarp in their warehouses. They did this because Carl would go looking for them on his frequent visits.

One wholesaler, though, refused to hide them. He had them front and center, where Carl could see them when he walked in with me. And this is how that conversation went.

Carl: What are you doing with that crap out there in your warehouse?

Ballsy wholesaler: Selling the crap out of them, Carl.

Carl: You can't do that!

Ballsy wholesaler: Why not, Carl?

Carl: Because they're *crap*!

Ballsy wholesaler: Really? *Why* are they crap, Carl?

Carl: Because I *say* so! *That's* why!

Ballsy wholesaler: You'll have to do better than that, Carl. Give me a good reason.

Carl: Because they're *crap*. You'd better get rid of them.

Ballsy wholesaler: Oh, I will, Carl. The contractors love them. I'll get rid of them, and then I'll order more.

Carl: You can't do that!

Ballsy wholesaler: Why not, Carl?

Carl: I told you why. They're crap!

I began to realize that Carl thought he owned this guy. He had called on him for so many years and the guy had always bought what Carl was selling. It got to a point where Carl began to think of the wholesaler as *his* customer. His and his alone.

But then along came the salesman from Grundfos and the salesman from Taco, both with compelling reasons why the wholesaler should switch brands. They *sold* him, which was something Carl had stopped doing a while ago. He thought he owned the guy at the wholesaler.

And that's the day the wholesaler got ballsy.

Carl never did get him back.

Nobody owns anybody in this business, Erin. Everyone has to earn what they want. They have to do this every single day. This will never change.

Everyone matters

Here's the greatest lesson I ever learned at a plumbing-and-heating supply house. I was still with the rep and our sales manager was teaching me how to make sales calls on wholesalers. "You've got to talk to the buyer," he said. "No one else in this place matters."

At the time, there was a huge supply-house chain called New York Plumbers. They had a big branch in the South Bronx, which they seemed to be heating with people. There were all these guys sitting at desks, doing the business of plumbing and heating. The buyer sat up in front of the room, like a high-school teacher.

The sales manager strutted in and I followed like his puppy. He breezed by all those guys at their desks, heading for the buyer like a torpedo. I scampered.

A rousing conversation, filled with jokes, laughter, and industry gossip, and then a stroll into the cavernous warehouse. Our sales manager wrote the order and it was a nice one.

On our way out, he treated the minions the same way he had treated them on our way in. Each was ignored as we strode out, order in hand. Hey, look at us! Who's better than us?

"Never waste your time with the little people," he said, and because I was young and stupid, I listened to him and did just that in the days that followed.

One day, I entered that big building in the South Bronx, walked by the little people and went right to the buyer. He wasn't there, though. One of the serfs was now seated at his desk.

"Hello," I said. "I'm Dan Holohan. Do you know where the buyer is?"

"He got fired," the guy said. "*I'm* the buyer now. I got a promotion."

"Well, it's nice to meet you," I said.

"Really? You've had many opportunities to meet me before, but you always chose to pass me by. I used to sit over there with the other guys." He pointed at the rows of desks. "Never even took the time to say hello, did you?"

"Well, it's nice to meet you," I said, holding out my hand.

"Get your ass out of my office," he said, going back to his paperwork.

I never again made that mistake.

Everyone matters, Erin.

My day as a potted plant

Erin, you know Medford, Massachusetts is the town your twin sister and Adam live in these days. You also know we have a Medford here on Long Island, and that we pronounce that name just as it appears – Med (like the Club) and Ford (like the car). However, in Boston, you and I have learned that the proper way to pronounce Medford is to pretend we have a mouthful of Sam Adams beer and to then sputter *MEHfah*. I've gotten used to this; although I sometimes pretend the beer is a Miller Lite, and not a Sammy, in honor of our Milwaukee-born Adam. It works just as well.

I have also struggled with Peabody (*PEEbidee*), where I have friends, and Worcester (*WUsta*), where your sister, Meg, spent four years at Holy Cross. I'm okay with Somerville, where Colleen and Adam used to live, even though I've heard this fine old town, former home of Daniel Stilson, referred to as Slumerville by citizens of Boston, but that was before gentrification.

None of which has to do with hydronics, but I'm getting there.

In the days that I worked for the manufacturers' rep here on Lawn Guyland, the International Telephone and Telegraph Company owned Bell & Gossett. This is an important part of the story of how I once spent a day as a potted plant in a looming tower overlooking Boston's Quincy Market, the memory of which continues to make me shudder.

ITT also owned Sheraton Hotels back then, and there was supposed to be this grand sense of corporate solidarity between all the ITT-owned companies, which extended to their reps, of course. This meant that if I was going to a tradeshow, and there was a Holiday Inn available across the street from the show, and a higher-priced Sheraton 25 miles away, I had to choose the Sheraton, even though this was more expensive and massively inconvenient. We were to keep things in the family. And when you're in the rep business, you can't be holier than the church.

Now knowing that, you would think that when Sheraton built a new hotel they would insist on using Bell & Gossett products, right? I mean we were all in the same family and wouldn't it be grand for ITT's bottom line if one division bought stuff from another division. After all, that's what had me driving miles to get to my bed after standing all day at that tradeshow.

But Sheraton viewed all of this as a corporate check valve, where the business flowed only one way. If we wanted to get our stuff into their hotels we were going to have to sell them.

The year I served as the potted plant, Sheraton was building a hotel out on Lawn Guyland. This is where things got tricky. The new hotel was to be in our territory, which meant we would be responsible for warranty service, should that be necessary. But the contractor awarded the job was from out of state, and that rep was trying to sell them B&G. The engineer, who had the ability to approve the change in the specs was at Sheraton's headquarters, which happened to be in that looming tower overlooking Quincy Market in downtown Boston.

You following all of this?

A friend from that fair city of Boston recently mentioned that there had been a "shock attack" and I was right away thinking about electrical wires and storm-related damage. I said, "*Shock* attack?" to which she replied, "Not 'shock,' '*SHOCK*' You know, like *Jaws*?"

You see how easily misunderstandings can start? That's what we had with Sheraton – a misunderstanding. We thought they should specify our stuff because we had to stay in their fancy hotels, but noooo.

So the folks in charge of the various companies concerned with all of this sent a delegation to Sheraton to sell them on the grandeur of our stuff. The owner of the Boston B&G rep firm represented his company. Bell & Gossett pulled out the biggest gun in their technical arsenal and sent Gil Carlson, who had dreamed up so much of hydronic science as B&G's Director of Technical Services. He's the guy who figured out that circulators should pump away from compression tanks. He also dreamed up primary/secondary pumping, and much more. He had a ridiculously fertile imagination and a brain far larger than mine.

My company sent a very-young version of me.

Why me? We were responsible for any warranty service (a minor function in this big picture), and I suppose they probably had one extra chair in the conference room. My job was to sit near the window and experience photosynthesis.

But wait, I'm getting to the juicy part.

Eastern Airlines used to run an hourly shuttle between LaGuardia Airport in New York and Boston's Logan. It was quite a deal. You didn't need a reservation, and if a plane was full, and they had one additional passenger, they would roll out another plane, just for that one person. Imagine that.

My boss told me to get a ticket the day of the meeting, which was to be at 10 AM and I was so excited because I had been on a total of one business trip involving an airplane up to this point. I would get to sit next to the Great Carlson and appear brilliant by association. All I had to do was keep my mouth shut. Such an honor.

A week before I was to be planted near the window, I bought a suit and a new pair of wingtip shoes. We both know that every girl's crazy 'bout a sharp-dressed man and I was hoping the engineers at Sheraton would feel the same about me.

I woke while it was still dark, put on the suit and the new wingtips, drove to the airport, hopped on the plane, and within an hour, as the sun was rising, found myself at Logan Airport. I got into a cab and told the driver where I needed to be. "That's by Quincy MAAAkit," he said and I nodded, hoping that this was true.

We get there fast. I pay him and quickly slide out of the cab, but in doing so, my new suit trousers snag a wire that's sticking out of the cab's upholstery. This tears an eight-inch-long, L-shaped hole, right down to the skin. The driver looks over his shoulder and says, "That's gonna be wicked embarrassing, khed." He drives off.

All the stores are closed, of course.

So I take off my new suit jacket, wrap it around my sorry lower-self and wander the streets, waiting for the meeting to start. In doing so, I manage to break in my new wingtips by raising water balloon-size blisters on both feet.

I'm now ready to go sit with the big shots.

I manage to get to the meeting by crab-walking sideways along the walls of the looming tower. I'm holding the slice-of-pizza-shaped gap in my drawers with my left hand as I shake hands with my right, but no one notices the oddness of this because I am a philodendron. Coffee is offered, which I politely decline, knowing what coffee causes.

Gil Carlson begins to lecture us for more than an hour on the finer points of centrifugal pumps, valves and controls. He is brilliant.

The Boston rep then has his say, and he, too, is impressive.

I sit there, smiling painfully and bleeding a bit onto my leather swivel chair.

The meeting breaks up. The Sheraton engineers tell us how impressed they are with all they have heard, and that they will take all of this into consideration – for the good of the family.

Eventually they will decide to hold the spec, which favors the competitor, who is cheaper. And that's what gets installed.

I made it back to Logan later that day, along with a thunderstorm, which has delayed all flights. I stand with my back to the wall near the gate for a good long time. I can't sit because, well, you know. And I can't walk because of the blisters. I stand in the corner, a miserable, wilted ficus.

Three decades pass and. I'm doing a seminar in that cursed Long Island Sheraton hotel. I'm retelling the story of that day to your mother as we move stuff from the car to the meeting room. As I bend to lift a heavy case of books, I feel something pull, but it's not the chinos. Nope, I just gave myself a hernia. Laid me up for six weeks. Hurt wicked *bad*!

Next time, it's the Holiday Inn for me.

Sheraton can kiss my flabby old ass.

Hydronics taught me about pricing

I mentioned earlier that there was this day during the summer of '88 when it dawned on me that in 12 short years all four of you would be in college at the same time. Kelly would be a senior; Meghan would be a sophomore, and Colleen and you, would be freshmen. And, as you know, that's exactly how it turned out.

This was scary stuff for old-school parents who saw their kids' education as their responsibility, *and* their priority.

I was working for the rep at the time, so I knocked on the owner's office door that summer and asked if some day, somehow, I might be able to buy into this company and get rich like he was rich. He smiled and said, "Absolutely not."

I explained about our growing daughters and our upcoming financial challenge. And then I asked what he would do if he was me and he gave me that magical advice.

"I'd definitely quit," he said.

So I did. And then I went home to tell your mom that all of our lives had just became that much more exciting.

"Where's the money going to come from?" she asked.

"I'm going to write a book about steam heating," I said.

"And how long will that take?"

"I figure about six months," I said.

"And how will you feed us between now and then?"

"I will do some seminars," I said. "And I will consult with people about their heating problems."

"Well, you'd better get to it," she said.

So I started to write *The Lost Art of Steam Heating*, which took three years instead of six months to complete. Hey, who knew?

Oh, and people weren't exactly lining up to hire me to do seminars in those days, so that left consulting.

"You're not actually going to touch anything, right?" your mom said.

"Gosh, no," I said. "I'm going to look, figure out what's wrong, and then write reports. The building owners can then get anyone they'd like to do the work."

"How much are you going to charge these people?"

"I figure fifty bucks an hour," I said.

"How did you arrive at that amount?"

"It seems like a nice number."

"Well, get to it," she said.

So here's what I was thinking: There are a lot of people in this world who are rich, cold and miserable. Many of them live in big houses right here on the Isle of Long, and they all have rich friends. Many of these houses are old and grand and they all have either steam- or hot-water heat. Oh, and the steam pipes are banging. The air vents are squirting. The heat is uneven. The circulators are making a racket. The valves are in backwards. The controls aren't controlling. The boilers are oversized or undersized. It's a regular hot mess.

The friends come over to visit and they see and hear all these things going on. They ask their friend, the mansion-owner, why he doesn't take care of these problems. The rich guy sighs and says that he would love to, but no one understands these old systems. Everyone he called told him to have the system ripped out and replaced, and that was out of the question because it would involve tearing up his fancy old house.

And that's where I came in.

They found me through a magazine article, or by word of mouth, and I went to see them. I listened to their tales of woe and asked myself, What can cause that? Then I worked my way through the checklists in my head and figured it all out. Often, it was a missing air vent. Other times, it was broken steam traps. Or it might be vacuum forming in a place where vacuum shouldn't be forming. And on and on like that. It doesn't take long to find the cause of the problem if you go about it in the right way. I'd spot it, explain it, and write a report. And then I'd give them a bill. And since I am an honest guy, and it did not take me very long to figure out what was going on, that bill would often be for just $50 or maybe $100. I would bring this money home to your mother and she would smile at me.

So I'm doing this locally for about a year and having a ball. I got to poke around a lot of very snazzy houses, and this rich guy that I helped would tell another rich guy, and that put the food on the table while I was writing the book.

One day, an attorney, who practiced building-management rather than law, called and asked if I could consult on a number of buildings that were having problems. I went to see a few of these buildings and the problems raised their heads and shouted at me. "Over here!" they said. It was like hydronic whack-a-mole. Easy to spot. Easy to bash. I'd dash off my report and send the attorney a bill.

But then he calls me one day and says, "Can you stop by my office? I need to talk to you about your invoices."

And you know what that usually means, right?

So I gulped and went to see him.

"What's up?"

"I need to talk to your about your pricing," he said. "I love your reports and so do the board members of the buildings you've visited. But then I show them your bill, which is usually for about $100, and that's a problem."

"What's wrong?" I asked.

"Well, as I said, they love your reports. You're solving problems, and the speed at which you work is great, but when they see your bills they question your skills."

"How so?"

"Well, Dan, quite frankly, you're not asking for much. They look at these bills for a hundred bucks, or fifty bucks, and then ask why I got a fifty-dollar guy for the job. Isn't there someone better?"

"That makes no sense at all," I said.

"It does if you're rich," he said. "These people smoke cigars that cost more than your hourly fee.

"Look, here's what I need you to do. Whenever you speak to me, I want you to send me an invoice for eight-hundred dollars."

"Really? How are you coming up with that number?" I asked.

"Because it's less than a professional engineer would charge, but it's enough to get their attention and their respect. They need to feel like I'm bringing them a true expert, and true experts charge like these people charge in their own professions."

"You serious about this?"

"You bet I am. You charge me eight-hundred dollars whenever you look at something and everyone will be happy."

So that's what I did. And having learned a great lesson about these particular rich, cold and miserable people, I began to do the same with all of them. I'd get a call. I'd listen to the complaint. Their fuel bills were higher than ever. Their pipes were banging. Some rooms were too hot, and others were too cold. Their friends were asking why they didn't do something about all of this. They were aggravated. They wanted solutions.

Oh, and how much do I charge?

"That will be eight-hundred dollars," I said.

"Wow! You must be great!"

"I'm as good as it gets, "I'd say, "And I'm all yours."

"Wow! You are the *best!*," they'd say. "When can you be here?"

And you want to know the toughest part of all of this? It was saying the number. I had to stutter it the first few times.

But that got lot easier with practice.

Pricing is a funny thing, and a lot of thinking needs to go into how much you charge. I've watched many contractors go out of business because they didn't think they had any overhead because they worked out of the house. Or they didn't think they'd ever have to replace that truck or any of their tools. They also didn't think they had to advertise or market. I've also watched a lot of contractors talk customers out of buying things that they, the contractors, couldn't afford to buy, which is crazy.

People value what a contractor or a consultant has to offer in ways that we often don't understand. Consider vodka for a moment (okay, maybe for more than a moment). It's a grain-neutral spirit, which means it has hardly any taste. It's also clear, like water. What makes one better than the other?

Perception.

Sidney Frank knew this when he introduced Grey Goose vodka to the market. He was going after Absolut vodka, and he knew that one way to do that was not to lower the price. But he also knew that another way to beat Absolut was to raise the price of his Grey Goose to a ridiculously higher level.

And people who could afford the high-priced Grey Goose flocked to it, even though Grey Goose and Absolut are about the same thing.

If a contractor or a consultant knows what he or she is doing, they're probably worth a lot more to most folks than they think.

But that's the thing. Are they *thinking*?

Perception

Ray Kottner had driven a cab on New York City's streets for more than 60 years when he decided to stop charging people. Ray drove a Checker Marathon cab, one of those classic New York vehicles that are but a memory now. When I was a boy, my biggest thrill was to be able to sit in one of the jump seats that folded up and down. We rarely took cabs, but I can remember every ride that we did take. Five or six people fit in the back seat of those beauties.

In 2006, Ray removed the meter from his cab but kept prowling the streets of New York. When someone flagged him down and asked where the meter was, Ray would tell them that the ride was free. He'd take them anywhere they wanted to go. No charge. People could tip, of course, and they did, often for much more than what the normal fare would have been. People can be that way sometimes, especially when confronted with an unusual situation.

I read this story in the newspaper back then and I cut it out and carried it in my wallet for a few years. It made me think about what things are really worth.

One year, your mother and I were traveling on some seminar trip. When we returned home, we saw the results of a huge Nor'easter that had blown through two days before. A bunch of shingles that used to be on our roof were now laying on our lawn. Not good.

Now, I'm of an age where I've gained the wisdom to know that men of a certain age do not belong on the top of tall houses that have steep roofs. This is a job for younger men who see themselves as being both bulletproof and immortal.

I looked up at my roof for a while and then decided how much it was probably going to cost me to have it all made right. I arrived at this figure by thinking about what the job was worth to me. It was all about how much I was willing to pay not to have water dripping through the ceilings, and not to have to ride in an ambulance. I also didn't want your mom giving me that look. You know the one.

So I called a couple of guys I know who do this sort of work. They're a father-and-son team and they get by okay in their small business. I don't think they'll ever be rich, or ever be able to retire comfortably. They go from job to job, just making it. They do wonderful work but the problem is that they base their prices on what their competitors charge. And those competitors are just like them. These guys all walk warily around each other. They create this condition called, What The Market Will Bear. And then I think they see the market as each other. If *they* can't afford it, *nobody* can.

Anyway, the father and the son arrived right on time and the son gamboled up the extension ladder and onto our injured roof. I stayed on the ground and drank coffee with the father. Every now and then, we looked up at the son. The father was also wise. Let the kid do the tough stuff.

When they were finished, I asked them what I owned them and they looked at each other for a while, and then at me, and then they decided on a price that was exactly one third of the number that I had arrived at in my mind when I had first seen the damage.

You know why? They were charging me based on how easy it was for them (the son, actually) to do the work. It was just shingles and labor. It wasn't like they were ever going to have to replace their truck or their tools or retire someday. It was just a couple of hours work and some shingles. How could they possibly charge a lot for that?

But here's the thing: I was willing to pay based on what it meant for me to have the work done. I didn't want to do it myself, but even if they had understood what the work was worth to me, I think they still would have charged the lower price because, in their minds, that's what the market will bear.

I paid them what I thought it was worth. I gave them three times what they had asked for. They looked at me like I was nuts, but they took the cash. Then they looked at each other and I could see something in the son's eyes that was not in the father's eyes. That was good.

Ray Kottner drove his free cab around New York City for a year and a half and got lots of press for what he was doing. The guy was a delight to see on the TV. He was great at the chat and he was smiling his way down every street, giving it all away, and doing better than he had ever done when he used to charge for the rides. Go figure.

Then, in July, 2007, an investigator from the Taxi and Limousine Commission spotted Ray taking a $10 tip from a grateful passenger. The investigator pulled Ray over, seized his cab, and made him to post a $1,500 bond to get it out of impound. They also hit him with $585 in fines because they said that he was no better than a thief for giving away rides for which other cab drivers were charging. He was allowing his customers to decide what his services were worth, and in New York, that's apparently against the law.

In May, 2010, Panera Bread opened a new store in Clayton, Missouri, just outside of St. Louis. Everything in that new store is free. There are no prices on the menu, but customers are encouraged to pay what they feel the food is worth. A nonprofit foundation is running the program, and if it's successful, Panera says they will expand the program.

So far, most of the customers (a mix of well-to-do and lower-income folks) have paid full price for the food, or they've taken a couple of bucks off what would be the full price. A few have paid half-price, but most have come up with the cash for what they think the food and drinks are worth. Some even pay more, and everyone seems to like having the choice.

So here's a question for you: If you didn't post prices, and someone came into your place of business, would they pay what you think is the correct full price for what you have to offer? Would they pay more? Or perhaps less?

What's it worth?

And the products that you sell, if you could name the price to own those products, not for resale, but for your own personal use, would you pay what you're charging others? And if not, why not?

What's it worth?

An interesting way of looking at things, isn't it?

What is something worth? And if you had the opportunity to decide the price, where would you place it? Give it some thought.

Would you make the price What The Market Will Bear, whatever that means, or would you make the price representative of what that product or service does for you, and means to you?

I didn't want to go up on my roof to fix those shingles. I'm too old for that sort of adventure. I knew what the job was worth to me. Trouble was, the guys doing the work didn't know the true valve of what they were selling, and that's often the problem. It's also the reason why contractors beat each other over the head in a never-ending quest toward the lowest common denominator, and the lowest possible price.

We're not spending nearly enough time thinking about what things are really worth to people. Given a free choice, most customers will pay more than you think they will pay, and even in New York.

On a lovely June evening in 2007, Ray Kottner was sitting in his taxicab, waiting to give someone a free ride, when his heart stopped beating.

I like to think he was smiling.

But is this cheating?

I've learned that there are many imaginative contractors in the heating business, and many have a fine way with words, along with unusual ways of sizing equipment, explaining stuff to customers, and being creative when problems arise.

For instance, I met a contractor who would quote every job at least twenty percent higher than what any of his competitors put out there. "It's because I like to make money," he said.

"Oh."

"Yeah, I do," he said. "Lots of money."

"But how do you get the premium price," I asked. "What makes you so special?"

"I sell only the square Btu, Dan," he explained. "Only the square ones."

"Huh?"

"Yes, square Btu," he repeated.

I must have been wearing my baffle face, so he grabbed a sheet of white paper and a pen and set to sketching.

"You see, Dan, in the old days, builders of tract housing would use these round boilers. These were vertical, fire-tube boilers and they were pretty cheap. We called them, Builders' Specials. They were junk, and not meant to last very long, but people didn't know what they were getting in those days. Everything was included with the house."

"I'm familiar with Builders' Specials," I said. He was drawing circles within circles on the paper.

"So then perhaps you know that when you place a round Btu in a round boiler everything fits perfectly. Round boiler, round Btu. See? Isn't that nice? It was a standard thing in the '50s. They stacked like pancakes."

"Huh?"

"Yes, the round Btu," he repeated. "Even Elvis had them."

"Wait a minute," I said. "British thermal units have no shape."

He smiled at me, as he would a confused child. "Of course they do, Dan. They can be either round or square. And the square ones are the only ones we use on our jobs. They cost more because of the sharp corners. Those are the only corners we cut on any job. That's why our price will always be twenty percent higher than the competition."

"I don't get it."

"Watch," he said, drawing a large square, and then a lot of smaller circles within the square.

"Now, Dan, as you know, most of the boilers made today are square, not round. And as you can see, when you put round Btu in a square boiler, you're left with all of these spaces between the Btu." He pointed at the spaces between the bunched circles with the tip of his pen. "That leads to inefficiency. Makes sense, doesn't it?"

"Um?"

He held up his hand to stop me and then made another sketch, this one of a big square with smaller squares laid out like patio blocks.

"But when you put square Btu in a square boiler, as you see here, those Btus will snug up against each other like patio blocks, leaving no gaps at all in between. And that, of course, leads to higher efficiency." He nodded with certainty and sincerity." And that's why our price is higher.

"You ever wonder why expensive Johnny Walker booze comes in square bottles, Dan? Same reason."

"And people go for this?"

"Why wouldn't they?"

"I'll have to give that some thought, " I said.

And all these years later, I'm still thinking about it.

Service vs. Products

Erin, you may remember when you were a girl that I was away from home a lot. I was doing the consulting, and we were paying our bills and taking care of you and your sisters, but it dawned on me that I was in the service business. If I didn't work every day, I didn't get paid. And when I added up the available hours in a week that I could work, I realized that there would always be a ceiling on how much I could make. This, in spite of the advice about the $800 from the building-management guy.

So I stopped consulting and focused on writing my first book, *The Lost Art of Steam Heating*. I had been working on it all along, of course, but the consulting was taking time away from the hours I could be writing. I figured that our family would have to take a few financial steps backward in order to move forward. It was the same realization I had when I was working for the manufacturer's rep and realized that you and your sisters would all be in college at the same time a few years down the road. I was never going to make enough money to afford that if I was working for someone else. I realized that my job was actually keeping me from making the money we needed because I had to go to it every day. So I quit.

Around that same time, groups began calling me do seminars. They knew me from my magazine writing and I was getting a reputation as someone who was fun to listen to. They'd call and ask how much it would cost for me to speak all day. I said it would be a thousand bucks, which seemed like a lot of money. Hey, it was more than $800, right? But the thing is, seminars are *also* a service, just like consulting. I knew that, but the thought of getting a thousand bucks for just talking all day was irresistible. Besides, I like talking.

So I did a bunch of local seminars and word got out that I was available. The seminars were easier to do than the consulting because I didn't have to figure out anything, and the time I had spent writing reports for clients, I could now devote to working on the book.

I did this for a while and started to get calls from all over the country. That was thrilling because I would now get to go places I had never been, and meet people I had never met. "How much?" they'd ask. "A thousand bucks, plus travel expenses," I'd say, and off I went.

I went to just about every state. I was seeing mostly airports and Holiday Inns, though. And I was spending more time away from home, and for the same money. I was a thousand-dollar guy, and I was getting tired. That's when it dawned on me that if I charged *two* thousand dollars instead of one thousand dollars I would make the same amount, but travel and work half as much. It also occurred to me that I might lose half my seminar customers if I charged more than a thousand bucks, but I'd still be ahead since I'd take home the same amount of money as before, have more time to finish the book, and most important, have more time to spend with you, your sisters, and your mom.

So that's what I did. By the spring of 1992, *The Lost Art of Steam Heating* was ready to go to the printer. I had decided to self-publish the book because I didn't think a publisher would be interested in a book about heating systems that no one had installed since the 1930s. I got together with a local printer, got the prices for the first run and was all set to go when our old van died. This was the van that I used to do seminars. I was traveling with a lot of equipment in those days and needed a vehicle that size. We hadn't been able to save much money in the three years we had been in business. Babies, as you well know, are expensive, so your mom and I had to make a decision. Do we buy a new van, or do we print the book? And since the van was actually bringing in money (we weren't sure the book would), we decided to put a hold on *The Lost Art of Steam Heating* in favor of transportation.

And this is where Al Levi comes in. I'd been good friends with Al, his brothers, Marty and Richie, and their dad, Irving for years. When I worked for the manufacturer's rep, I would help out those guys with problem steam- and hot-water jobs. Their company, OSI, is here on Long Island. They were mainly a fuel-oil dealer at the time. Since then, they've branched into gas service, plumbing, air-conditioning, mechanical contracting, and electrical work. They pretty much do it all.

Al knew that I was writing the book and he asked me one day if I was going to publish it posthumously. Al's a guy who likes to get things done. I told him that the book was ready but I had to spend the money we had saved for printing on the new van, and that it would be a while before I'd be able to bring the book to life.

"How much do you need?" he asked.

"Seventeen-thousand, five-hundred dollars," I said.

Al reached into his pocket, took out his checkbook, wrote me a personal check for the total amount and said, "Pay me back when you can." He didn't even ask me to sign a paper. I paid him back six months later.

That's a friend.

And he helped in other ways. I was trying to figure out how much to charge for *Lost Art*. How could I put a price on the years of research and writing I had put into that book? I had never done anything like this before.

"Charge thirty bucks," Al said.

"Why thirty?" I asked.

"Because if I was walking a tradeshow and saw you selling that book, I'd want it. But I would first consider if the price you were asking would cut into my beer money. Contractors think that way, especially at tradeshows. I'd spend thirty bucks on that book."

So that's what we did. The book's been through dozens of printings since then and at one point, we raised the price to forty bucks because printing costs had risen. I asked Al what he thought about that. He said, "If people will pay thirty, they'll pay forty." He was right. He usually is.

I took the first shipment of books in July 1992. We kept them in a public-storage locker because your mother and

I were still working from home in those days. A group in Boston had hired me to do a seminar in a hotel near Logan Airport. Your sister, Meghan, was 12 that summer and I asked her if she wanted to take a trip. She jumped at it.

We drove to Boston in the new van. I had bought my first car phone, which came in a bag with a handle. It looked like a toiletry kit. The phone actually had a coiled wire, just like a house phone. I wanted it because it made me feel like I had made it in business, even though I hadn't yet. But I didn't want to actually use the phone because calls cost twenty-five cents a minute.

Meg loved the idea of having a phone in a car, though, and I can still see her smiling. It was 1992. What 12-year-old wouldn't want a phone in the car?

We spent the night in the hotel after going to dinner, and we both got up early the next morning to set up for the seminar. I had boxes of *Lost Art* up front, and during the first break, I mentioned that I had written this book and it was available for thirty bucks. Meg was my helper that day and what happened next made her eyes go wide. Mine, too. Every person in that room rushed forward with cash money in hand. We sold every copy. They asked for more.

I finished the seminar at five o'clock and loaded the van. Meg was in the passenger seat. Before I drove out of the parking lot and started the long drive home, I took all that cash out of my pocket and dropped it on her lap. All these years later, I can still hear her giggling as she tossed those bills in the air. "Daddy," she said, "can we afford to call Mom and tell her about this?"

"Sure, Meg," I said. "Give her a call."

And that was the moment I knew we were all going to be okay.

Seventeen more books followed *Lost Art*, and each took time to research and write. I started charging more for my seminars, following the same logic as before. It became a matter of convincing groups that I was not an expense; I was an asset they could use to make money. Just about every group I have ever worked with made a good profit on the seminar I did for them, and many had me back again and again.

By the time I wrapped up my seminar career in January 2016, I was charging $7,500 for a 5-1/2-hour seminar, plus travel expenses. The groups still made money. Hydronics taught me that people value education and entertainment, and if a speaker can combine those two elements, large crowds will gather. And they did.

But more important, was the discovery that a book is a *product*, not a service. The books contained the words I was saying at each seminar, but I didn't have to be there to read those words. The books, these products, gave me the luxury of time. I didn't have to travel, as much as I did with consulting and seminars. I had more time to read, to learn, to write, and that led to more products.

The contractors who came to my seminars were in the service business. Most of them were one-man shows. The smarter ones realized that *their* product was their people. They'd spend time grooming good people, whose services they could then sell as products.

Spend some time thinking about that.

And when you meet younger people who are growing, encourage them to think about what they're good at, and what they're not good at. I believe that before a person reaches the age of forty, at the very latest, he or she should have this all figured out. If you're still weak in an area at that age, you're not going to get better. Find someone who can do that task for you. Focus on your strengths. Build those strengths.

We stared our business when I was 39. I knew then that there were only two things I was really good at: I could tell stories. And I could bring people together.

And Erin, if you look closely at everything I have done in my career, it all revolves around those two things. The books, magazine articles and seminars are about story. HeatingHelp.com is about bringing people together, and mainly through story. The members who post the Wall have plenty of those to share, and so do you and I.

One last thought about pricing. Focus on the value people place on what you do. If they don't yet see that value, you haven't told enough stories about what you're going to do for them, how you're going to improve their lives. Why they should hire you. How they will profit from the experience.

Come up with a price and say it. Just look them in the eye and say it. If they want you, great, but understand that not everyone can afford you. Those people will ask you to lower your price. And if you do that, you'll be confirming what they suspect - that you were trying to cheat them in the first place.

No, just give your price and leave it at that. Don't budge. They'll decide what happens next.

An association based in Maine called me about 10 years ago. They wanted me to drive from Long Island to Augusta,

Maine and speak to a large group for the whole day. At the time, my price for that trip was $6,000.

"Six-thousand dollars!" the woman in charge said over the phone. "I could get the Rolling Stones for that much."

"What do the Rolling Stones know about hydronics?" I asked.

"Well, can you come down in price?" she asked. I could see that coming.

"I can't do that," I said, "but how about if I give you seven-thousand dollars worth of education for just six-thousand dollars? And I'll do it all in the same amount of time."

"How is that possible?" she asked.

"I'm a professional," I said. "Have you ever seen a square Btu?"

They hired me.

Hydronics taught me about troubleshooting

I was telling you about Al Levi and how he kick-started my book-writing career with that loan. Before Al became a business consultant and a writer for *Plumbing & Mechanical* magazine, he and did a lot of troubleshooting for his family's business. I dubbed him, Ace Troubleshooter, and I nicknamed his brother, Richie, The Man Who Can Fix Anything.

The three of us would visit a problem job, figure it out, fix it, and move on. Al would say, "Well that's done, kina hora." I asked what that expression meant, and Al explained that it was a Hebrew phrase that kept away evil. Like when a Jewish mother says, "My daughter? She should grow up and marry a rich doctor, kina hora."

I love this stuff.

Another thing I learned from the Levi family was that once we troubleshot a job and solved it, none of us should ever say the name of that customer out loud. To do so would bring the evil eye onto the job and we'd be back there again.

So none of us would ever say, "How are things going at that Murphy job? Everything still running okay?" Rather, we'd say, "Hey, remember that job? The one with the noisy circulator. Big guy with the red hair and the belly? How's that one going? Hear any more from him?"

Get it. *Never* say the name out loud. Or, heaven forbid, the address. Addresses are worse than names. The evil eye uses GPS and a jet engine.

I did this for years when I worked for the manufacturer's rep, and for more years as a consultant to the Rich, Cold and Miserable, and when I was done with that, I did a lot of it just for fun. It gave me a good feeling to solve something that is stumping others, and besides, I could write about it.

I did have an advantage, though, because I wasn't doing the actual work, so no one was yelling at me. I was there to help. I was showing up with an open mind, a fresh pair of eyes, and a bright flashlight.

Hydronics taught me that, when faced with a problem, the first thing to do is to identify something that was undeniably true. For instance: There is no heat in the kitchen. Or, that circulator is leaking. Or, the boiler rotted out after just three heating seasons.

This undeniable truth becomes home base. It's there. It's real. We can come back to it if we get confused.

The next step, of course is to ask the key question, which is, What can cause that?

And this is where the open mind comes in. Some troubleshooters will take short-cuts and say, "Nah, that's not possible. Can't be that." And I always wonder how, if we have no idea what's causing the problem at this point (which is why we're there), how can we possibly say it's not this or that without first checking.

So troubleshooting is a lifestyle you need to embrace if you're going to do it. You won't solve them all, and some solve themselves before you can (I hate those), but you'll do better than most on those problem jobs if you follow that formula.

I spoke to a plumber once who was having a problem with a hot-water system. He set the fill pressure at 12-psi but the gauge kept rising to 20-psi. Now there are a lot of things that can cause that. For instance, the compression tank may not have the proper air charge, or it may be the wrong size for the job. The feed valve may be bypassing and overfilling the system. If there's a tankless coil in the boiler, it may be leaking domestic water into the boiler water. You run down the list. You keep your mind open. You find the solution.

You know what this guy did? He scrapped the boiler and installed a new one.

Because the pressure was rising.

And then he had the same problem.

You know what he told me? That manufacturer makes lousy boilers.

What can cause that response?

A lack of knowledge.

Cardboard Apps

These days, I don't know many people in this business that don't have all the world's knowledge in their pocket. They're forever checking their smart phones for this and that. Just the other day, someone asked me if I knew of a good app for sizing gas lines. I wondered why the guy just didn't use a paper version for that. Remember? We used to have these charts. Still do, in fact. But then I realized that paper is so 20th Century.

Not that I'm trying to get in touch with my inner fogie here, or go all Luddite on you. I love today's technology as much as anyone, but I still keep a dusty copy of Merriam Webster's Collegiate Dictionary on the shelf over my desk. Sure, I haven't opened in it years because it's much easier and faster for me to Google a word I need to check, but that book has a such a nice maroon color, and it smells like old knowledge, so I'm keeping it.

My nine-by-12 office is home to the dead these days. Their books, some dating to the early-1800s, gaze down on me. I open them often to stay reacquainted with their writers. These are my old friends and they are remarkably patient with me. They never ask for attention. They just stand side-by-side at attention and wait until I need them, and they are always there for me.

Over there in my three filing cabinets, there are handwritten and typed notes, written by the dead. Much of those notes have to do with job proposals and tricks of the trade as it was in days gone by. There is also a lot of old product literature in those cabinets and the photos in that literature are of a time long gone, but when I sometimes see the machines in those catalogs still operating in the field I always smile. We live in a heating museum.

One of those folders in the cabinet on the left contains a bunch of what I think of as cardboard apps. These are the sizing calculators the Dead Men carried in their pockets when telephones still had slots for nickels.

Here, for instance, is a 5-1/4" round, Hot-Water-Capacity Calculator from the John Wood Company. They note under their name that they've been around since 1867. How about that?

The calculator has three circular sections and these instructions:

1. Locate on outer dial your laundry equipment.

2. Set opposite the laundry equipment the kitchen equipment you have.

3. Set the number of people in your family opposite the number of baths.

4. Read gallons opposite Personal Factor. This is for peak hot-water requirement of family. To determine size heater you require, see table on back of calculator.

That's simple, but it only allows me to have five people in the family, which made me wonder because, back when contractors were using this cardboard app, people probably had more kids than they do today, so I'll set that one aside and look at this other cardboard app from A.O. Smith. A.O. allows for eight people in the family (which may be the key to their success). Their cardboard app, which is, when folded, exactly the size of my iPhone, tells me to:

1. Select appliance and bath column for your home.

2. Match Dot to that column.

3. Read gallons required for number of people in your family.

Isn't that easy? And I don't have to plug in either of these or get within range of a signal to use them.

In 1959, General Industrial Co. of Chicago, Illinois (phone number LOngbeach 1-5871) gave away a four-inch round, honest-to-goodness slide rule. It's not for sizing water heaters. It's just a slide rule and I'll bet if you handed this to a teenager he or she wouldn't be able to tell what it is, even though it says Slide Rule right on the front.

Or how about this one from Waterfilm Boilers, Inc. of Jersey City, NJ? It was 1953 and they were selling Koven Trimrad baseboard radiators. They gave away a plastic-and-cardboard app that was about the size of a Samsung Galaxy S5. It calculated heat loss and sized the baseboard. All you needed to do was dial in the cubic contents of the room, the square footage of glass, and the square footage of the exposed walls. No questions asked about what was inside the walls, or what sort of glass made up those windows. They probably wanted to make life too simple for the contractors, which may be why most folks have never heard of them nowadays.

In 1954, American Standard came out with a 6-1/2" round Profit and Overhead Calculator. Watch this:

Step 1. Set the total of all overhead expenses opposite Total Sales in the little window. Read the Overhead Percentage. Turn the wheel over.

Step 2: Set the red arrow Total Direct Costs (Labor and Materials) for job. Add to this the Overhead Percentage from the other side, your desired profit, and you have the Selling Price of Job.

Think they knew how to figure all the overhead in those days?

Me neither.

American Standard also had a heating calculator (it, too, arrived in 1954, a big year for cardboard apps). Theirs was better than the one from Waterfilm Boilers because you had to slide to whether the building had single- or double-glass windows, and you had to consider infiltration. Once you slid all of that into place, you'd select both your boiler (there are five choices!) and your Heatrim baseboard radiators. This one is about the size of two pieces of white bread, side by side. Nice.

In 1956, American Standard kicked it up a notch with their Residential Comfort-Conditioning Calculator (Round of applause!). Now consider how many houses were going up in 1956 when all those babies were booming. This cardboard app goes into much more detail when figuring the heat loss. It's still the size of the white bread, but now they want to know a lot more details about construction, which makes sense since the contractor was probably using this one for new homes rather than old homes.

Crane, not to be outdone, offered a cardboard app (two-slice-white-bread size) that asked questions similar to American Standard's and then came up with how many feet of their cast-iron baseboard you'd need to use.

I figure this one got used less often since we both know that the way baseboard really gets sized is to measure the walls and then install the baseboard to fit along those walls.

And then, of course, there was Bell & Gossett's System Syzer, credited to my teacher, the late, great Gil Carlson. When I was working with the contractors in New York City and Long Island, I would not leave home without that delicious, dessert-plate-sized, plastic app. I used it constantly and now I've learned that B&G has replaced Gil's Wheel with an electronic app, and that's nice, but I'm keeping my old one because it works just fine and comes with many sweet memories.

So there.

As each of these cardboard- and plastic apps showed up, I'm sure contractors were thrilled. Heck, I still smile every time I look at them. I think about how many hands must have touched these things before they came to me, how many jobs they helped size, and how many problems they helped solve. How much time they saved.

And not one of them needed a battery. Nice.

Learning how to use that System Syzer

In 1974, when I shifted from the plumbing to the heating side of the manufacturers' rep business, one of the older salesmen took me aside and taught me about the marble.

"When you're sizing circulators, or even when you're just looking at a hot water job," he said, "you should imagine that you're inside the pipe, rolling from one end to the other like a marble." I nodded and smiled. This was something that I could see in my mind's eye. "And whenever you get to a tee," he continued, "just ask yourself which way would you go if you were a marble."

"How will I know which way is right?" I asked.

"You'll feel it," he said.

He was giving me the essence of what engineers call delta-P, or pressure differential, and I liked his way because I really *could* feel it.

He also showed me how to use the Bell & Gossett System Syzer, and that tool eventually became my

American Express Card of Heating. I wouldn't leave home without it. The salesman also showed me how to size circulators in a commonsense way, and I liked that, too.

I was on the phones then, taking all those calls each day. Many of them went like this:

"Hello, this is Dan. How may I help you?"

"Yeah, listen. I got this pump and it ain't working. I got to get a new one and I need it in a hurry. There's no heat."

"What can you tell me about the pump?"

"It's red."

"Uh huh, and what else can you tell me?"

"It's broken."

I'd try to coax more information out of the guy. What was on the nameplate? Oh, there was no nameplate? How about on the motor? Could he get the horsepower rating? Can't read that either, eh? OK, how about the size of the flange? Or the length of the circulator from one end to the other? And the centerline between the flanges?

Often I'd be able to look in the old B&G catalogs and find what I thought might be the right one for the job, but this was making the big assumption that the circulator that was there now was the right size for the job, and that's a big assumption to make. After all, the circulator was broken, and maybe the reason why it was broken was because it was the wrong size.

So I'd think about that marble. Which way would I go if I were rolling through the pipe? I liked to think of my marble as being large enough to touch the inside walls of the pipe. Big enough to feel the friction as its sides rubbed against the insides of the pipes. Friction loss. Delta-P.

And there was also flow rate to consider, of course. I knew by this time that heat traveled on flow like a passenger on a train, and the more flow there is, the more heat there can be. You could see all of this on that beautifully simple tool, the System Syzer.   On it, Gil Carlson showed the normally used maximum flow rates for copper and iron pipes of various sizes. You could design for flows beyond these, of course, but you'd probably wind up with excessive pressure drop and velocity noise in most cases. If you stayed within Gil's limits you'd be safe. I liked being safe. So did the contractors.

Gil's wheel told me not to try to move more than 4 gpm through a 3/4-inch pipe. The folks who make baseboard convectors show that same limit, by the way. That's good enough for me. If I needed more than 4 gpm, I'd move up to a 1-inch pipe, which can handle up to 8 gpm.

When a contractor would call and tell me about the broken red circulator, and he didn't have any other information, I'd ask him what size pipe served the circulator. I'd figure that the circulator shouldn't try to pump more than that pipe could handle. Here are the limits I'd use:

- 1/2-inch pipe is good for 1-½ gpm
- 3/4-inch pipe is good for 4 gpm
- 1-inch pipe is good for 8 gpm
- 1-1/4-inch pipe is good for 14 gpm
- 1-1/2-inch pipe is good for 22 gpm
- 2-inch pipe is good for 45 gpm

And so on. If the contractor could tell me the pipe size, I could tell him the flow rate. Was I oversizing? Nope, I was sizing up to the maximum flow you could move through that pipe without having a problem. Did the job need that much? Can't tell for sure, but I was thinking that if I were the original designer I would size my pipe just this way. I'd use the smallest possible pipe to get the maximum flow needed, along with the best possible economy for the building owner. If the job needed 45 gpm, why would I use a main larger than 2 inch?

But pump head is another matter. I learned that, while I had to figure my total flow on the needs of all the circuits that the circulator would serve, I would only have to base the pump head on what the flow would see while traveling through the highest-pressure-drop circuit. If my circulator was serving a two-pipe, direct-return system with five circuits, it would only have to worry about the worst-case scenario, which was usually the longest of the five circuits.

Direct-return is sort of like a ladder. Figure the left side of the ladder is the supply; the right side is the return, and the rungs are the circuits. If I put in a circulator with enough head to make it up the left side, through the highest rung on the ladder, and back down the right side, then the circulator would have no trouble at all flowing through the lower rungs while it was at it.

It's sort of like saying that if you're able to drink five beers without falling down, then you'll also be able to drink less than five beers without falling down. That analogy work for you?

Good.

So once we figured out the circulator's flow needs (based on the size of the pipe it served), I'd ask the contractor what the longest circuit was. Then I'd allow 6 feet of pump head for every 100 feet of length in that circuit. Again, this is from Gil's System Syzer. When you're at the maximum normally used hydronic flow rate through a pipe of any given size, the head loss is going to be 4 feet per 100 feet. To this we have to add 50 percent to allow for the additional pressure drop through fittings, valves and other components. If I add 50 percent to 4 feet per 100 feet, I wind up with 6 feet per 100 feet. Easy.

The contractor would tell me the length of the longest (highest-pressure-drop) circuit, and that would give me the two things I'd need to size the circulator over the phone - flow and head. If he didn't know the longest circuit because all the pipes were hidden behind the walls and ceilings, I'd have him go outside and measure the length, width and height of the building. Then I'd imagine the longest run of pipe that I could put in that building.

I'd go from the left-hand corner of the building to the far end, then up to the top, across the top to the other side, down that side, back to the right-hand corner of the building, and finally, back to where I was standing. I'd base my pump head on that worst-case run, bumping off all the corners, and then I'd select it from the pump curves in the manufacturer's catalog. And if my point of operation fell between a pump that was larger and one that was smaller, I would always pick the smaller one.

I did this for the 19 years I worked for the rep and I never once got a pump back. Was I oversizing? Not at all. I was sizing based on the existing piping on the job, pipe that someone else had sized based on the heat-loss of the building. I figured that if the pipes were the wrong size, someone probably would have noticed that long before the pump I was replacing had failed.

It's a simple method, based on common sense, and it works.

Learning to think like air

Not long after we started in business, a caretaker called and asked if I would be willing to consult on a problem hot-water-heating system in "the biggest house you will ever see."

Who could say no to that?

The house, I soon learned, was the mansion at Duke Farms in Hillsborough, New Jersey, and the only resident of that house was Miss Doris Duke, only child of James Buchannan Duke, and heir to the American Tobacco Company fortune, as well as many other opulent things. And as large as it is, the mansion shrinks into place on the 2,700 acres of manicured gardens that surround it.

How's that for a lawn?

This is the family that endowed Duke University, which also has a very nice lawn. J.B. Duke knew how to put up significant buildings, designed to laugh at bad weather and hard times, and Doris Duke carried the torch he passed to her very well.

When I arrived at the house, and after I managed to get my slack jaw to close, I met the in-house plumber, who also doubled as the heating guy. He explained that Miss Duke was at her place in Hawaii because the heating in the mansion wasn't heating, and also because, well, she could. I nodded in understanding and continued to gape.

I asked if anyone else lived there and he said, "Just the staff." I nodded. "There are a hundred and five of us," he said. I nodded again – slowly. "Miss Duke employs a full-time professional in every trade you can imagine," he continued.

"That must be something," I said. "I mean working here."

He sighed. "Well, it's a very good job and I enjoy it, but do you have any idea what your life would be like if your entire focus from day to day involved pleasing one grand lady and being at her beck and call?"

I thought of your mother, Erin, and nodded again. "Yes, I can."

"Let's go inside," he said.

The main room contained everything but the Great Gatsby and Daisy, but what drew me were the bronze floor grates. Each was about two-feet square, and each puffed lukewarm air. I checked the temperature of the air with an electronic thermometer. Not good. The plumber chattered on about how the air coming from the grates was much hotter last year, but this is the best he could get from them now. "And nothing has changed," he said. "I don't understand. I have the boilers running up to 200 degrees but this is all I can get out of the grates."

Nothing changed. I hate when they say that. If nothing changed, I wouldn't be there.

We went to the basement, which could have hosted a bowling league. They had several boilers, all running with big circulators. I could tell by the size of the pipes that the system had once operated on gravity alone, which would have been normal for the time. The big pipes reached out and entered large sheet-metal ducts. I smiled because I'm a fan of indirect heating. It's how the rich got their fresh air back in the day. Fuel bills and income tax were not concerns.

I opened a sliding metal door on one of the ducts and saw the big, cast-iron indirect heaters looming in there. This architects who served the rich back in the day didn't want to burden them with radiators. Radiators were for the servants' quarters. The rest of the house drew its warmth from the hot air that wafted over these huge indirect heaters and rose upward through those bronze floor grates toward majestic ceilings. There was no return-air ductwork in most indirect systems. The air just leaked out of the house through loose windows. Fuel bills? Meh.

I noticed that someone had placed an oscillating fan inside the ductwork, just before the indirect heater. "What's this for?" I asked the plumber.

"I put it in there. I'm trying to blow the heat upstairs," he said. "It doesn't seem to be working, though, and that's what's got me stumped. Heat rises."

"Actually, it doesn't," I said. "Hot air rises."

"Well, same thing, right?"

"Not exactly," I said. "Heat radiates. Hot air will rise, but only if cold air can take its place.

"I don't get it."

"Come here; I'll show you." I followed the large sheet-metal duct back to where it met the foundation wall. "Where does this go?" I asked.

"Outside," he said.

"Where outside?"

"I don't know," he said. "I don't do outside. I do inside."

So we went outside and looked for a grate that would allow in the outside air. That's how these systems worked. They brought in 100 percent outside air that grabbed the heat from those huge hunks of cast iron inside the ductwork. Keep the wealthy healthy with lots of fresh air. We looked here and there but we couldn't find that grate, so we went back to the basement and measured in from the corner of the foundation to the spot where the sheet-metal duct met the wall. Then we went back outside and measured in from that same corner.

Where there should have been a grate there was only pachysandra, which was doing just fine in the cold weather because they have great gardeners at Duke Farms. You'd expect that from a place that's three times larger than New York City's Central Park.

"Was this groundcover here last winter?" I asked the plumber.

"I don't know," he said.

"You don't do outside, right?"

"Right."

So I waded into the greenery and stomped around on it for a while.

"The gardeners aren't going to like that," the plumber said.

"It's okay," I said. "I do outside."

And that's when my stomping made a hollow sound. I smiled. "Got a shovel?" He went to get one and I waited, and while I waited, I thought like air. How would I get into the house? He came back in a few minutes and handed me the shovel, I dug down a few inches and hit clear plastic. I moved some more of the dirt out of the way and saw the metal bars of the grate. "Time to get the gardener," I said.

When the gardener showed up, I explained what we were doing and how the air wouldn't move across the red-hot indirect heaters because there was no fresh air coming into the house. He understood but then explained how ugly those ground-level grates were and how they had decided to cover them all with sheets of clear plastic, topsoil and pachysandra. "That's why the house is cold," I said.

The gardener pointed to the plumber. "It's his job to keep it warm. It's my job to keep it green."

"The problem's outside," I said. "He doesn't do outside. You do."

And we went around like that for a while, Mr. Inside vs. Mr. Outside, until the gardener reluctantly agreed to remove one of the plastic sheets, just to prove me wrong. He scraped and grumbled while we waited, and then he lifted the edge of the plastic and I watched dead leaves get sucked past the grate and into the hole. Nice.

We went back inside and took the temperature of the now-hot air that was rising like a phoenix into the gorgeous rooms. Even nicer.

Lesson reinforced: Air won't move unless there's other air to take its place.

Second lesson learned: Sometimes the butler didn't do it. Sometimes, it's the gardener.

Learning not to bleed the air that isn't there

I learned this the hard way, and more than once. If, when bleeding air from a radiator, you don't not get any air, but only water, STOP BLEEDING! This is not an air problem; it is a balancing problem. There is no heat because not enough hot water is flowing that way. If you persist in bleeding air that is not there, you will eventually drag hot water from the boiler to the radiator, which will make you feel smart and (temporarily) satisfied.

If you don't get any air, it ain't an air problem.

Stop bleeding.

Learning about altitude

And in similar way, if you're bleeding a radiator and you're not getting any water, that's why you don't have any heat. Where there is no flow, there is no heat. And you can't have flow if you don't have water.

Either there's not enough fill pressure to lift water into that radiator, or something is blocking the water from flowing into that part of the system.

Go wander around and be nosey. That's where the fun is.

Learning about late-'70s ghosts

After the '73 OPEC oil embargo, boilers began to get smaller and smaller. The goal, of course, was to save fuel, and boiler manufacturers figured that if a boiler held less water, and was made of less metal, it wouldn't take as much fuel to get the water up to temperature.

We called these "flash" boilers because they seemed to work that quickly, but they brought with them an unusual problem. When we zone a building with circulators, we have to use flow-control valves after each circulator to prevent ghost flow. That's flow that's not supposed to happen, but does anyway. Cool name, isn't it?

A flow-control valve is a check valve with a heavy check. That weighted check stays closed when the circulator it serves is off. That prevents the hot water that's in the other zones from creeping into the zone that's off through a ghost flow. Heat doesn't rise. Hot water does.

These low-water-content, flash boilers came up to temperature so quickly that the rapidly expanding heated water now had the power to lift the weight inside the flow-control valve and overheat the zone that was supposed to be off.

Your grandpa was service manager at the manufacturers' rep at the time and this was a big problem for him and Richie the serviceman (who hated everyone). We serviced what we sold for the first year and the contractors were taking advantage of our commitment to that promise. Calls came in daily.

We asked the engineers at Bell & Gossett for their thoughts. They studied the problem and told us that it was caused by a thermal burp. Cool name again, right? They said that the same would happen if someone installed the flow-control valve too high above a modern boiler. They suggested we wrap solder around the weight in the flow-control valve to make it heavier. We suggested they do something to stop the problem. They suggested the solder again.

And that worked on some of the jobs, but not all of them, so your grandpa and Richie got together with a local machinist and had him make us some heavy inserts to take the place of what the factory supplied. These worked every time, but I cringe when I think of the extra pump energy that we wasted to push them open on a call from the thermostat. I'll bet each one of those brass inserts weighed a pound.

Their goal was to silence the complaints, though, and grandpa and Richie sure achieved that with a little ingenuity.

It's often more about people than it is about product.

Learning to listen to customers

Most customers aren't technical when it comes to hydronics, but they know what they see and hear, and they know what's normal within their buildings, and what's not.

An old-timer told me about how he would listen for the leaks in the copper tubing buried beneath the slab of a radiantly heated, Levittown house. He would crawl around the floor with a doctor's stethoscope, but as you can imagine, that's tough work. You need quiet and you need good knees. Most contractors have neither.

So he's crawling a house one day, listening away, when the homeowner starts asking him why he's doing what he's doing. He stops and explains that he can hear the leak if it's quiet (meaning, if she would just shut up), and that the hot water would be flowing sideways instead of in a straight line through the pipe where the pipe is leaking.

"Oh, I can show you where that is!" she said.

"Really?"

"Sure! Get up and sit over there." She puts him in a kitchen chair and leaves the room. She comes back with a bucket of water and a mop. She wets the mop and mops the kitchen floor.

"I don't get it," he says.

"Watch," she says, walking to the thermostat and giving it a push.

The contractor sat there for a few more minutes as the heat came up. Then he watched in amazement as the floor dried in a pattern over the pipes.

"See this over here?" she said. "That's new."

The floor was drying in a circle where the water was leaking.

"From that day on," the contractor told me, "I always listen. They may not be technical, but they sure ain't stupid."

Again, it's often more about people than it is about products.

Learning where not to put a thermostat

I once helped a contractor who had a problem with a house that went cold every afternoon at the same time. A little while later, things went back to normal. The homeowner would call the contractor and he would show up, only to find everything as it should be.

"The guy says it happens at three o'clock," he said.

"Maybe we should go there at three o'clock," I suggested.

"Yeah, that makes sense," he laughed.

What we saw made both of us laugh. The homeowner had hung a new mirror and it was in the perfect spot to bounce sunlight onto the thermostat on that other wall, and always at three o'clock during the winter. You had to be there to see it. You would have laughed, too.

Not that I'm immune to making such mistakes. When we added the dormer to the house, my heating contractor buddy asked me where I wanted the thermostat.

Knowing that your aunt Missy was prone to mess with the thermostat, I told my friend to put it in our bedroom, which faces due East, and which has that lovely circle-top window. Facing east.

On winter mornings, when the sunlight hits the upstairs thermostat, the heat goes off. Your mother questioned my judgment about the location I chose. I told her it was a new system of solar-setback, the latest in thermostat technology.

She rolled her eyes.

Speaking of Missy. As you know, people with Down syndrome can do some peculiar things for their own reasons, whatever they may be. When you were at college, Missy got in the habit of opening all the windows in the house during the winter. She would do this after your mother and I went to sleep, and since it was winter, we would notice it pretty quickly. I would ask her why she did this and she would deny doing it. But her eyes would waggle, you know, like they always do when she'd lying?

"Your eyes are waggling," I'd say.

"Don't bother me," she'd say.

Each month, her social worker would stop by and we would have a meeting about Missy's goals. Your mom and I told the social worker about the windows and we brainstormed a solution. We all decided to tell Missy that if the house got too cold from open windows during the winter, we were going to have to send all our money to the oil company. And that meant there would be no money to send her to camp next summer.

Made sense, right? We put finding a solution to the problem in her self-interest.

She got it, of course. There were no more open windows.

Then I woke up sweating one night in February. The house was nearly 90 degrees. I checked then thermostats and they were all pegged on the maximum setting. I turned them down and tried to go back to sleep.

The next morning, I asked Missy if she had touched the thermostat. She told me she wanted to go to camp next summer.

Okay, follow the logic:

If the house is cold, I can't go to camp.

Therefore, let me make the house hot so I can go to camp!

See? People, not products.

Which brings me to my favorite misplaced-thermostat story. I wrote this in 1995 when you were 14 years old. It's as true as can be, and I smile each time I reread it. I hope you enjoy the experience as much as I did.

Only Gus touch!

Here on Long Island they've turned nearly all the "Blob" diners into grandiose castles. They've taken all those wonderful stainless-steel restaurants that once looked like railroad cars and built over them so that now each looks like OZ.

People of Greek extraction own most of these diners and when you enter they whisk you to a table and rush over with glasses of ice water. After the ice water the menus arrive, and the menus are huge. Most have at least ten pages. On the typical Long Island diner menu you'll find everything from rye toast to roasted wild boar. Place your order and a scurrying waiter returns in minutes with more food than you can handle. You could eat yourself into a coma at one of these places. I've never figured out how they can keep so much food back there. And they never close.

I sat in one of these food factories on a hot and humid night last August with The Lovely Marianne, my sweet wife. We were on our way to pick up one of our four teenaged daughters from a place where young boys leer and slobber. We drank coffee, ate rice pudding and contemplated our place in the Universe.

"It's freezing in here," The Lovely Marianne said, wrapping her little hands around her coffee cup.

"That's heat transfer, you know," I said.

"What?"

"The way you're holding your hands around the cup." I touched the back of her hand with my finger tip. It felt soft. "The Btu are passing from the hot coffee, through the walls of the cup and into your hands." I smiled. She gave me a look that could curdle milk. I continued, nonetheless. "The walls of the ceramic cup, however, act as an insulator, my love." I stroked the tiny hairs on her forearm. "A metal cup would be better."

"Stop it," she said.

"Stop what?" I asked innocently.

"You know what."

"You don't like the way I'm stroking your arm?"

"That's fine. It's the other thing."

"You don't find heat transfer interesting?" I asked, innocently.

"Certain kinds of heat transfer, sure," she said with a wicked smile, "but not this, you bozo."

"They could take all the food out of the freezers and it wouldn't spoil in this place," I said. "Maybe that's what they're planning to do?"

"I think they just want to turn the tables over faster," she said.

"Well, let's give them this one, okay?" She nodded and stood up. I took one last gulp of coffee and we headed toward the cash register.

The owner, an elderly man who looked like Anthony Quinn in *Zorba the Greek,* stood behind the cash register and looked out over the shivering people of OZ. He wore a short-sleeved shirt and a wide smile.

"Mighty chilly in here," I offered.

He pointed to the five thermostats mounted on the wall next to the cash register.

"Seventy degrees," he said, and I started to giggle because this was the first time I'd noticed that all his thermostats were behind the cash register. No wonder the place felt like a coal mine.

"Something is funny?" he asked, the smile drooping into a frown.

"Oh no!" I said. "It's just that you have five thermostats and they're all mounted next to the front door."

He smiled and smacked himself in the chest with his big Zorba hand. Then he gestured grandly toward OZ and said, "This *big* place! I have zones. Five zones!" He pointed to each zone with a meaty finger and gave me that look SOMEONE IN THE KNOW gives to an idiot. "Most people, they don't understand about such things," he explained. "Big place! You zone to make more comfortable. Look! Big place, eh? I work hard for big place. Work for years. Used to have Blob diner, but no more! Now have BIG PLACE WITH ZONES!"

"It's wonderful," I said, "but whenever the door opens, the thermostats click on."

He shook his head and laughed slowly. "Heh, heh, heh." In three short bursts his laugh told me how remarkably stupid I was. He shook his head again and pointed to the thermostats. "Seventy degrees. You see? *Seventy degrees.* This is good!"

"Don't you think the thermostats would work better if they were actually *in* the zones there were supposed to be controlling," I offered.

He smiled even wider. "This is what stupid heating contractor want to do," he said. "You know what happens when thermostats are in room?" He waited.

"What?" I asked.

"Customer touch! Waiter touch! Waitress touch! Busboy touch! Cook touch! Wife touch! Daughter touch! Son touch! Everyone touch!" He pointed to everyone in the auditorium-size diner and then back toward the row of thermostats. People stopped talking and turned his way. "ONLY GUS TOUCH!" he proclaimed to the room, smacking himself on the chest again, just like Zorba. People looked at each other. Forks moving toward mouths stopped midway. "ONLY GUS TOUCH!" he shouted again.

"I see," I said.

"Can we go now," The Lovely Marianne asked.

"How was rice pudding?" Gus asked my beautiful bride.

"Chilled to perfection," she said with a shiver.

"Good!" Gus lit up the room with a final smile. "You come back soon, eh?"

"Soon as I warm up," she said.

"Good!"

We walked to the car, and before I could speak, she said, "Don't start, okay?"

"But it's everywhere, my little flying squirrel! Don't you see? Heating and cooling are an all-encompassing pursuit once you make it your life's work. It's a people sport. It's everywhere!"

"*Don't,*" she warned, giving me a look she usually reserves for slobbering boys who come seeking young Holohan women. "Don't start."

"Want me to turn on the heater?" I asked, turning the ignition key.

"No."

"Want me to tell you how the heater works?"

"No!"

"Heating is interesting, you know," I said.

"It's gonna get hotter in here if you don't stop," she said.

"You know that radiator in Jerry Seinfeld's apartment? You know, the one on the show? *Seinfeld*?"

She wasn't about to bite, so of course, I kept it up. "It's in his living room? Right under his window? You know the one, my sweet wife, my little steam trap?

"WHAT ABOUT IT?!"

"Well, that's not a *real* radiator, you know. There has never been such a radiator. You can tell by looking at it. It's not a column radiator, and it's not a tube radiator. It has this big boxy section near the bottom. I suppose it could be a Clow radiator. They used to make these Clow radiators with gas burners built right into them. When the steam was off you could light the burner and boil the condensate that sat in the bottom of the radiator. I suppose it could be one of those. I've seen those in the field. It amazes me that people still have those around. You could set fire to your curtains with one of those Clow radiators. Do you want me to show you one in a book when we get home, my little spider monkey?

The Lovely Marianne gave me that special look again. You know, the sort of look that makes you suspect you're about to enter a long tunnel with a bright light at the end of it. Like in a near-death experience?

She's crazy about me.

Learning not to deadhead a pump

One day, a contractor called to tell me about a large, base-mounted pump that he had installed in an office building. "I put in what the engineer specified," he said. "But this one is real noisy. I think we may need a new one."

"What sort of noise is the pump making?" I asked.

"It's shrieking like a jet taking off from Kennedy airport," he said.

"Sounds like velocity noise," I said.

"What's that?"

"It's what happens when a pump is too big," I explained. "The pump tries to shove too much water through the pipe and that's what makes the noise."

"But an engineer sized this," he said.

"They're human," I offered.

"I think we need a new pump," he said.

"Maybe not."

So I met him on the job and we put some gauges on this pump that was about the size of small pig. I took the difference between the suction and discharge pressures and found that point on the pump's performance curve. Sure enough, this one was way oversized and it had the velocity noise to prove it.

"I still think we need a new pump," the contractor said.

"Maybe not," I answered. "Let's make a system curve here."

"What's that?" he asked, and using my System Syzer, I showed him how to do this.

"We may be able to trim the impeller," I said. "We'll put it on a lathe and make it smaller. It's not my first choice as far as efficiency goes, but it will probably cure the noise problem."

"You sure we don't need a new pump?"

"Yep!" I said with supreme confidence.

Well, he thought that I was so bright that he didn't even notice the wet spots behind my ears. He just started asking me all sorts of questions and I was basking in the glow of the attention he was paying me. I felt like such a grown-up.

Needless to say, I wanted to answer all his questions, but first I had to find a quieter place so this is what I did:

1. I shut off the big pump.

2. I closed the isolation valves.

3. I removed the gauges.

4. I put the plugs back in the gauge tappings.

5. I restarted the big pump.

Unfortunately, Step 5 was suppose to be, I opened the isolation valves.

I restarted the pump should have been Step 6.

But these things happen.

So there we were, the contractor and me. We're standing just outside the boiler room. I'm talking; he's listening. We did this for what felt like maybe seven minutes, but might have been a bit longer. It's hard to say. But it was right around then that we heard the explosion.

"What's that?" he said, and it was just about then that I knew for certain what had happened because I had read about this in a book. Turns out you're not supposed to run a pump with the isolation valves closed. Energy in equals energy out, and if that spinning impeller can't move the water, the energy of motion quickly turns into heat. And that leaves you with one very scary butter churn.

"What the heck was that?" the contractor asked again.

"Beats me," I said (which is exactly what you would have said!). "Let's take a look."

We opened the door and my sphincter muscle did the mambo. Picture a rather large impeller spinning in space. The cast-iron volute is in chunks and stuck in the wall. I look at the contractor; he looks at me. He says, "Didn't I tell you we needed a new pump?"

To which I instantly agreed (which is exactly what you would have done).

Later, I went back to my office with my tail between my legs. I knocked on Walter Bosch's door. Walter was our resident engineer, a graduate of the Merchant Marine

Academy. He had, let's just say, a very colorful vocabulary. I sat down and told him what had happened to me and he laughed until he got tears in his eyes. And then he called me dirty names, all of which I had earned.

But Walter also had a way of turning your disasters into teachable moments and engineering lessons. He wrote up a memo to all of us in the company, which I have saved for all these years because it made such a powerful impression on me. Here is the gist of what he had to teach us.

"Recently, I was asked if a relatively large pump could run in a shut-off position for a full, eight-hour work shift. My response was, 'Hell, no!' The person doing the asking quantified by explaining that there might be a couple of hundred feet of three-inch pipe connected to the pump. I said, 'Don't do it!'

"I once attended a pump seminar sponsored by Chemical Engineering *magazine. One of the speakers, the chief engineer for a major pump manufacturer, gave us a quick-and-dirty formula for calculating the temperature rise in the volute of a pump running with the valves shut off. Here it is:*

$$\text{Temperature Rise (°F)} = \frac{5.1 \times BHP \text{ (at shut off)}}{\text{Volute volume in gallons} \times \text{Specific Gravity} \times \text{Specific Heat}}$$

"Let's assume the pump in question contains about seven gallons of water and has a 40-HP motor. Throw in 200 feet of three-inch pipe containing another 76 gallons of water:

$$\text{Temperature Rise (°F)} = \frac{5.1 \times 20 \, BHP}{76 + 7 = 83 \text{ gallons}} = \begin{array}{l} \textit{1.23 degrees} \\ \textit{per minute} \\ \textit{of operation} \end{array}$$

"Now, 1.23 degrees per minute, times 60 minutes, times 8 hours equals 590°F temperature rise. Neglecting the initial water temperature at saturation, we would approach 1,400 psig inside the casing. Pumps don't have that much safety factor!"

Then he gave us some other examples of this phenomenon. The one that stuck in my mind was the simple Bell & Gossett Series 100. Run a Series 100 with the valves closed and you'll get a temperature rise of just over 50 degrees per hour.

Amazing, right?

And consider a two-horsepower, Bell & Gossett Series 1535. That's the little close-coupled, end-suction, base-mounted pump you see on so many cooling towers all across America. Run that pump with the valves closed and you'll get a temperature rise of 1,590°F *per hour.*

Hard to believe, isn't it?

Yeah, I thought so, too.

Learning about steam-to-water heat exchangers

I visited an engineer who worked for the City of New York. He worked at a pitted drafting table in a green room that occupied about an acre of New York City real estate. He shared this green room with about a hundred other City engineers. Green is supposed to be a calming color.

We were looking at a plan for a new heating plant in a City-owned building. The plan called for a steam boiler that was about the size of a cape-cod house. It came complete with all the stuff you'd expect to find around a steam boiler of this size. Above the boiler hung a steam-to-water heat exchanger that was as big as a two-man submarine.

"What's the deal with the heat exchanger," I asked.

"We're heating the building with hot water," the engineer mumbled without looking up from the blueprint.

"I can see that," I said, "But the building is only three stories tall." I was telling him something that he, of course, already knew.

"Uh huh," he muttered, still staring at the plan.

"So why are you using a steam boiler?" I asked out of genuine curiosity. "The building's only three stories tall." He looked at me from over the top of his reading glasses. "Why don't you just use a hot water boiler," I persisted "If you use a hot water boiler you won't need the heat exchanger, the boiler-feed pump, these steam traps, the temperature regulator, the strainers." I pointed at all the unnecessary gear on the blueprint.

The engineer smiled at me. "Do you understand steam heat?" he asked gently. I nodded. "Do you understand the people who take care of steam heat?" he pressed on.

"Not sure what you mean," I said. He smiled and stood up from the drafting table.

"The people who take care of steam heat are used to doing things a certain way." His eyes took on a look you get only after spending a lot of years in a green room. "These people blow-down low-water cutoffs. They flush mud legs. They set pressuretrols. They watch pressure gauges. They clean strainers. They scrutinize gauge glasses. They pop relief valves. They're members of a trade union. If we put in a hot water boiler, we will be denying these people the pleasures they've come to expect from a New York City boiler room. "And if we deny them these pleasures," he continued, "they will get aggravated and do bad things. We don't want them to do bad things so we give them what they expect, which is a steam boiler. Do you understand"

"Sort of," I said.

"Good!" He went back to looking at the plans.

Often, it's more about people than products.

In another part of New York City there's a housing project that stretches for blocks. This is a place where thousands of people live together as total strangers. New York City heats these buildings with hot water, and here too, they use a steam boiler and a steam-to-water heat exchanger. How come? Because the buildings are very tall and high-pressure, hot-water boilers can get pretty pricey and require special people to watch over them. The engineers could have used steam, but few people want to heat directly with steam nowadays, so they did it with a heat exchanger. That also kept the union guys in the boiler room happy.

What the engineers wound up with in this case were a couple of boilers that were as big as two-story buildings and a steam-to-water heat exchanger that looks like a Greyhound bus.

I visited the boiler room on a frigid January morning when the thousands of strangers who live in the connected high-rise buildings were freezing and screaming. The water flowing through their radiators wouldn't get any hotter than 150-degrees, which just doesn't get the job done in January.

Now, before I go any further, I have to tell you how this system works:

The boiler sends steam to the heat exchanger, which hangs in space like a steel dirigible. Condensate from the heat exchanger's shell drips into the return side of the boiler without benefit of a boiler-feed pump. This is okay because you don't need a boiler-feed pump when your heat exchanger is that close to the boiler and your boiler pressure is only 2 psi or so. All you need is gravity, and they had plenty of that. There is no steam trap on the heat exchanger because, without a boiler-feed pump, there is no need for one.

On the water side, big base-mounted pumps whip the lukewarm fluid out of the heat exchanger and send it flowing under the city streets to the mechanical-equipment rooms of the high-rise buildings. These are the primary pumps.

Secondary pumps in the mechanical rooms of each building snatch hot water from the primary flow and send it skyward toward the radiators. These pumps are also pretty impressive to look at.

Everything worked as it should on the day I was there, except the 150-degree water was too cool to heat human beings. Nevertheless, a small army of men in overalls went from apartment to apartment bleeding radiators. They didn't get any air when they bled those radiators, but that didn't stop them from bleeding. They bled because that's what people in overalls do when there's no heat. They bleed.

When I got there, the boiler room was filled with official-looking guys. Each had an electronic thermometer and a clipboard. These folks were busy probing the pipes and taking temperatures here and there. After a few hours of data collection, this is what they decided: The water, at 150 degrees, was too cool to heat human beings on that particular day.

Their solution was to raise the steam pressure. They raised the steam pressure because that's what people with clipboards do when there is no heat. They had it up to 13-psig when I arrived, and the only thing that kept them from pushing it higher was the 15-psig relief valve setting. They had reached the limits of this particular technology.

"There's no air vent on the heat exchanger," I mentioned, after poking around the boiler room for a while.

"What are you talking about?" a guy with a clipboard said.

"If you were air, could you get out of the shell of that heat exchanger?" I asked, pointing up. They looked. The condensate return line left the heat exchanger and dropped straight into the bottom of the huge boiler. "There's no way for air to get out," I said. "The steam can't get at the whole tube bundle because air is in its way. Steam and air won't mix. You're probably using about a quarter of the exchanger's capacity. That's why the water isn't hot enough."

They weren't buying this.

"This system has worked fine for years," one of them said.

"Do you ever shut the boiler off?" I asked, looking at the vacuum breaker in the exchanger's shell.

"Never!" they said in unison. "We use it year round for domestic hot water. We never shut it off."

"Never?"

"NEVER!"

"Well, somebody must have shut it off. The shell's full of air. Steam can't get in because the air can't get out. That's why the water isn't getting hot."

"That can't be it," one of the clipboard guys said.

"Why not?" I asked.

"Because it's worked for years."

"But it's not working now," I said.

"It's worked for years!" he insisted.

"But when you don't know what's causing the problem, how can you discount any possibility?" I asked. "Aren't you violating the first rule of troubleshooting?"

"Which is?" the clipboard guy asked, giving me a look that could set asbestos on fire.

"To remember that we're all human. And then to check everything off the list of possibilities." I said. "Right now, it's acting like it's bound up with air, and that's certainly possible if the boiler had shut down, even for just a little while."

They still weren't buying it so I asked one of the boiler room guys if he would take a wrench and clamber up on top of the big boiler. When he got there, I shined my flashlight on this union that was on the heat exchanger's condensate drain line. I told him to loosen it. He did, and a ferocious rush of air came spewing out of the exchanger's shell. Steam shot across the heat exchanger and the water temperature shot up almost instantly.

"There you go," I said.

"But we never shut these boilers off," the guy with the clipboard insisted. And for the first time, he turned to one of the boiler-room guys for confirmation. To this point, no one had spoken to any of the boiler-room guys, so naturally, they hadn't offered any information. It's like that in NYC. Clipboard guys with ties hardly every talk to boiler-room guys in blue jeans. And vice versa, of course.

"You ever shut this boiler off?" the clipboard guy asked.

"We shut it off for a half-hour last week to do a repair," came the answer.

And that's all it took to fill the shell with air. A lousy half-hour. The vacuum breaker opened as the steam in the shell cooled and turned to condensate. A vacuum formed and the vacuum breaker went to work, sucking in great gobs of air. And once the air got in, it couldn't get out because there was no air vent in the condensate-return piping.

I had them add a main vent to the discharge side of the shell. It should have been in there from the start, but someone in the green room had missed that small detail.

Which is easy to understand. We're only human.

And speaking of humans, we sure can be angry at times. The older I get, though, the more I realize that getting angry is a waste of time. It's better to laugh, and this business sure provides enough chances to do that.

Here's another heat-exchanger story for you, Erin. This one happened when you were still a baby and I was working for the manufacturer's representative. I knew enough then to keep my mouth shut and pay attention.

There was this steam boiler in Manhattan that was feeding a steam-to-water heat exchanger that we had sold. The boiler-feed pump, which we had also sold, was overflowing and the contractor had a telephone, so he used it. Your grandpa sent Richie, who was very capable with the tools, and who knew every curse word ever muttered, as well as some of his own making. Walter Bosch, our mechanical engineer, decided to join Richie. He was as good as Richie was with the cursing. I went along to be quiet and learn.

We got into Richie's Chevy station wagon and headed for the City. Richie cursed every driver around him as Walter and I listened, appreciating the verbal virtuosity and creativity of the man who hated everyone, and when we were about 20 minutes from the job, Richie had decided that whatever was wrong with this job was the contractor's fault. Richie was superb at that. He hated everyone who bought our products, but he was very good with the tools.

Anyway, we got to the job, met the contractor (whom Richie brushed by) and headed to the boiler-feed pump. It was vomiting hot water out its receiver vent and all over the floor. The contractor made a comment about the quality of our products, which caused Walter to glare and Richie to growl. I just watched and kept my mouth shut.

Richie picked up a wrench, which caused me to take a step backward, but he used it on the receiver's float valve instead of the contractor. The float valve was holding. Its job was to maintain a minimum water level so the boiler had feed water for the first start-up. Once the condensate returns from the system, the receiver wouldn't need the feed valve again. A bad feed valve could cause what was happening, but this time it wasn't the culprit. Richie mumbled some words that were made of acid and barbed wire.

"Excuse me?" the contractor said.

"Nothing wrong with the product," Richie said, and then mumbled some more. Richie could have made Lil Wayne blush.

"Let's look at that heat exchanger," Walter said. It was the shell-and-tube type, and it was sitting on a rack about six feet above the steam trap and condensate-transfer pump, which moved the condensate from the heat exchanger to the boiler-feed pump. There was a steam regulator on the feed line to the heat exchanger, which is normal for this set-up. Walter later explained to me that the reason why the heat exchanger was mounted as high as possible over its steam trap was because, when the steam regulator closed, the only pressure available to shove the condensate through the steam trap was the weight of the water in the vertical pipe between the heat exchanger's outlet and the steam trap's inlet. That made sense. I mean a steam trap just sits there. Condensate won't move through it unless there's differential pressure. The trap's outlet connected to a condensate receiver that was vented to the atmosphere, so all we needed was a few feet of stacked water on the trap's inlet side to build weight and we were good to go.

Walter watched the transfer pump, which was quickly cycling on and off, even though the steam regulator was closed at the moment. That seemed like a lot of condensate. Or was it?

And that's when Walter noticed the pipe plug. It was screwed into a three-quarter-inch tapping in the shell of the heat exchanger. Next to that plug was a large, bright-red sticker that read, INSTALL VACUUM BREAKER HERE!

"Sir, do you see this?" Walter asked the contractor.

Richie snarled. I watched in wonder.

"Yeah," the contractor said.

"Please read it to me," Walter said.

The contractor smirked. "It says, INSTALL VACUUM BREAKER HERE!"

"And what is this?" Walter asked, touching the pipe plug.

"Pipe plug," the contractor said. "That's the way it came."

"Why didn't you do what the sticker demands?" Walter asked.

"I didn't have a vacuum breaker," he said. "Besides, plugs cost less and don't leak."

Richie reached down into a bushel basketful of dirty words I had never heard before. They drooled from his mouth like lava.

"Richie," Walter said, "please pull the tube bundle. Dan, help him."

"Wadda ya doin' that for?" the contractor asked.

"To show you what you did," Walter said. "They teach this in the Merchant Marine Academy."

Now pulling a tube bundle from a shell-and-tube heat exchanger involves a lot of nuts and bolts, but it was worth it because when we slid it out and looked at the curved end of the tubes we saw the holes. Those tubes looked like someone had taken a hammer and chisel to them.

"There's your problem," the contractor shouted. "You make lousy heat exchangers. Look at those holes! And this thing is just a few weeks old. Piece of crap leaks!"

Walter nodded. "Yes, the water from the hot-water system is leaking into the shell of the exchanger. That's what's flooding the boiler-feed pump. The transfer pump is just dumping that water into the feed-pump's receiver. As I said, they teach all this at the Merchant Marine Academy. They call it basic physics. It involves stuff like atmospheric pressure and gravity. You know about gravity?"

"You're gonna pay for this," the contractor said.

Walter gave the guy a Jack Nicholson smile. "Dan," he said, "there's a deli downstairs. Go get me a bottle of water and a straw. We'll wait for you."

I did what I was told and was back quickly. The contractor looked more annoyed than ever. Richie was deep-breathing. Walter took the bottle of water and the straw. He unscrewed the cap, slipped the paper off the straw, dipped it into the bottle, placed his finger over the top of the straw, pulled the straw out of the bottle, extended his hand with the straw so it was in front of the contractor's face, lifted his finger, and just smiled as the water slid out of the straw and onto the floor. Then he did it again. And again. "Atmospheric pressure and gravity," Walter said. "Basic physics."

Richie mumbled words that even Lil Kim wouldn't say.

"What's your point," the contractor said.

"My point is that my finger is the vacuum breaker," Walter said. "When I lift it, the water leaves the straw. If I don't lift it, the water stays inside the straw, or inside the shell of the heat exchanger. And when water, which we call condensate, stays inside the exchanger, the steam is going to find it the next time the steam regulator opens. And that steam is going to hammer that water off the back of the steel shell. Then the water is going to bounce back and smash into the tube bundle at the exact point where the tubes are curved and at their weakest. That's why the tube bundle is leaking and that's the source of your problem here. And notice I said *your* problem."

"You mean all of this is because of that pipe plug?" the contactor said.

"Yes," said Walter. "That's why the factory puts that sticker on the shell. It reads, INSTALL VACUUM BREAKER HERE!"

"Who's supposed to pay for this?" the contractor asked.

"You are," Richie hissed.

"Why me? I didn't know."

"So true," Walter said. "You *didn't* know. So just think of the cost of the new tube bundle and the vacuum breaker as tuition."

Richie had much more to say once we were back in the Chevy. He got that contractor out of his system and then went back to cursing the other drivers.

I figured that contractor was never going to buy another product that we represented. There were plenty of other choices for him. Walter and Richie were right in what they were saying, but sometimes you win the battle and lose the war. I'm sure that as the years went by, that contractor told everyone he met that we suck more than that vacuum breaker. Even though the mistake was his.

Often it's people, not products.

Learning about more ghosts (with primary-secondary)

The guy had told his architect to have a corner of his basement dug out so that he could play half-court basketball with his two kids.

The ceiling was 14 feet above the parquet floor and there was an electronic scoreboard hanging on the wall that would have made Michael Jordan smile. Down the hall there was a theater, a mahogany bar with lots of stools, a workout room, and a wine cellar. And that was just what was in the basement.

Oh, and he also had ghosts.

The contractor who installed the heating system in this yuppie wonderland had pulled out all the stops. The owner had asked for the best that was available and that's pretty much what he got. The boiler room looked like a collaborative effort between NASA, Bill Gates, and Leonardo da Vinci. It took my breath away when I first saw it. Four boilers stood side by side along the wall. The pipes lined up with military precision in a primary-secondary fashion. The controls were in charge and knew exactly what had to be done. It was everything I would have assembled if I had all that money.

"Feel this pipe," the contractor whispered, glancing nervously toward the boiler-room door. We were standing in front of a long primary manifold. There were 20 pairs of secondary lines coming off the bottom of the manifold. Each dipped down a foot before turning up toward the ceiling and then heading out toward the far reaches of this mansion.

I grabbed hold of the secondary line and winced. "Ouch! Is the circulator on?"

"No," he said nervously. "Now feel this return line over here. It's even hotter, and this circulator's off, too. I'm pretty sure the primary pump is pushing water up into the secondary circuits. Here, feel this one over here." He led me to a pipe on the far side of the boiler room. I reached up and grabbed it. It was hot. "That's a return line," he said.

"How could it get that hot unless the primary pump is doing it?"

This was one of those times in life when the reality of the job supersedes what you read in textbooks, but I just couldn't see it in my mind's eye. The supply and return tees to each secondary circuit were so close together. They were practically touching each other.

"I'm not so sure about the primary pump," I said. He rolled his eyes in frustration. I pressed on. "I mean, if you were water, and you were flowing through this primary main and you got up to this first tee, wouldn't you go straight through into this second tee?" I pointed at it. "It's only an inch away. Why would you go through the bull of that first tee, all the way up through that long circuit, and then back through the bull of the second tee? It just doesn't make any sense. Water's always going to take the path of least resistance, and in this case, that path of least resistance is such a clear choice. It's only an inch away, for Pete's sake."

"Then how come the pipe's so hot all the way over there?" he asked, hitting me in the puss with the reality of the situation. I hate that.

"I don't know," I admitted.

"It's gotta be the primary pump," he insisted.

"I don't know. I think it's probably ghost circulation."

"How can it be ghost circulation?" he asked. "I've dropped every secondary circuit a foot below the primary main. Hot water rises. How can it go down?"

"I don't think a foot is enough of a drop," I said, feeling the hot pipes again.

"Well, what would be enough of a drop then?" he asked. "Should I go all the way to the floor? The reason I did the heat traps was to avoid having to use forty flow-control valves. Am I going to have to take all of this apart and install flow valves?"

"Maybe."

"I still think it's the primary pump," he insisted. "It's gotta be pushing up into the secondary circuits. Look at how fast it's moving."

"Then why are some of the returns getting hot?" I asked. "I mean, feel this one over here." I grabbed hold of a return line, about ten feet away from the primary main. It was red hot. "The supply line for this same circuit is lukewarm, but feel this side."

"It's gotta be the pump," he insisted again.

And we went around and around like that for a while and got to the point where we were just staring at the equipment. Jobs like this one require a great deal of staring.

Finally, I suggested that we drill and tap the supply and return side of one of the secondary circuits and put some pressure gauges on it. My thinking was that we could get a pressure reading on the two gauges with the primary pump off. Then we could start the primary pump to see if the gauges changed. If the primary pump moved water through the secondary circuit, the gauges would show a difference in pressure from supply to return. If the gauges didn't move, that meant that the movement of heat that we were feeling was happening by gravity circulation alone. It was ghost flow.

We spent a half-hour getting the thing set up and then we started the pump. The gauges held rock-steady. We looked at each other and knew for sure that what we were seeing was a ghost.

"It can move that fast?" he asked.

"I guess so," I said, hardly able to believe what I was seeing. If you were there with us, I'll bet you would have thought it was a pumped flow as well. It was moving that fast! But it didn't seem to care whether it was doing it on the supply or return side, and that's what was so strange.

So we learn. He wound up installing 40 flow-control valves and the problem went away. Neither of us knew how low a heat trap would have to be to effectively stop this radical a ghost gravity circulation, so we took what seemed the safest path. We wanted this one to go away once and for all.

And it did.

That day, when I got into my car and tried to back out of the rich man's driveway, he pulled up right behind me in his Bentley. He got out, slammed the car's door, which sounded like a bank vault closing. I stepped out and mentioned that I was just leaving, but his car was blocking me in. I had never met this guy before, and he didn't know why I was there.

"You'll wait," he said, brushing by me.

So I sat in my car until he returned, which took a good long while.

Having money doesn't mean that you have class, Erin. That's worth remembering.

Smokey and the Band-Aid

You and your sisters had a great education. Not everyone is that fortunate. Many in this industry get their diplomas through the School of Hard Knocks, where the tuition can often be high.

And then there are some in this business who take those Hard-Knocks courses, pay the high tuition, but still refuse to learn from their mistakes.

Which brings me to another story.

Smokey currently resides in Ol' Stony Lonesome, but when he was with us, he was magnificent in his thick-headedness. As is the case with some in this trade, Smokey was born with the entire world's knowledge already in his head and didn't feel he ever had to ask for advice. He would take on heating jobs with the total confidence that comes with a thick skull, and when things went south, he would continue to move in the wrong direction because that is the nature of a man who already knows everything. Physics, biology and mathematics mean nothing to such men.

Smokey believed that cigarettes were harmless because his father had had an uncle who had smoked until he was nearly 90 years old, and if it was possible for that man to smoke for so many years without ill effect, then all the doctors in the world were wrong. For Smokey, the exception was the rule, and he saw himself as that exception.

Smokey used one match in the morning to get himself lit off and this was only because he had to sleep for a bit at night. If he could have kept last night's last cigarette burning through the wee hours, he would have used its still-glowing butt to get himself going at first light, but no one makes such a cigarette, so he used the one match and sucked smoke all day, as though it was a religious calling. He was the only man I have ever met who could out-smoke Gil Carlson.

Smokey asked for my help one day, but in a way that fit his character, meaning that he didn't actually ask for help (men who know everything require no help). He merely called to say that I really needed to see this horrible air separator, which was never able to vent all the air from this heating system that he had just installed because it wasn't as good as the ones they used to make.

"It vents whenever the pumps are running," he said. "It's never finished. I hate it, and you should hate it too. You should write about it in the magazines and tell everyone to stop buying this air separator because it never stops venting. It can't get the job done."

"Where is all this air coming from?" I asked.

"The air separator is making it," Smokey said, and there was not a trace of doubt in his voice. The man was born with his mind made up.

So we got together on the job, which had radiant tubing in a concrete slab. It was Smokey's first radiant job, but that was not a problem because Smokey already knew all there was to know about radiant-floor heating. "You put the tubing in the concrete," he said. "You heat the water, and you pump it through the tubing. The building gets hot."

Case closed.

It was around 9:30 in the morning, and Smokey was bashing his second box of Marlboro's for the day onto his left palm to tamp down the tobacco before tearing at the cellophane with his teeth.   "These pumps suck, too," he said. "I want you to tell people about them. Tell them not to buy them."

"Why?" I asked.

"Look at how many you need to get the job done!" he said.

There were six of them, and Smokey had bolted them together, flange to flange, and on the return side of this cast-iron boiler. This, it turns out, was his Band-Aid.

"You get a special on these circulators?" I asked.

"That's how many you need to get anything moving through the tubing," he said. He lit another Marlboro and left the stub of the last one burning on the edge of the boiler.

"How much tubing do you have on this job?" I asked.

"I don't know," he said, "probably more than a thousand feet."

There were no manifolds. The boiler had a 1-1/2" supply, which Smokey had reduced to 3/8" after leaving the air separator (which never seemed to be able to finish doing its job). The single tube then entered the concrete floor like a deep-space voyager and eventually returned from the concrete on the other side of the boiler, where it connected to an air vent that was the size of a can of Budweiser. The first of the six circulators followed. From there, it was a hydronic daisy chain of pure pressure. It looked like the Six Flags of heating.

"You don't believe in radiant circuits, do you?" I said.

"Wadda ya mean?"

"A thousand feet of tubing, broken up into, say, five 200-foot circuits?"

"Too many chances for leaks," Smokey said.

"You buried more than a thousand feet of three-eighth-inch tubing as one long piece, didn't you?"

Smokey lit another Marlboro, spit a fleck of biomaterial, and nodded. "Yep, that's how it's done."

"That's why you need all these pumps," I said.

"I know," he said. "One's not strong enough. You should write about that. The manufacturer sucks."

"Oh, I will," I said. "And that's quite a boiler bypass."

Smokey has piped a half-inch copper line from the supply side of the boiler to the suction side of his circulator railroad. There was a ball valve in the line for balance. It was closed.

"Gotta protect the boiler from low temperature," Smokey said. "I know all about that."

"I'll bet the boiler comes up to temperature quickly."

"Like a rocket," Smokey said. "But you're here for that lousy air separator. Listen to that thing."

It was whooshing, all right. It was nearly as loud as the Budweiser-size air vent on the suction side of Smokey's circulator sculpture. He was staring at the air separator and shaking his head. "Garbage," he said, exhaling a cloud of smoke, which I watched swirl right into the big air vent.

"Have you ever noticed," I said, "how blowing and sucking sound about the same?"

"Wadda ya mean?" Smokey said.

"I mean how air, when moving quickly through a hole, makes about the same sound, whether it's going this way or that way. Blowing or sucking? Ever notice that?"

"Can't say as I have," Smokey said.

He lit another smoke, blew out, and once again, the huge air vent sucked it right in.

"Do you know about the point of no pressure change? How it's at the place where the compression tank is? And if you pump toward that point with a big enough pump, or with, say, six pumps piped in series, stem to stern like what you have here on your Band-Aid, you're going to get quite a negative pressure on the suction side of that pump. Or pumps."

"Huh?"

"Blow some more smoke that way," I said, pointing toward the vent. He did. The vent sucked in the smoke nearly as quickly as Smokey was blowing it out.

"Wow!" Smokey said. "A system after me own heart!" He let loose a laugh, which turned into a hacking cough.

"Now watch over here," I said, pointing at the air separator. He did. "You won't see the smoke come out because this isn't a hookah."

"Huh?"

"You're sucking in air because you're pumping at the point of no pressure change with lots of pumps in series. The combined pump-differential pressure is greater than the system's static fill pressure. That's why the vent is sucking. The air is probably eating this boiler. The air separator is trying its best to get rid of the air that the vent is sucking in," I said. "Sucking and blowing."

"I hate that thing," Smokey said, giving the air separator the finger.

"Under the circumstances," I said, "I think you should be thanking it."

"I hate it. You're not going to help me get even by writing about this, are you?" Smokey snarled.

"I will when it's time," I said.

"When's that?"

"Someday," I said.

And now it's time.

Learning about pump cavitation

When Gil Carlson would come to New York City to speak at an ASHRAE event, my old boss would ask me to sit with him and keep him company during the day. This was difficult because Gil was a good listener, and by this I mean that he didn't talk that much, or at least not to me. Now that I'm older than he was then I realize that he probably didn't speak to me because he didn't have much to say to a dopey kid.

So I would ask him question after question. I might say, "Mr. Carlson, how did you come to realize that circulators in closed systems should always pump away from the compression tank?"

He would answer, "It's just something I've always known." And he would smile.

And then I was left to come up with the next dopey question. And this would go on all day long. It the reason why I can now stand in front of big groups of people and speak nonstop for hours and hours. Dead air is inspirational.

As you know, I'm not an engineer, and what I know of engineering came to me by way of books, listening and paying attention, and it arrived mostly years after the days I was trying to get Gil to those ASHRAE meetings on time.

I'd sit and listen to his lectures, mostly in a state of utter confusion because Gil would launch into this stratospheric ballet of math and charts and graphs. It was only his visual stuff that stuck with me – the word pictures, and fortunately, there were enough of those to make me want to learn more.

At one point during one of these talks Gil put up an overhead slide that read N.P.S.H. and he asked, "Does anyone know what this acronym stands for?"

An engineer in the front row answered, "Net Positive Suction Head."

"Well, there's that," Gil said. "But it also has *another* meaning? Anyone?" And at this point he once again became a hydronic lighthouse, beaming that maniacal grin of his across the room. And sitting once again, he repeated, "Anyone?"

No one answered. Gil lit yet another cigarette, smiled, and said, "It stands for NOT (he underlined the N with his crayon) PUMPING (he underlined the P) SO (and so on) HOT!" And then he beamed out another of those wild smiles and the place went nuts.

This is how I came to understand N.P.S.H.. I learned from Gil that there are two kinds. First, there's N.P.S.H.A., which stands for Net Positive Suction Head Available, and then there's N.P.S.H.R., which is short for Net Positive Suction Head Required. The first is what you find on the job; the second is what the pump manufacturer determines the pump needs.

But now I have to back up a step and ask you to consider the shape of a centrifugal-pump's impeller. It has a hole in its center, which we call the "eye" because it acts like the eye of a hurricane. Water enters the circulator through the impeller's eye. Branching out from the eye we have a bunch of curved vanes, and these end at the outer edge of the impeller.

When the impeller spins, it takes the water that's within the eye and flings it outward along those curving vanes to the edge of the impeller, and from there toward the outlet of the circulator. The instant this happens, there's going to appear at the eye of the impeller a pressure that's lower than the pressure that's at the edge of the impeller. Water in the circulator's suction line will rush in to take the place of the water that's no longer within the eye of the impeller, and since you can't compress water, and because the system is completely filled with water, the whole big wheel of water turns.

I hope I painted a good word picture there.

Okay, now imagine what happens if we clog the circulator's suction line with debris so that when the impeller throws the water from its eye, not enough new water can enter to take the place of the missing water.

Think of a pump that's serving a cooling tower. Imagine there's a lot of crap stuck in the pump's inlet strainer. Or think of a boiler-feed pump, where the condensate is red-hot and close to the boiling point. What if the impeller tosses out that hot water and there's not enough new water to take its place?

In both of those cases (cooling towers and boiler-feed pumps) there often isn't much positive pressure available to enter the suction side of the pump. The level of water in the cooling tower, or the boiler-feed pump receiver, probably isn't that high. And since both those systems are open to the atmosphere, the only positive pressure you have going for you is the weight of the water above the inlet to the pump. Subtract from that positive pressure the pressure drop through a strainer and the approach piping and you wind up with N.P.S.H.A. That's what's available (it's also the reason why we put strainers *after* the pump on cooling towers).

And that brings us to the pump manufacturer. They'll test each pump to see how much Net Positive Suction Head the pump will *require*, and they publish this on their pump curves. If what the pump requires isn't available then you smack right into Not Pumping So Hot.

Most engineers (other than Mr. Carlson) call this "cavitation," and here's what that's all about.

Water boils at 212 F., but only at sea level. If you go to Aspen, Colorado, you'll be able to boil water at 197 F. When pressure drops, so does the boiling point of water. When an impeller spins, the pressure at its eye drops and if there's not enough N.P.S.H. available, the water will reach the point where it flashes to vapor. This isn't steam because we're not adding any more Btu; it's just vapor, but it's still going to ruin your pump (and your day).

The vapor bubbles form at the eye and get flung along the impeller vanes toward the outer rim of the impeller, where the pressure is high. The bubbles then collapse under the higher pressure and the surrounding liquid water screams in to fill up the spaces formed as the bubbles cave it. The water hits the edges of the impeller with incredible force. It's enough to quickly chew up an impeller and wreck the pump. Standing on the outside, it sounds like the pump is moving gravel. What you're hearing is the sound of the water colliding with and wrecking the impeller.

Oh, and note how the cavitation happens only when there's not enough N.P.S.H. available. To make this happen in a closed, hot-water heating system, you'd have to have a pump that can produce a differential pressure that's greater than the system's static fill pressure, and you'd have to be pumping right at the point of no pressure change (the location of the compression tank). This is rare, and the reason why we don't see much cavitation in hydronic-heating systems. You really have to screw up to make it happen, but that doesn't mean you won't be successful.

For instance, set up a two-temperature system (say low-temperature radiant along with high-temperature radiators) and use a three-way mixing valve to get the lower temperature. It's possible to pipe this in a way so that when the three-way valve goes to bypass it isolates the secondary (radiant) pump from the system's compression tank. The moment that happens, the radiant pump will cavitate, and if no one notices, it will die in a hurry.

That's why it's best to use a three-way diverter valve rather than a three-way mixing valve on this application. When the diverter valve shifts, the secondary circuit will still have the benefit of the compression tank, which is in the primary circuit. It's a small detail, but it can save your secondary circulator.

Now Pursue Smarter Heating!

Water, water everywhere

With hydronics, you can't get away from water, and some of that water is quite special.

I read a news story about a heating technician who had gone to Madonna's digs in England to repair one of her radiators. She has those classic European panel radiators and each has its own set of valves. The techs had shut off the radiator and were draining the water from it when the maid showed up and screamed. Turns out, Madonna is a disciple of Kabbalah, which concerns itself with the mystical aspects of Judaism. Part of that belief system involves Kabbalah water, and Madonna had had her heating system filled with that very expensive version of H_2O. After a rabbi blesses this water, it is supposed to have the power to return to its primordial state of completely positive, healing energy.

How about that?

The maid was concerned about spillage because Madonna had spent about $10,000 on the stuff, which proves, once again, that it's very good to be crazy rich.

So, Erin, no matter what anyone tells you, remember that all water is not just water. You and I learned this as young Catholics. We go to church and bless ourselves with holy water. The nuns reinforced that teaching for me with a 12-inch ruler. You had it easier but this is another of those times when the worth of something depends on the value we assign it.

I also read that Guy Richie left Madonna in 2008, right after she insisted on filling their swimming pool with Kabbalah water. Big price for that. Guy had had enough.

I was at a trade show in Atlantic City and I was thirsty, so I looked around for a water fountain. The one I found was right next to a machine that sold water. I stood there for a while and thought about how, in the United States of America, you can sell absolutely anything to just about anyone if you do a good enough job of describing the thing's virtues and value.

The brand of water in the machine was Dasani, a product of the Coca-Cola® Bottling Company. I went to their Web site to see what made this water better (and certainly more expensive) than common tap water, which was free for the taking, and right there next to their big, expensive machine. The Dasani site explains that the good folks at Coca-Cola begin with "the local water supply" and filter it. Then they add a special blend of minerals "to make it taste crisp." In other words, it's filtered tap water in a plastic bottle - for two bucks. Oh, but they also provide nutritional information on the label, for those who are health conscious. This is good to know: Dasani water contains:

- 0 calories

- 0 fats

- 0 sodium

- 0 carbohydrates

- 0 protein

This is because it is *water*. Nevertheless, it is very special water. Otherwise, why would it cost two bucks?

I think about water all the time. Your mother and I were visiting the good folks at Lochinvar in Nashville,

Tennessee, and they put us up at the Gaylord Opryland Resort, which is like Disneyland for country fans. There was a boat ride inside the sprawling property that lasted about 10 minutes. It was one of those things you just had to do.

We waited on line, bought our tickets and got on. The attraction here was that the water flowing in that make-believe river had come from all the waters of the world. The folks in charge gave us a list of all the rivers, streams, oceans, bays, sounds, and every other imaginable body of water on the planet that had contributed to that upon which we floated. It was a World's Fair of Water.

I looked over the side of the boat as we motored along. It looked like regular water to me.

But it wasn't. It was *special* water.

In 2010, the Cumberland River, which is also made up entirely of water, overflowed its banks and wrecked the resort. It also changed the magical mixture of the resort's famous stream. I like to think that the Cumberland River just got pissed at the attention the stream had been getting and decided to take it out.

Gaylord had to start all over again.

I often wonder why contractors don't sell the idea of filling heating system with special water. Call it what you will. Who's to know?

I'll bet they could get a nice premium for that.

Hey, Madonna went for it.

Troubleshooting circulators

The Bell & Gossett Series 100 circulator had an oil-lubricated, 1/12th horsepower motor that was nearly as big as a football. It connected to a cast-iron, spring coupler that connected to an oil-lubricated bearing assembly, which also held a mechanical seal. The steel impeller inside the cast-iron volute was wide and would pass lots of system debris. And you could fix this thing forever.

Few contractors put shut-off valves around the Series 100 in those days, and changing a bearing assembly was always an adventure for Richie (who hated everybody). Richie had neither the time nor the patience to drain the water from an entire heating system, so when he had to change a bearing assembly, he would always try to catch it on the fly. This involved preparing the new bearing assembly, gasket and impeller in place and ready to go. Richie would then remove the four bolts on the old bearing-assembly, while holding it in place. He'd next take a deep breath, yank the old one from the pump's volute, and with a quick sleight of hand, jam the new bearing assembly into place without spilling too much water.

We called it "pulling a vacuum," but it was really the fervent hope that there were no open air vents at the top of the system that would allow the atmosphere into the vertical pipes, which would then imitate Walter Bosch's trick with the straw and the two-buck Dasani water. The atmosphere is rather heavy and it loves to shove water out of vertical pipes whenever possible.

I watched Richie do this a bunch of times. When it worked, he'd turn into a rooster. But now and then, it didn't work. Richie would yank the old bearing assembly and stare in horror at the old gasket, which was torn in half, and stuck to the volute. Richie would then say words that would make a pirate blush, put down the new bearing assembly, grab a knife and scrape furiously at the remnants of the old gasket.

And that's when we heard the music. You remember that scary theme music from the old movie, *Jaws*? You know, when they shark is coming. DA-DUM. DA-DUM, DA DA DA DA DA DA DADUMMMM!

Well, the sound in this case was GLUB-GLUB. GLUB-GLUB. GLUB GLUB GLUB GLUB GAGLUBBB! And out would gush the hot water, which turned Richie into a Loony Tunes character. I loved every moment, but acted suitably concerned and offered help.

"GET THE HELL OUTTA MY WAY!" Richie would scream, and I would.

At one point, an oil-heat serviceman told me how he used a Nerf ball to keep the water inside the system when he was changing a bearing assembly. Oil-heat servicemen changed a lot of bearing assemblies on Long Island. He'd pull the old bearing assembly, and jam the Nerf ball into the volute. It would suck up some of the water and not let in any air. "I could go out to lunch and that water would still be in the pipes," he told me.

I passed this trick on to Richie, who told me that guy didn't know his ass from first base.

If the idea wasn't Richie's idea, it was a lousy idea.

Another thing learned working with the Series 100 and other circulators that had bearing assemblies was that when they start, there's a forward thrust of the impeller that can separate the mechanical seal. That meant that when we were changing a bearing assembly and installing the impeller on the new bearing assembly, we had to put something solid under the spring-coupler end of the shaft. If we missed that subtle detail, there would be a bit of play in the shaft when we made up the impeller nut. The forward thrust on the first start would separate the mechanical seal, leading to a leak. Water would get into the bearing assembly and it would be time to replace it all over again.

I think this often-missed detail is one of the reasons why water-lubricated circulators, when they arrived in the late-'70s became popular so quickly. That wasn't the only reason, of course, but it was probably one of them. A mechanical seal can't leak if the circulator doesn't have one.

Bell & Gossett decided to change the cast-iron coupler to red-plastic coupler at one point. The thing looked like a toy and the installers responded by not buying the product.

B & G switched to a steel coupler and some of the customers came back, but others grumbled because the steel just didn't have the heft of the cast iron.

Then they switched the steel impeller to plastic, but they didn't call it plastic. They called it glass-impregnated poly-something-or-other

There's a power in words.

But in this case, the contractors saw it as plastic, like the red coupler (even though the impeller was milky white) and stopped buying the product.

That seems so strange nowadays, when so many hydronic components contain plastic parts, but back then, they equated plastic with cheapening the product, and the

Series 100 had been around for so long, they considered this a true insult. Many felt abandoned.

So being their rep, and since a rep cannot be holier than the church, I set out to show the integrity of glass-impregnated poly-something-or-other impellers. I did this by arranging to have Counter Days (or Daze) with several willing wholesalers. This involved me showing up early with bagels, coffee and my display table. On that table I had a hot-plate, a pot of water and the glass-impregnated poly-something-or-other impeller. I boiled the water and dropped in the impeller. I had brought along a pair of tongs from our kitchen for the all-important impeller-extraction procedure, so I could hand the thing to a contractor and show its integrity after having been in the hot pot.

But that's not the way it worked out. The first guy in that morning grabbed a bagel and then stuck his other hand right into the boiling water to grab the impeller. He let out a shriek and did the Dance of Pain across the floor. The countermen loved it.

"That's hot!" he shouted.

"Yes," I said. "It's boiling water. Our new glass-impregnated poly-something-or- other impeller can sure take a lickin' and keep on tickin'."

"You hurt me," he said, and promised never to buy our product ever again.

After awhile, the folks in the field accepted it, though.

Something else was brewing at the time. One of our big customers was the Long Island Lighting Company. They sold electricity and natural gas to a lot of people, and they also serviced heating systems. The Series 100 attracted them because of its serviceability, but here's the funny part: LILCO wouldn't change any parts. If a coupler broke, they changed the entire circulator. Same went for a broken bearing assembly, or saggy motor mounts. Their thinking was that if one part breaks, another part may soon also break, so let's save the potential repeat call by changing the whole works.

My old boss absolutely loved this way of thinking because, instead of selling replacement couplers, bearing assemblies, and motors, we were selling whole circulators, and a lot of them. But we were also allowing LILCO to redefine this forever-reparable work of engineering as a throwaway product.

Ah, but the sales were glorious!

What they didn't see coming, however, were the water-lubricated circulators from Taco and Grundfos. Once we embraced the idea of changing the entire circulator instead of rebuilding it, we opened the door to all throwaway circulators. Grundfos and Taco were about to clean our clock.

A few years went by and I was in Boston at an association meeting. A contractor was chatting with Ken Fagan, who worked for Emerson Swan, the local Taco rep.

"What's the replacement part for a Series 100 bearing assembly," the contractor asked Ken, which I thought was strange, Ken being the Taco guy and not the B&G guy.

"Oh, that's a 007," Ken said, giving him the model number of the very popular water-lubricated, one-piece circulator that cost half as much as a Series 100.

"Okay, thanks," the contractor said.

And it was then that I knew things would never be the same for oil-lubricated, three-piece circulators with motors the size of footballs.

And it hasn't been.

Considering pump curves

Again, not being able to be holier than the church, I had to continue to sell what our factories were sending us, and in those days, Bell & Gossett wasn't having much success with small, water-lubricated circulators that could compete with Taco or Grundfos. For a while, they tried making arrangements with European circulator manufacturers to bring their product to the U.S., rebranded as B&G's, but what often happened was that once we made some headway, the European manufacturer would decide to enter the U.S. market with the same product, under their own name, and at a cheaper price. It was, as you can imagine, frustrating.

So I went back to the Series 100 and looked for what made it special. I focused on its relatively flat pump curve. Pump curves show the relationship between flow in gallons per minute vs. system resistance to flow, or what we call Total Dynamic Head (which has to do with friction, not the height of the building).

The Series 100 runs at 1,750 rpm, which gives it that distinctively flat curve. Flow can shift a great deal one way or the other without building much head pressure building. The water-lubricated circulators, while less expensive, all ran at double the speed of the Series 100, giving them a much-steeper performance curve. When zone valves closed, slowing the flow of water, these circulators would back steeply up their curves, building pressure. In most cases that wasn't an issue, but certain zone valves didn't care for the higher head pressure when they were trying to close, and when they finally did close, they did so with a bang that would rattle the pipes and scare the homeowner. It was a common enough problem that some of the Honeywell salespeople were advising contractors who were having the problem to disconnect one of the springs that brought their popular Honeywell zone valve to closure. This worked sometimes, and didn't work at other times.

I made a big deal about this in *The Problem Solver* newsletter, and that kept a lot of contractors loyal to the Series 100 for a time as B&G continued their quest to come up with a viable water-lubricated circulator.

This high-pump-head situation also showed up on larger jobs, where there were usually much-bigger, base-mounted pumps. We had represented Danfoss since the early '70s and were selling a lot of thermostatic radiator valves. These valves are non-electric and have limits on the pump head against which they can close. It becomes a battle between the hydraulic pressure created by the pump and the pressure exerted by the expanding chemical inside the thermostatic radiator valve's operator. When enough TRVs close on a day when the weather is mild, the big pump will back up its curve. And if that curve is steep rather than flat, pressure will build. Build enough pressure and the hydraulic force gets to be great enough to shove open all the TRVs that have closed on room-air temperature. The result is over-heated buildings.

We were holding the bag with that one. We had sold the valves, promising temperature control, and the tenants weren't getting what we had promised. Often, the pump that was in the building before we arrived with the TRVs was oversized (a very common problem in New York City). It wasn't our pump, and we would have to convince people that it wasn't the TRVs, but the oversized pump that needed fixing.

That was never easy.

These days, with smart circulators that run on ECM motors and take their cue from system conditions at any given moment, slowing the flow and not building high-head, the problems I've described are no longer problems.

It's nice when pumps are smart.

Troubleshooting no flow

Many Long Island houses, built in the '50s, have diverter-tee systems, with copper pipe and steel convectors. Lots of these houses heat with fuel oil, and the oil companies do the service, often for little or no money. That's a Long Island tradition. Buy oil from us and we'll give you a free (or very-low-cost) service contract. The price of the service is built into the price of the oil, of course, These companies couldn't stay in business if it wasn't, but customers around here like playing that game. It makes them feel they're getting something for nothing.

These are mainly tract houses, all the same and assembled without much thought about future service. There aren't that many service valves because service valves cost money, and the builders of tract housing did their best to keep costs down.

So when an oil-heat technician has to service a hydronic system with diverter tees, he will do all that he can not to drain that system because filling it up again can be a big problem. He'll put a purge hose on the return side and open the feed valve. The water will flow through the main, pushing air ahead of itself, but it often won't flow through the branch circuits.

Back in the boiler room, it seems that the system is filled with water. No more air is coming out of the purge hose. But when the tech goes upstairs, the rooms are cold.

The radiators are filled with air.

Bleeding those convectors is a maturing experience. Most are behind heavy furniture and the covers are painted shut. And if the tech can get the cover off, there may not be a working air vent on the convector, so they'll do what they can not to have to go upstairs.

I told you earlier about William Henry, the long-gone fellow who gave us Henry's Law. That's the law that has to do with the way a gas will dissolve in a liquid, depending on pressure and temperature. The more pressure you put on a liquid, the more gas it will hold in solution. Vice versa, of course. And the hotter the water gets, the less air it will hold in solution (and vice versa). I don't think the oil-heat techs knew of William Henry, but they somehow figured out that if they raised the system pressure, and at the same time, lowered the system temperature, when trying to get these diverter-tee systems restarted, the air would dissolve into the water and the convectors would get hot.

Not everyone's an engineer, but these guys sure knew how to get the job going so they could move on to the next one.

And the lesson learned was, where there is no flow, there is no heat.

Speaking of which, I once looked at a big heat exchanger that wasn't doing what it was supposed to be doing. We pulled the head off the thing and found a pair of welders gloves splayed across the tubes. It looked like two big hands, trying to stem the flow. And it was getting the job done.

I wonder if some guy is still looking for those gloves.

Another time, a contractor found a nickel stuck inside a copper elbow. One day it was turned this way, another day that way. Flow. No flow. Heat. No heat.

Tough to plan for that one, eh?

And then there was the wholesaler who sold the sample boiler that had been on the customers' side of the counter for a couple of years. A contractor bought it and installed it, not considering what might be inside that boiler after it had sat where it had sat for so long.

He found out.

Troubleshooting compression tank problems

First the old-school tanks. They hang from the ceiling. They've been there for a very long time. They have no diaphragm. The larger ones have gauge glasses so we can see the water level.

If you're losing the air cushion out of those, suspect that gauge glass. According to the folks who make gauge glasses, you're supposed to keep the valves closed unless you're checking the water level inside the tank. That's because the valves that make up part of the gauge glass have packing glands. The upper valve sits in air, not water, so the valve-stem packing dries out. The air that's inside the tank is under pressure. It creeps out through the dry packing and leaves the system. The system pressure drops. Someone adds water to the system (or a feed valve does the job automatically) and the water goes into the only place it can go, that being the tank because the rest of the system is already full. The water level rises; the stem packing gets wet and doesn't leak.

The system water gets hot and expands, but with the now-diminished air cushion inside the tank, the expanding water has hardly anywhere to go. So the pressure builds and the relief valve pops.

Keep the valves on the gauge glass closed. The only reason they're open is because people are too lazy to get a ladder when it's time to check the water level inside the tank. If someone keeps opening those valves, close them again and then break the glass. If they fix the glass and open the valves again, break the glass again. You can break it faster than they can fix it. Sooner or later, you'll wear them out.

If an old-school tank is losing its air and it doesn't have a gauge glass, check for pinholes in the top of the tank. Look, too, at how the tank connects to the system. There should be a Bell & Gossett Airtrol Tank Fitting at the bottom of the tank. This device stops gravity circulation between the tank and the system piping. The cooler water in the tank will absorb the tank's air charge. This is Henry's Law at work. If there's gravity circulation in the line connecting the tank to the system piping, the cooler water with the dissolved air will fall into the system piping and enter the flow of hot water. The cooler water that left the tank will get hot and give up the air it carried from the tank, and that air will wind up in a radiator.

Someone will bleed the radiator; the system pressure will drop. Fresh water will enter the system and go straight into the tank. Now there's not enough room for expansion of the hot water, so the relief valve pops.

You can have as many compression tanks as you'd like on a hydronic system, but you have to connect them all to a manifold, and then connect the manifold to the system piping at a single point. This becomes the point of no pressure change for the circulators. If you have multiple points of no pressure change, your circulators will get very confused and start doing some wacky things with their pressure differential, which can cause system problems.

If your old-school tanks are losing their air and everything else looks good, look for a big radiator that's filled with air. It can pretend to be a second compression tank, and a second point of no pressure change. It will set up a condition for the circulators where they'll establish a point of no pressure change somewhere between the tank and the air-bound radiator. Water will then leave one "tank" and enter the other "tank." The result is usually an old-school tank that just can't hold its air.

If you're using more-modern compression tanks, the sort that have diaphragms, know that those diaphragms are semi-permeable membranes, and that the air that's supposedly trapped behind the diaphragm forevermore really isn't. Air will move right through that rubber membrane by osmosis, and an average rate of 1 psi per year. The air winds up in a radiator and someone will vent it. Fresh water enters and the relief valve pops because there's not enough air on the other side of the diaphragm to allow for the expansion of the heated water.

Amtrol invented the Extrol tank. Their original tanks used dry ice for the air cushion. They figured the trapped carbon dioxide would stay put, but then learned that it moves across the diaphragm by osmosis. They introduced the Schrader valve as a solution. Take the water pressure off the tank before you check the air pressure, though, or you'll get a false reading.

Tank manufacturers don't broadcast that business about the migrating air, but if you ask them, they'll tell you it's true. Tanks lose at least one-psi of air pressure every year.

It pays to keep asking questions, especially when you're troubleshooting.

Troubleshooting feed valves

Usually, these simple devices either feed or they don't. Troubleshooting involves changing the ones that don't work, but the bigger question is, should we leave them open or closed. The feed valve's job is to, well, feed. You figure out the height of the hydronic system from the point where the feed valve is to the highest hydronic component. You take that height in feet, divide it by 2.31 to convert it to pounds per square inch, and that tells you how much water pressure you need to fill the system to the top. And since you'll need some pressure at the top so you can vent air from that point, you'll add a couple of psi to what you just came up with. Simple.

But here's the thing. Since hydronic systems are closed to the atmosphere (or at least they're supposed to be), you shouldn't need that feed valve again unless you drain water from the system, which may make you wonder why people buy them in the first place, right? I mean some of the feed-valve manufacturers tell you to shut the valve once you're done filling the system. In fact, they do more than tell you; they plaster their installation-and-operation instructions with WARNINGS, which threaten us with portents of personal injury and/or death should the valve remain open. And let's face it, that's enough to make even Chuck Norris nervous.

But what if we close the feed valve and the air vents finally finish doing their job on those far-out circuits (such as those long, secondary radiant circuits that we love so much) and the system pressure drops a bit. Now we have to go back to fill the system by hand, and that costs money. And since we'll be adding cold water to the system by doing this, and since cold water contains air, we'll probably have to go back more than once. Gosh.

And we don't want to leave the fill valve open and defy the manufacturer's instructions (and all that implies); but we also don't want to have to keep going back to the job because that's just going to eat up the profit and aggravate people.

Flip a coin?

But before we do, here's an example of why some manufacturers issue those warnings about leaving the feed valve open. This is a true story. A house on a slab had baseboard heat and part of the copper loop dipped into the concrete to get by the front door. That pipe that went into the concrete floor developed a leak, which sent the water down, not up. It leaked for a good long time with nobody noticing because there was no vapor barrier under that slab. The water just drained away. The fuel bill went up and so did the water bill, but the homeowners just took that in stride because it happened gradually, as do so many things in life.

One day, the local water company decided to work on the main in the street. They went around the neighborhood, leaving notes in all the mailboxes, explaining that the water would be off for the day. The couple living in the house on the slab were at work and they didn't get the word. It was winter and the circulator was running while they were at work. There was no low-water cutoff on this boiler. The installer had depended on the open feed valve to keep the boiler and the system full, but with the city water shut off, the boiler ran dry. The thermostat kept calling for heat, and the burner kept running. Soon there was hardly any water in the boiler. The burner kept running, though, and the boiler got hotter than the hinges of Hell.

At the end of the day, the guys working on the water main were done and they opened the valves. Ice-cold water spewed from the feed valve, hit the red-hot metal, flashed into steam, blew up the boiler and took down the house. No one was home, which was a blessing, but this is one of the reasons why you'll see those warnings in the feed-valve instructions.

We learned from events such as this that all boilers need, and must have, a low-water cutoff. It's madness not to have one.

I tossed this open-or-closed question up on the Wall at HeatingHelp.com one day. Lots of people had plenty of points of view, and I read and considered each of them. And then Bob "Hot Rod" Rohr wrote this:

"If you have a rubber-tube radiant system, you either have a working fill valve or you may have to return every

heating season to add a shot of fill water. For some reason, many of those systems tend to need a boost of pressure every year.

"I've tested some to 100-psi (tube only) for 24 hours and they held, but over the summer they drop enough to prevent boilers with low pressure switches from operating.

"I suspect that for every disaster story of a fill valve left on, you could find one for a fill valve left off. Vacation homes are a classic case of freeze-up due to low-pressure lockouts that could have been prevented if the fill valve was allowed to do what it was designed and intended to do.

"It's your choice and there are plenty of arguments either way you go. It's a sad day when lawyers dictate hydronic installations. Which is the lesser of the two issues?

"Some auto-fill valves come with a knob to regulate flow. Once the system fills and purges you can adjust the flow to provide some make-up without flowing 4 GPM in the event of a break, and maybe that's a compromise?

"A large radiant job can take days to purge all the microbubbles, I'd advise leaving the fill on for a few days or a week, or you may be returning every day to top it off, only to meet an unhappy, no-heat customer.

"Perspective varies depending on whether you're manufacturing, selling, or on the receiving end of the unhappy-customer calls. They just want the reliable heat and domestic hot water you promised and billed them for.

"Maybe the tank-fill systems with alarm contacts tied into a phone dialer would be another answer. But whose phone number should we use?"

Good question, and a bad situation no matter how you look at it.

What Pumping Away taught me

I don't know if I ever told you the story of how my book, *Pumping Away - And other really cool piping options for hydronic systems* came to be. It was 1994 and you were 13 years old at the time, as was Colleen. Meghan was 14 and Kelly was sweet 16. I was working on my third book, which was to be the one I called, *How Come? Hydronic heating questions we've been asking for 100 years (with straight answers!)* That was to be my tribute book to Dead Men such as R.M. Starbuck, who had written these wonderful question-and-answer books for the trade when the hydronic industry was young. I was enjoying the format of dreaming up questions for myself and then finding the answers. I asked everything I could imaging my reader might ask.

One day, the mailman arrived with an envelope that contained a note from a contractor and a check for 20 dollars. He wanted to buy my book, *Pumping Away*. I had used that expression at seminars and in my magazine writing, but I had not written a book about it. I was including the concept in *How Come?* but I had never thought of writing a book called *Pumping Away*.

I looked at your mother and she looked at me. It was just the two of us in the business back then. She said, "Write a book called *Pumping Away*."

"Why?" I said.

"Because I'm not sending this check back."

She has a way about her.

So I took all the stuff I had written about the proper location of the circulator in a hydronic system and how the compression tank determines the point of no pressure change out of the Q&A format that it had taken in *How Come?* and put it into a conversation between my reader and me.

I took the book to our graphics artist and asked her to design it. She looked at it and mentioned that there wasn't much to it. I looked at it again and asked what she could do about that. She said he could bump up the font size to give the book more pages. I said okay and she went to work.

Even though it wasn't planned, that book became a huge bestseller for us, and over the years I've gotten so many comments from contractors about how much they like the big font. Makes it easier to read. I always smile when they say that.

Lemons to lemonade.

The main point of the book is that in a closed hydronic system, the point where the compression tank sits will always be a point of constant pressure. If you pump away from that point, you'll be adding the circulators differential pressure to the system's static-fill pressure, giving you an overall increase in system pressure, which makes it easier to get the air out of the system.

The reverse gives you the opposite. If you pump toward the compression tank, the tank's pressure will stay the same and the circulator's differential pressure will show up as a drop from the system's static pressure. The lower pressure causes air bubbles to grow, making them more difficult to get out of the system.

Bottom line: If a contractor pumps away, he won't have to go upstairs to bleed the radiators.

I've probably explained this thousands of times to contractors over the past decades. It's a hard concept to learn if you try to learn it with numbers. That's the way my old teacher, Gil Carlson, taught it. I never got it until I could see the pictures in my mind's eye, and imagine myself as the flow of water, the pressure inside the tank, the difference in pressure the circulator was producing to create the flow. I had to think like a marble. Then it became clear.

And once I got it, I did my best, in writing and in person, to help others get it.

But to this day, there are contractors who refuse to believe it because someone taught them to do it another way when they were young. To do it the way I suggest means they have to change a habit, and also admit to themselves that they were wrong.

And a lot of people have a tough time with both of those things, Erin.

One more thing. When I was done with *Pumping* Away, I wrote this dedication:

> ***For the Associates,***
> ***Kelly, Meghan, Colleen, and Erin***
> ***Young, and strong, and . . . beautiful!***

When we were all younger and having fun running on the Bethpage bike path and in those local 5-K races, I taught you how to pace yourself, how to reserve your strength, and how to match your breathing to your pace. We'd run at the same pace day after day and progress slowly.

And as we ran, I would say, "Young" (breathe), "and *Strong*" (breathe) and . .

And then you young women would say, "*Beautiful!*"

And we did that again and again and again until you all believed in your hearts that you truly were.

And you still are now, only more so.

Hydronics taught me that (most of the time) you can't make this stuff up

So there's this ordinary guy out on a service call. He's on Long Island; he's in a basement; he's adjusting an oil burner. It's a single-family house. He has to go out to his truck a few times for this and that. The lady has a snarling Chihuahua that has the run of the house. She tells the service guy that the dog is okay, that he doesn't bite, that he likes to be in the basement and that he, the service guy, should just do his work and not bother the dog.

Easier said than done, right? The guy is sitting on an upended bucket, with a box wrench in his right hand and a part of the oil burner in his left. The dog is yipping, baring his teeth, quickly advancing and retreating in that annoying, little-dog way. The guy is doing his best to ignore the dog, but that's not easy to do and the dog knows it. He lunges in and nips the service guy on the meaty part of his right hand. They both let out a yelp.

The dog backs off and growls. Our guy gives him a look that should have nailed him to the wall, but it didn't. This dog has chops. He races in again with the teeth and our guy instinctively snaps the box wrench in his direction. "Get outta here!" he hisses.

"So what happened?" I asked.

"I accidentally hit him right between his big eyes. He went down for the count."

"Hurt?"

"Dead."

"Gosh."

"Yeah."

"So what did you do?"

"Well, he wouldn't fit in my toolbox, so I used the toolbox to sort of flatten him out."

"You're serious."

"Yeah. Then, once he was pretty flat, I put him inside my jacket, under my arm, and zipped up."

"Oh, my."

"And when I was done, I walked out with him."

"You say anything to the lady?"

"I told her that I went out to the truck and I think the dog might have scooted out between my feet. Hard to keep track of a dog that size, you know?"

"What did you do with the body?" I asked.

"I drove about three blocks; rolled down the window and tossed him like a Frisbee. Done."

As I said, you can't make this stuff up.

You don't have to.

A contractor told me about how he kept going back to the same job to put air into the compression tank. On his last visit, he passes this kid coming up the basement stairs with a partially inflated balloon.

"That needs more air, son," he says.

"I know," the kid says, "but there's no more air in the tank."

I love it when they tell me these stories.

Another contractor kept getting callbacks on this burner that would run when he was there and stop running as soon as he left. Seems someone had wired the burner in series with the basement light switch. This is one of those times where it doesn't pay to save electricity by shutting off the lights on your way out.

It's a grand industry, Erin, filled with mechanical mayhem and a good amount of laughter. Keep listening. These folks have much to tell us.

Oh, and watch out for Frisbees.

Hydronics taught me how to size systems

This brings me to a story about this house in a very wealthy section of New Jersey. The new owner was frustrated because every 10 days or so, a large fuel-oil truck that had 18 wheels grumbled up his street. The driver would stop, pull a long hose that was as thick as my thigh up to the oil tank's fill pipe, plug in, and whistle as the oil gushed from the truck to the tank. The new homeowner hated this man.

So he hired me to see what I had to say about him saving some fuel dollars. He was open to any suggestion. Should he stick with oil, or should he switch to gas? Should he keep the boilers he had, or get new ones? Should he have the whole system repiped? Should he burn down the house? Hmm, what to do?

I met him at his house, which was smaller than Versailles, but not by much. The oil truck was there. He asked me what I wanted to do first and I suggested we take a tour of the place, mostly because I'm nosey, and never pass on an opportunity to poke around in the stuff that rich folks like to accumulate.

We went from room to room and I ogled and gawked. The place had gravity hot-water heat and any of the cast-iron radiators could have held down the Graf Zeppelin.

"Can we go to the basement?" I asked.

"Sure," he said. "Wait 'til you see these boilers?"

"You have more than one?"

"There are two," he said. "And they're big."

"And they're connected to the oil truck," I said.

"Yes," he said, "there's that."

We got to the basement, where my legs suddenly stopped working because this place had horizontal mains made from eight-inch, screwed pipe. It was a thing of beauty and I thought, once again, about the men who installed this big stuff. What size wrenches? Where the heck did they stand? How'd they do this?

I was getting all sentimental and sloppy over my trip through time, when the homeowner gently reminded me about those boilers, so we walked a while through the basement and that's when I came upon the two Ideal Redflash boilers. Once again, my legs stopped working. These two had once burned coal, but were now connected to the big truck outside. Each had a rating of 500,000 Btuh, and both burners were firing.

But then, *firing* doesn't quite do what was going on justice. These beasts, each of which was the size of a minivan, now had tons of sand where the coal grates used to be. The burners, each bigger than the Fourth of July, hung from the cast-iron doors and vomited fire deeply into the bowels of those boilers. We could have toasted rye bread on the jackets.

I shut off the burners and carefully opened the door of one of the beasts. You could yodel in this boiler and get an echo. You could cremate your spouse in this boiler and no one would ever know. You'd probably get a No. 10 smoke for a few minutes, but other than that, you'd be in the clear.

"Has anyone done a heat-loss calculation on the house?" I asked the homeowner.

"Yes," he said. "The salesman from the oil company did one."

"Oh."

"Yeah, it didn't take him long," the homeowner said.

"Did he go from room to room and measure the walls and windows and whatnot?" I asked. "Did he check the attic?"

"No," the homeowner said. "He just wrote down what was on the two labels and then gave me this quote." He took a sheet of paper from his folder. The quote was for a single boiler, rated at 1,300,000 Btuh.

"One boiler?" I said.

"Yeah, the salesman said that it's crazy to have two boilers. There's twice as much stuff to break down. He also said he knew that this would be the right size for the house because these two boilers have been here for all these years, and they've served the house well."

"But he's quoting 300,000 Btuh over the total load of both boilers," I said.

"I know," the homeowner said. "The salesman mentioned that it's an old house, so it never hurts to have a little bit extra."

"Oh," I said.

So I did what the salesman should have done, which was a heat-loss calculation. That's the only way we were ever going to find out the actual heat loss of the house. Anything less is just a guess.

And here's what we learned: The total load for the house on the coldest day of the year was 375,000 Btuh. That other boiler was a stand-by. Why was it firing all the time? My guess is that a service tech turned them both on one day and they stayed turned on. The abnormal became the normal. Happens all the time.

The homeowner decided to fire the oil company, which didn't surprise me.

"They see my house as a vending machine," he said.

I made him a sketch of how I'd like to see all the main gravity lines tied together into a primary loop. "Stop by a local supply house and ask them if they have in stock four, eight-inch-screwed by two-inch-sweat reducers," I said. "And don't take no for an answer. They'll try to jerk you around because you're a homeowner. They've got them back there somewhere."

Just kidding.

So with the supply-and-return gravity mains connected (with flanges and copper tubing, not reducers), I sketched how to use two boilers, with a combined load of 375,000 Btuh, on secondary circuits. I included a couple of bypass lines so the flue gases wouldn't condense. This story goes back to before we had condensing boilers; otherwise, I would have suggested those. Condensing boilers love those old, high-volume systems.

He had a gas contractor install all of this, and I followed up with him during the following winter. Most of the time, he ran just one of his new, relatively tiny, boilers, which is better than running a single 1,300,000 Btuh boiler. Right?

The homeowner was happy. So was I.

I think laziness was what cost that oil company the business. The salesman didn't want to take the time to do what a professional should *always* do when replacing a hot-water boiler, that being a proper heat-loss calculation. The salesman must have thought that if he went to the trouble to do the calculations, and then didn't get the job, he would have wasted his time.

But you can see where that got him.

Thing is, I've been telling this story at seminars for a very long time, and contractors still come to me during the breaks to argue with me. They can't afford to do heat-loss calculations on every job. It takes too much time. They'll go by the label on the old boiler. I was making them feel guilty. I have no idea what they're up against.

I'll mention that a proper heat-loss calculation will nearly always give them a smaller boiler than one they might size by the Label Method, and that a smaller boiler mean a more-competitive price, and more closed sales. They'll argue with me about this too. It takes too long to do. They don't have the time.

"So how's business?" I'll ask.

"It *sucks*," they'll say.

So I think I'll just keep telling them about the rich man and his Redflash boilers, and that big oil truck that doesn't stop there anymore.

And while we're guessing

Tom parked his truck down the street from the McCabe's house and eyeballed the distance between him and the front door. He figured it was somewhere between 100 or 150 feet, give or take. Close enough, he thought. He opened the truck's door and hopped out. He held his arms straight out in front of him and positioned his open palms so that his fingers obscured his view of the house. Then he closed his left eye and sighted down his arms like a rifleman. He dropped his left arm. "Don't need lefty on this one," he said to himself. "Looks like about a five-section boiler to me, give or take. Five fingers equals five sections. That's about right for this neighborhood." Tom whistled as he hopped back into his truck and drove the rest of the way to the McCabe house.

Mrs. McCabe answered Tom's knock and smiled. "I'm here to size up that boiler for you," he said.

"Oh yes, come right in!" she said. "Will you be able to give us a price today? We'd like to get this work done as soon as possible."

"No problem," Tom said. "I'll have the price for you in a few minutes." She opened the door wider and stepped back. "No, that's okay, ma'am. I don't need to come inside. It's easier for me to do the engineering from out here. I'll knock again when I have the price. I just wanted you to know that I was here."

"Okay," Mrs. McCabe said. "You're the expert."

Tom walked to the corner, looked over his left shoulder and sighted down the edge of the house. Then he paced across the front lawn to the opposite corner of the house. He kept the line as straight as possible as he walked, stepping over the garden hose, the lawn sprinkler and the bushes alongside the front walk. "One, two, three, four, five," he mumbled as he counted his paces from one side of the house to the other. Tom knew that each of his paces was about three feet, give or take, and that his rule of thumb measurement was nearly as accurate as you would get with a tape measure, but who has time to lay a tape across a lawn nowadays? And besides, none of this is rocket science.

Tom reached the corner of the house, multiplied the number of paces it took him to get there by three, made a mental note of that, and then turned to his left and paced down the side of the house. When he got to the corner of the house, he made another mental note, and then glanced upward. "Two stories," he mumbled. "That's about twenty feet, give or take." He added that into his mental arithmetic and came up with the cubic volume of the house. The shape of the roof was a triangle, of course. Most roofs are, but he always treated them like rectangles. A rectangle is close enough to a triangle when it comes to figuring heat loss. And let's face it, it never hurts to have a little bit extra, especially with an older house.

He multiplied his cubic volume number by a factor that he uses for homes that are located south of the Long Island Expressway and that gave him his boiler size. He walked back toward the street so that he could count the vent pipes on the roof. "Two baths," he mumbled, and then he added his rule-of-thumb load for domestic hot water. He glanced around the yard for anything that might indicate that a lot of kids lived here. He liked to throw in a bit more load if he saw swings and slides or skateboards and bikes but the McCabes didn't seem to have any children, so he went with the numbers he already had.

Adding it all together, he came up with a four-section, cast iron boiler. He clucked his tongue and made it five-section boiler, just so that it would agree with the Finger

Method. It never hurts to have a little bit extra with an old house. Then he walked back to his truck and put his price together.

Tom has a rule of thumb for figuring prices. This, he has found, saves him time. He charges by the Btuh. In this case, the boiler was 175,000 Gross Btuh. For jobs south of the Long Island Expressway, Tom charges 1-1/4 cents per Btuh. That would make the price of this job $2,187.50. Jobs north of the Long Island Expressway go for 1-1/2 cents per BTUH because that's where the rich folks live, but Tom hardly ever gets to quote on those jobs. It's out of his marketing area.

He was going with Gross Btuh pricing on this job because Mr. McCabe didn't appear to be at home. When both husband and wife are home they will often beat up Tom on the price. When this happens, he usually has to drop to the boiler's Net Btuh ratings instead of the Gross ratings for the pricing. The difference between Gross Btuh and Net Btuh on a hot water job is 15 percent. On a steam job, it's 33-1/3 percent and that hurts, but what can you do? Fortunately, this was a hot water job. Or at least he thought it was. The house wasn't that old. It was probably hot water.

He knocked on the door and handed Mrs. McCabe the Gross Btuh price. He had written it in pencil on the back of his business card. She looked at the number and then at Tom. "You sure you don't you need to go downstairs and look at the old boiler?" she asked.

"Nah," Tom said. "I've seen a million houses like yours. I know what's down there. After a while, it's all rule of thumb, ya know? This is a good price I'm giving you. Trust me."

She looked at the business card again. "I have to ask you, and I hope you don't take this the wrong way, but my husband said that I have to ask."

"Ask what?"

"Can you come down on the price?"

Tom sighed and looked at his fingernails. "Well," he said, how about if I knock off about two hundred bucks, give or take. How would that be?" His rule of thumb when it's just the wife or the husband is to try dropping to the nearest round number before going all the way down to the Net Btuh number. People, for the most part, like round numbers. How about if we make it an even two grand?" Tom said. "How would that be?"

"But you said you'd come down two hundred dollars," Mrs. McCabe said. "If you bring the price to two thousand dollars that's only a discount of one hundred eighty-seven dollars and fifty cents. I'll have to check with my husband."

Tom, not being the sort of guy who lets chump change get between him and a job, said, "Okay, how about if we just call it nineteen fifty? Would that do it for you?" Tom also likes round numbers. It makes the accounting easier.

"Okay, that sounds better," Mrs. McCabe said. "I'm sure my husband will agree. Nineteen hundred and fifty dollars it is. May I have a new quote?" She handed Tom the business card. He crossed out $2,187.50 and wrote $1,950. He added his initials and handed the card back to her. She looked at it and smiled. "So when can you do the work?"

"Oh, let's figure next Monday or Thursday, more or less," Tom said. "One of those days should be okay with me. That be okay with you?"

"Okay," she said. "Do you know what time you'll be here?"

"Figure morning or afternoon. I can't say for sure at this point. This business isn't an exact science. We have to play it by ear, ya know? Ride with the tide and go with the flow. Ya know?"

"Okay," she said.

Tom walked away a happy man. He didn't have to drop to the Net Btuh level on this job. That would have cost him an extra hundred bucks, give or take. "Cash in my pocket," he mumbled as he got into his truck.

He had five more estimates to do that morning. More or less.

About that pick-up factor

That's the difference between the Net rating and the Department of Energy Heating Capacity rating, or what we used to call the Gross rating. Gross is the amount of heat that leaves the boiler and heads toward the radiators. Net is what's left over for the radiators, after the pipes between the boiler and the radiators get hot.

When hydronic heated stared back in the 19th Century, everyone used a pick-up factor of 1.56 for both steam- and hot-water systems. That's because those jobs used very large pipes. This was the time of gravity-hot-water heating, and vapor-steam heating.

In 1945, when heating equipment became available again after the war, the industry dropped the pick-up factor for both steam- and hot-water systems to 1.33. Then, in 1967, they lowered it further for hot-water systems, making it 1.15, where it remains today. My guess is that the Hydronics Institute was looking at competition from furnaces right around that time, and also the popularity of smaller, copper tubing and copper fin-tube radiators. Both called for a lesser pick-up factor for hot-water systems. But can you see how if someone is replacing a boiler in a building built in, say, 1920, there might be an issue with that pick-up factor, especially if it's a hot-water system? This is why boiler manufacturers talk so much these days about piping their boilers with primary/secondary pumping. Without that, or the special boiler-bypass piping they may also recommend, the new boiler will probably use more fuel that the old boiler ever used.

It's the butterfly effect. A decision made in 1967 ripples through the decades and can have a huge effect on a boiler replacement done today.

History matters.

And so does baseboard

I've often joked about what I call the Long Island Heat Loss calculation. It comes from there being so much copper-fin-tube baseboard here on Long Island. I suppose we can thank Mel Dubin, founder of Slant/Fin, for that. Mel once told me that he located his factory on Long Island because he wanted to be as close as possible to Levittown, with its 17,000 radiant-heated houses on slabs. He knew that buried copper tubing, installed in a hurry during the '50s wasn't going to last, and that his baseboard would be the logical alternative.

And Mel was right.

Erin, the house you grew up in, and where we still live, has wall-to-wall baseboard. It was the easiest way for the contractor to install it for the previous owners back in 1970. I've also joked that if Slant/Fin made baseboard with hinges, the contractors would have continued the loops right across the doorways.

We heat with fuel oil. As you know, there's no natural gas in this neighborhood. There aren't as many fuel-oil companies as there were when we first moved in, but the ones that are still around continue to want our business. They call and ask if they can send an expert over to show us how we can save money on fuel. I always say sure because I love to watch what these salesmen do.

They get here, see the two huge loops of baseboard, downstairs and upstairs and then measure it all. They multiply the total linear footage by a factor they've worked out and then give me a quote on a boiler that's about four times larger than the heat loss of our house.

They believe the boiler has to support the radiation. I believe the boiler has to provide enough heat to satisfy our home's heat loss on the coldest day of the year. I also believe that if a house is over-radiated, we can take advantage of that by running a properly sized boiler at lower temperatures, depending on how cold it is outside.

The salesmen who sizes based on the linear footage of baseboard will never get my business, even though it's easy for them to do it that way.

The other thing about baseboard is the lengths to which it might go. I know that in a single loop there should never be more than 25 feet of element if it's half-inch, and never more than 70 feet of element if it's three-quarter inch. Go beyond that and the rooms at the end of the loops will be chilly on those colder days because the water traveling through the baseboard will have deposited most of the heat it was carrying in the rooms it visited earlier.

But this idea of sizing to the radiation persists. It makes sense in a steam-heated building, but not in a building heated with hot water.

I talked about this for decades. Wrote about it, too. People in the hydronics industry still argue with me.

How come?

That's the way they were taught.

Again. Go figure.

High-temp hydronics in the '60s

When President Eisenhower signed that Interstate Highway Act into law after World War II and started the blossoming of the suburbs, the bottom fell out of the hydronics business because furnaces will always be cheaper than boilers.

As we rolled into the '60s, the hydronics industry responded by doing a lot of research into high-temperature hydronics. They figured that if the water left the boiler at temperatures of, say, 250 degrees F., they could use smaller radiators as well as smaller pipes, valves, fittings, and circulators because they'd be working with a much-larger temperature drop across these systems.

They were right, of course, but high-temp systems needed circulators that could deal with that high temperature. On commercial jobs, where the temperatures rose well above 300 F., those big circulators needed little heat exchangers to keep the mechanical seals from failing. And if a pipe should burst, you had instant steam in the rooms with the people.

Jim Roche, who once did the teaching for Burnham, told me that when he was first married, he was looking to save money. Since he worked for Burnham, and since Burnham made cast-iron baseboard radiators, he figured he could get those at a discount. To save money, he sized for high-temperature, which called for fewer linear feet (a nice savings there!), and he installed it.

"The first thing I noticed," he said, "was that the copper tubing connecting the baseboard changed colors from the heat. And whenever we had a birthday party for one of the kids, we noticed that the balloons would explode if a kid got anywhere near the baseboards with one. It wasn't the easiest stuff in the world to live with."

But it was the hydronic industry's response to the furnace.

When OPEC shut off our oil in 1973, everything changed. Americans scurried around, looking for ways to lower the heating bills in the face of rising fuel costs. Solar thermal became a big deal (as long as the government subsidized it). We also saw devices that would block the flue when the burner stopped running. These left some bad memories, and as I recall, some dead people.

Oh, and people also got creative. They would vent clothes dryers indoors by running the exhaust through an old pair of pantyhose, forgetting how flammable that lint is. They also diverted their heating pipes into their fireplaces to pick up the heat from the burning logs. Steam explosions followed, of course.

Meanwhile, in Europe, those in charge began passing laws that would drive down the maximum allowable temperature of the water. This led to the rediscovery of hydronic radiant heating, which became even more popular with Thomas Engel's invention of PEX plastic tubing, and large-surface radiators that became a favorite of architects because they came in so many exotic shapes and colors.

This was not your grandpa's business anymore.

And as the water temperature dropped, modulating/condensing boilers began to appear, as did smarter controls and smarter circulators with ECM motors, and nothing was ever the same again.

Change happened so quickly in Europe because they drove it with strict legislation. Suddenly, a boiler that would last only 10 years instead of 60 years was acceptable. I once questioned this while at a boiler factory in Germany. The engineer said, "In ten years, we will have something better. Then they will buy that."

He had no doubt about this.

I think it may take Americans a bit longer to get used to that sort of thing, unless we start to see energy legislation similar to what they have in the European Union.

And I figure that will happen right after the pigs start flying.

Jim Roche again

During his classes, Jim would mention that we size for the coldest day of the year, and that on that day, the burner should never shut off. He asked if any of us had ever seen that happen. Silence.

He also said that the reason we zone heating systems is because we like to keep some zones cooler than others. And with that in mind, we should be able to size the boiler to be smaller than what's needed on the coldest day of the year. Then he said that he would lob 10 percent off the size of the boiler, per zone, up to three zones. That would reduce the size of the boiler by 30 percent in the typical house. He'd been doing this for years and years and had never had a problem.

When he retired, it was a very sad day for the hydronics industry.

What is high-efficiency?

Our friend, Jenni, was visiting from Scotland and she had never been to Central Park, so I took her there for a long walk, a ride on the carousel and some wine at the boathouse. We sat outside.

We were about three sips into that sweet part of the day when this ancient, cantaloupe-size, gnarled head rose out of the green water, about a yard away from our feet. It opened its cave of a mouth and Jenni screamed. I shoved my chair back and gaped. The waitress walked over and smiled. "Turtle," she said. "And if you think that's something, you should see the fish that are in this lake. They look like they're left over from a nuclear war."

But despite that, and as you know, the Central Park Boathouse is lovely, and it is also filled with wonder.

My contractor buddy, John, was having lunch there one day. He was sitting at the bar and he ordered the tuna sandwich. After a while, the waiter brought it to him and John noticed that the fish was very pink. In fact, it looked just like salmon.

"I ordered the tuna," John said to the waiter.

"Yes," the waiter answered and then scurried away.

John looked again at the fish and then asked the bartender to take a look. "What sort of fish do you think this is?" John said.

"That's definitely salmon," the bartender said.

"Yeah?"

"*Definitely.*"

So John caught the waiter's eye and motioned for him to come over.

"This is definitely salmon," John said. "I don't like salmon. I ordered tuna."

The waiter looked at the sandwich and said, "Yes, today the tuna is salmon." And he scooted away.

Isn't that delightful? It's so wonderfully efficient! If you don't have what the customer wants, just change the name of what you *do* have and call it what they actually asked for. Today the tuna is salmon. Brilliant!

Which gave me an idea.

You see, John is a very good contractor and he does his best to give his customers superb advice. He's also a great listener. Lately, he has been listening to many of his customers as they tell him that they want high-efficiency. The higher the better. They say this because high-efficiency is all the rage in America. These days, you can't throw a bagel in New York City without hitting someone who wants high-efficiency.

They're tripping over each other.

But high-efficiency comes with a price that's higher than normal-efficiency (whatever that is), and because of that higher price, high-efficiency is now a subjective term that is open to broad interpretation, and perhaps even reinvention. I believe it's now time to ask this question:

What exactly is high-efficiency higher than?

For example, let's say you own a building that has a hydronic heating system. Your boiler is 30 years old and you're not happy with your fuel bills. You're in the market for high-efficiency, not because you want to save the planet, but because you've had it with the big fuel bills. So you call a contractor, perhaps someone like John.

"A lot of my customers call and say they want to replace their boiler with a high-efficiency model," John tells me. "So I go and look at the job. I work up a price, and as soon as they see this price, they ask me if there's something cheaper that's still high-efficiency. I think, compared to what? And then I consider what they have right now. I tell them sure there is, and I quote them on normal-efficiency (whatever that is). And that's almost always what they choose."

Get it? Today, the tuna is salmon.

"Maybe you should just begin with lower-efficiency (whatever that is)," I say to John.

"But that's not what they're asking for," he says.

"But that's where they're winding up."

"That's true," says John. "But they asked for the tuna, not the salmon."

"But what if today the tuna is normal-efficiency," I say. "You could be putting the fish in efficiency!"

"Hmm," says John.

It's such a subjective term, this high-efficiency. The customers all want to hear about how much fuel they'll save once a contractor is done with the job, but I don't know many contractors who will put that in writing because customers are crazy. Some of them like to leave the windows open during the winter. If you put a number on the savings they're going to remember that as they breathe the fresh wintry air and look at their still-too-high fuel bills.

And let's remember that there's an entire system connected to that new high-efficiency boiler. What shape is that system in right now? Is it balanced? Properly sized? Is everything beyond the boiler room working? How are the controls? Are all the valves in good shape? Are they going to let you fix the whole system so that everything talks to everything else, or are you just installing that new boiler?

I'm thinking that the only way to really prove savings in any building is to install the new high-efficiency equipment and then keep track of what happens during the next year or so. But who will keep track of this? Will it be the building owner? And is he or she just tracking the amount of fuel burned? Does that define high-efficiency? Just fuel savings? If that's all it is, we could keep the old equipment and shut it off for part of the day. Hey, nothing is more efficient than a burner that's not running.

But shutting down the system will probably affect human comfort, right? So should human comfort come into play when we're talking about high-efficiency? And if we do that, who is going to step up to be the Standard of Comfort? Some folks like it warm while other folks like it cooler. And now we're really talking systems, which includes the building envelope, windows, doors, insulation, controls, piping layouts, terminals units, circulators, and on and on. We're not just talking about a high-efficiency boiler when we're talking about human comfort.

So how do you test for comfort? Do you conduct polls? Who will pull that together? Do we need to get Gallup involved in this? And who's going to pay for all of this?

This is getting complicated. Maybe high-efficiency is a comparison of the building we're working on to a similar nearby building that we're not going to work on (if there is such a place). If you can make an improvement in your building you get bragging rights. But how can you prove that things got that much better once you were done? Will the folks in the other building show you their fuel bills and tell you about their level of comfort? And what if they decide to make changes to their building, but at less cost than what you charged? Maybe they just sealed the cracks and made some adjustments to the burner, or gave their boiler a good cleaning. If we're going to define high-efficiency as a comparison to some other similar building, any improvements they make will take away from what you achieved. So subjective, this high-efficiency business.

Perhaps high-efficiency is really just a state of mind, based on how much the customer wants to spend and how he or she perceives the return on the investment. Whatever they get is probably going to be better than what they have now. Is that high enough?

Beats me, but who knows what the tuna will be tomorrow?

Hydronics taught me to relearn and explore radiant

When I went to work for the manufacturer's rep, I read about radiant heating from the 1950s in the Bell & Gossett Handbooks I found in desk drawers. There were a lot of numbers in those handbooks, but I needed pictures and stories.

Years later, I discovered the Englishman, T. Napier Adlam and his wonderful 1947 book, *Radiant Heating, Radiant Cooling and Snow Melting*. He worked for Sarco, known today for their steam products, but in '47, they were at the forefront of radiant research, and all of it was there in Mr. Adlam's book, with lots of pictures and plenty of stories. He's the guy who made me really get it for the first time.

Each morning, as I sit here at my desk in the room where you once slept, I give a moment's thought to the broken copper pipes that are buried in the concrete slab just below my feet. The guy who lived here before us abandoned that old radiant system in 1970, just 20 years after the crew had hastily installed it. We live in one of those houses built during the Levittown era. Levitt put up 17,000 houses in a year and a half (that's 30 houses a day!) and I don't believe he was thinking too much about the details of the floor-heating systems. They went in fast and they were cheap, and both of those things were very good back then. As a result, we now have baseboard radiators.

I think about those long-gone installers, though. Imagine working that quickly? You put the pipes on the ground and you pour the concrete. Done.

I also think about the other long-gone people who designed and installed those earliest radiant systems, both here and across the ocean. There were the Romans and their hypocausts, of course. You've probably heard that they were the first ones to think radiant. I see remnants of those systems whenever I'm in Europe. You can't wander far over there without stumbling into a Roman ruin or two. They put up stone walls and floors and left spaces behind and beneath them, through which they vented their fires. Make a rock hot and it stays hot for a good long time.

The Chinese were doing a similar thing back then with their kang heaters, and much of rural China still uses these stone tables to stay warm. A kang is a raised stone platform with a space below for the hot gases to pass to a chimney. During the day, they use the platform as a sitting- and dining area. At night, they put away the chopsticks and spread out the bedrolls. Kang heaters worked well enough to stick around for thousands of years. Got something today that's going to stick around that long?

In 1965, when the Beatles left Liverpool for New York City to play that big concert at the brand-new Shea Stadium, the Liverpool Cathedral had just been completed. This place looks like it's been there since the Middle Ages, but they only started working on it in 1920 and had to pause for World War II, which is understandable. They chose a radiant heating system for the cathedral in 1920, and that makes it one of the oldest of the modern radiant era. It's similar to the Roman hypocaust, but instead of venting products of combustion under the floor, they heat air and circulate that through stone ductwork just below the surface. It gets the job done. I read where 36 hours after shutting off the oil burners, the temperature in the cathedral had dropped by only one degree Fahrenheit.

Hot rocks rock.

Another thing they learned with the cathedral was that radiant systems don't heat the air within the spaces they serve. That saves fuel because the air temperature at the ceiling doesn't get that hot, so there's less heat loss through the roof. At one point, they measured the temperatures four feet above the floor and 97 feet above the floor. There was only a one-and-a-half-degree difference in air temperature between the two elevations. Hardly any convection at all.

Liverpool is a great place for radiant-heating history. There's a huge building on the River Mersey called the Royal Liver Building. This place opened in 1911 and it had 119,000 square feet of radiant walls. Big enough for you? This is the world's first hydronic-radiant job. It was also the world's first reinforced-concrete building. This best part of this story is that the electric-motor-driven circulator for hot-water heating systems won't arrive until 1928. So we have this enormous hydronic radiant-heating system that was, most likely, running on De Laval centrifugal pumps, driven by the waste steam from the building's power plant. In that way, it's like The East River Homes, where I lived as a boy. They built that in 1911, too.

And those radiant panels in the Royal Liver Building looked a lot like the European panel radiators of today, but they were actually metal trays that contained hot-water pipes. They filled the trays with the same stuff they used to finish the floors, a stone-like material called durato, which was similar to terrazzo. Once again, it's all about hot rocks. That system served the huge building until 1970, when they replaced the radiant panels with modern panel radiators.

The following year, over in London, the Brits opened the Third Church of Christ Scientist, which had radiant pipes in the ceiling. That was a first. And that same year, they also put hot-water pipes into the domed, plaster ceiling of the new Bank of England, also in London. They ran 180-degree water through those pipes, which is not something you can do with a radiant floor.

Well, actually you can do it (and I've seen it done) because this is America and many of us do what we want to do. It's just not going to be one of your better ideas.

But I digress.

Speaking of America, not to be radiantly outclassed (even though we had to wait a couple of decades), our first modern hydronic radiant system arrived in 1930 and it was also a ceiling system. Are you surprised to learn that the Brits were again responsible? They installed this system in their lovely embassy near Dupont Circle in Washington D.C. A few years ago, I was doing a seminar in the area and one of the guys taking the class told me that he had recently worked on that system. I like to think it's still up and running. I'd also like to confirm this by calling the embassy and inquiring about their current HVAC system, but in these wacky times, that might cause Daniel Craig to show up at my house.

In 1933, and again in England, scientists discovered (and by delightful accident) a new plastic they decided to call polyethylene. They had been super-pressurizing chemicals in an autoclave when the whole works blew up, leaving behind a destroyed laboratory, some very surprised scientists, and polyethylene. Unable to make the stuff again under normal conditions, they decided to repeat the explosion a few years later, and there it was.

Turns out it was the introduction of oxygen while at high pressure that created the magic and polyethylene went on to play a large role in the laying of undersea cables and the development of radar, which really helped out a lot during the Battle of Brittan.

After the war, a number of companies tried using polyethylene tubing in place of copper for buried radiant systems. It seemed like a natural replacement for copper but the problem with polyethylene is that it's a thermoplastic, which means it gets mushy when heated. That goes against the whole concept of radiant heating. Also, the radiant-system controls of the time were crude three-way valves that sometimes got stuck in the too-hot position, and that made most installers shy away from plastic pipe.

With one grand exception, that is. I have an intriguing magazine article from 1957 that asks the question: Plastic Pipe – Is it Practical for Panel Heat? The article gives all the pros and cons and then tells the story of a plastic-pipe, snowmelt system that Bell & Gossett had just installed under one of the sidewalks at their Morton Grove, Illinois plant.

When I first read this, my heart pumped faster because if that system is still in operation it would probably be the oldest plastic-based radiant system in America, and possibly the world. So I called a friend at B&G and he asked around. Turns out no one knew about it. I sent them the article. They asked around some more. They called retired people. They looked all over the place for old records and files. Nothing. If it's still there, no one knows where it is.

A shame to lose that one, eh?

But back to the Beatles. 1965 rolled around and they were heading for Shea Stadium, and as they were, Thomas Engel was getting a patent for a brand-new type of plastic. He called the new stuff PEX. It was a very-improved version of polyethylene.

Thomas Engel had found a way to get the carbon atoms in polyethylene to hold hands with each other, which stopped the material from getting mushy when heated. Eureka!

When I met Thomas Engel in Sweden on November 28, 1990, he said, "The paths of life are frequently this strange." He said this after mentioning that if a shoe factory had been present in his vicinity at the time he invented PEX, we would perhaps today be walking around on shoe soles made of cross-linked polyethylene.

But it was chickens, not shoes, that put PEX on the map. Professor Engel explained, "In our neighborhood, there was a chicken farm, and one day I was asked whether I could make pipes of this material, which could be laid in the ground. In this way, the hens would have a larger amount of heat and would lay more eggs."

Chickens. Gosh. Jean Simon Bonnemain would be proud.

"In 1965, I was together with various scientists of the Phillips Petroleum Company in Bartlesville, Oklahoma, and we were discussing the cross-linking of polyethylene. It was possible at that time to cross-link polyethylene by means of highly active radiation. The problem, however, lay not only in the extremely expensive, and somewhat dangerous, equipment, but also because this method of cross-linking was feasible only for wall thicknesses of up to

0.5 mm. The important uses for cross-linking polyethylene would, however, always be for thick-walled parts, having a wall thickness of one to 10 mm.

"I began my studies using an extruder and I very rapidly found that this technique was not feasible. This was followed by lengthy experiments with laser beams. Finally, I decided in favor of a compression method, with intermolecular friction, telling myself that the cross-linking of the molecules would have to be easier if I could heat them rapidly and bring them closer together by high pressure, so as to then cross-link them in the presence of a catalyst. Years of intensive research followed, finally culminating in success. The result was a handful of glittering white plastic, which came out of the autoclave.

"With this small treasure in my pocket, I flew back to Phillips Petroleum in the U.S., where we carried out analysis. We found I had actually obtained 97% cross-linking. And as a result, the thread-shaped chains of molecules connected directly to each other. We heated the polyethylene and the plastic simply would no longer melt into a shapeless mass. The joy was immense, but what was to be done with this new plastic, and into what could it be fabricated?"

He then explained how he traveled from one chemical company to another in the hope of selling a license, but the answer was always the same: "That's marvelous, but what do we do with it?"

Enter the chickens, just strolling down the path of life. They led Thomas Engel to Wirsbo (now Uponor), and to the laying of pipe under the turf of Olympia Stadium in Munich for the 1972 Summer Olympics (another first).

The first OPEC oil embargo followed in 1973, and we began looking at low-temperature, hydronic radiant heating as a way to save energy.

Thomas Engel had no advanced degrees. In fact, he never finished high school. At 19, he walked out of the American POW camp at Ingolstadt, Bavaria. He worked as a dishwasher, drove a taxi, labored in a furniture factory and in construction. And then he began to experiment with polyethylene, which he had read about during his years as a prisoner of war. That led to his invention of Engel-method PEX. He went on the get 120 patents, but preferred selling rights or licenses to his inventions rather than become a manufacturer. He was a millionaire before he was 30.

His licensee in the U.K. during the early-'50s was a collector of A.L. Brequet timepieces. Brequet died in 1823, and many consider him to be the finest watchmaker of all time. Thomas Engel was so taken by Brequet's art that he became a collector himself and went on to write the book, *A.L. Breguet, Watchmaker to Kings, Thoughts on Time*. He also made incredible watches of his own design, some of which have sold at Christie's for more than I paid for my car.

And you'd think between the PEX and the timepieces this would be enough for one life, right? Especially coming from a guy who had no formal education.

I came across an article from November 2013 the other day. It was about Engel. He had solved the permanent-magnet motor puzzle and wanted to give away his discovery because mankind needs affordable energy. His motor is spinning in Lucerne, Switzerland.

Lukas Weber wrote the article "It just keeps running and running" in the German newspaper Frankfurter Allgemeine Zeitung. He says that Engel's motor gets its power from neodymium magnets, the strongest permanent magnets known. Neodymium is a rare-earth element used in electronics.

"Magnets made out of this material are used in nuclear spin tomography and in wind generators; they drive water pumps of heavy trucks and keep tools steady," Weber writes. "Several suppliers of these magnets have assured us that the power of the magnets doesn't diminish — even after years of use."

Engel theorizes the power of the magnets can be converted into rotary motion. His brass machine resembles a small lathe. Magnets are attached to the disc rotor and the shaft turns in ceramic bearings.

"A disc magnet fixed at the correct angle and distance from the rotor, but which itself is able to rotate (Engel calls it the mirror), can affect the rotor magnets," Weber writes. "There is attractive and repulsive force, depending on the orientation of the pole, the rotor can thus be set in continuous motion as long as the mirror keeps rotating. The mirror's rotation regulates the speed of the rotor. The mirror hangs in a kind of outrigger. Two electric wires connect to the lower end with crocodile clips. There is a tiny electric motor that rotates the mirror."

Weber wondered if it is possible to do without electricity in the motor, but Engel said no. The electric motor only has eight milliamperes at nine volts; it's only a control mechanism. The power from the magnets at the shaft is much greater.

Weber continues: "The rotation is about 400 rpm. We don't have an instrument to measure mechanical power. So we are having to use the finger brake. It is difficult to stop the rotation by grabbing the shaft. With a bit of dexterity, one can turn the mirror by hand and set the rotor in motion. There is hardly any resistance when turning the mirror. The output felt at the shaft is clearly greater than the input needed to give the impulse. Of course measurement was only done with human sensors."

Another possibility is to put a second rotor on the opposite side, Engel noted. A screwdriver held between the mirror and the operating rotor results in the screwdriver oscillating between the magnets without touching them.

Weber notes that scientists are skeptical of Engel's results. Markus Münzenberg, a professor for experimental physics at Göttingen University, said that it is "impossible" for a motor to produce more energy than it uses. Professor Ludwig Schultz, the director of the Institute for Metallic Materials in Dresden, noted that while it is "possible" for magnet configurations to attract and repel other magnets, "the potential energy would periodically bleed off without there being a gain in energy."

When Engel's invention is likened to a perpetual motion machine, the inventor says that no such thing exists.

"Engel is convinced that his machine uses the enormous energy which is inherent in quanta, those inconceivably small components of atoms first described by the physicist Max Planck in the early part of the last century," Weber says. "He therefore calls his machine a quantumdeviation apparatus. He says it has to be further developed. He next wants to attach a small generator to the shaft and show that his motor delivers more electricity than is needed for its control. If he could do that, we'd really have some sensational news."

The paths of life are frequently strange and brilliant people are often seen as somewhat crazy at first. But they're often right.

Thomas Engel came to the end of life's path last April. He was 88 years old.

How I explained mean-radiant temperature heat to Mama and Marie

Erin, you know I like my coffee black. Your mother, on the other hand, takes hers with skim milk, no sugar. We were away for a few days last summer, and the morning after we returned, I checked the milk in the fridge to see how it had faired during our absence. I unscrewed the cap, stuck my proboscis into the hole, sniffed deeply, and then made that face. You know that face?

"We need milk," I said.

"So get in the car and go get it," your mother. "I want my *cawffee*!"

The lady is crazy about me, even after more than four decades of wedded bliss.

I drove over to Pathmark, parked, dodged the homicidal drivers in the parking lot, and made my way toward the skim milk. If all went well, I would be back home in no time at all and The Lovely Marianne would be pleasantly caffeinated.

I was looking for the correct milk with the proper date when a woman about my age, who was shopping for yogurt, whined to her daughter that she was freezing. They were wearing shorts, tee shirts and flip-flops – the summer uniform of Long Island.

"I'm friggin' *freezing*!"

"How cold do you think it is right here?" I asked. They looked at me, and then at their purses, and then at the yogurt. And I'm a friendly guy, not at all scary. No piercings or facial tattoos.

"Feels like about sixty, doesn't it?" I said, because sometimes I just can't stop myself. I am of an age.

"I don't know," Mama said. "What do you think, Marie? How cold? About sixty?"

"Yeah," Marie said. "Sixty. Whatever. Can we go now?"

"I'll bet it's a lot warmer than that right here," I said.

"No friggin' way," Mama said.

We never stop being classy here on the Isle of Long.

"Where you going next?" I asked. "I have to go get a thermometer. I'll catch up."

Marie gave me a look that could grind glass. Mama said, "Cereal aisle. I have to get my raisin bran. It keeps me regular, ya know?

"Oh, I know."

"C'mon, Marie." Marie gave me that look. You know that look?

Anyway, I scurried over to the housewares aisle and picked up an electronic meat thermometer. It cost 12 bucks but I wasn't going to buy it; I just needed it to check the temperature. I pushed the button and sure enough, it was seventy degrees. Next stop, raisin bran.

Mama and Marie were trying to decide between Post, which was on sale and the Pathmark brand, which was a few cents cheaper. I showed them the thermometer. "See?" I said. "It's seventy degrees."

"Sure, it's warmer here," Mama said. "It's the dairy aisle that's cold."

"I'll bet you it's the same temperature back over there as it is here," I said.

"No friggin' way!"

"Ma! Can we go?"

"Really," I said. "I'll bet you a dollar." And what Long Island mother could resist that?

"Let's go see," Mama said.

"MAAA!"

I kept my eye on the thermometer as we turned into the dairy aisle. It was pegged at 70. We stood in front of the yogurt for a few minutes, Mama, Marie and me, all of us watching the thermometer. "You owe me a dollar," I said.

"Double or nothing in Frozen Foods," Mama said.

"You're on." Hey, it was just one aisle over. No biggie. And the best part was the temperature of the air in that aisle was also 70 degrees. "Pay up," I said. Your mother was going to be so proud of me. Mama would be buying the skim today.

"Not so fast," she said. "Let's go again. There's no friggin' way the temperature by the roast chickens is seventy degrees."

"MAAA!"

"You go to Atlantic City a lot, don't you?" Mama smiled and nodded.

So we went to see the roasting chickens, turning languidly on their rotisserie. "I'm getting a hot flash," Mama gasped.

I showed her the thermometer. "It's seventy degrees. You lose," I said.

"AWWWW!"

"MAAAAA!"

"Did you know your body is a radiator?" I asked.

"You talking about my flashes?" Mama said.

"No, all the time," I said. "You're a radiator."

"Ain't that a Katie Perry song?"

"*Firework*, Ma," Marie said. "Baby, you're a *firework*, not a *radiator*."

"Oh, whatever."

"When we were in the dairy section and the frozen-food section, our bodies were giving up heat to the cold surfaces around us," I went on about all of this because, well, that's what I do. I have no life. "But the air was the same temperature as it is by the raisin bran. And now you'll notice that just the opposite happens here by the chickens."

"Let's move. These chickens are killing me," Mama said, so we headed down the magazine aisle. "Whew! That's better." She picked up a copy of *People* and fanned herself. "I can't believe George Clooney got married."

"Did you know that you felt warm by the chickens because the rotisserie acts like a heat lamp? The air doesn't get any warmer, but we do. You feel cooler now, right?"

She was waving George Clooney and his bride like mad. "Yeah, much better now."

"That's because your body isn't just a radiator; it's also a fan-coil unit."

"A what?"

"A fan-coil unit. Like a blower in a warehouse."

"MAAAA!"

"You lose about one quarter of your body heat when you fan yourself like that, even though the air temperature doesn't change. Here, look." I showed her the thermometer. Still 70 degrees.

"Who the hell are you, mister?" Marie said. "You some kind of Bill Nye the Science Guy, or something? Can we go, Ma?"

"Aspettare, Marie. This is getting interesting."

"And you lose another quarter of your body's heat through evaporation."

"What's that mean?"

"Well, when it's cold outside, you can see your breath, right?" Mama nodded. "That's evaporation. When water evaporates from us, we feel cooler. It's like when we sweat."

"Men sweat," Mama said. "Women *glow*."

"MAAA!"

"What type of heating system do you have at home?" I asked.

"Honeywell," Mama said. "I got one of those round heating systems. Goes on the wall. It's beige. I twist it when I flash."

"If you had hydronic radiant heating in your house you would never experience what heating engineers call Cold-70. The Mean Radiant Temperature all around you would be perfect and you and Marie would be in a state of pure bliss."

"Oh my gawd, Marie! *Bliss!* We haven't felt that since the day your father walked out. I could use some bliss."

"You should call a good heating contractor," I said.

"Let's go, Ma. Really. You two are making me nervous."

So I went home to your mom, anxious to tell her about my two new friends and the glories of Mean Radiant Temperature, yet again.

"Where's the skim milk?" she asked.

I got in the car and drove back to Pathmark.

Hydronics points in new directions

Over the years, I've asked industry colleagues where the hydronics industry is. They'll shake their heads and ask what I mean. "If you had to get in your car and drive there, where would you go?" I'd ask. "Would you go to a manufacturer? An industry association? A trade show? A Web site? Where is it?"

No one has ever given me a good answer to that question, and I don't have one myself.

It used to be that we all looked forward to the spring because that's when the trade shows kicked in. A good show was a place to get together with old friends and make new ones. It was also the place where we learned about what the manufacturers had come up with in recent months.

Nowadays, we get that news almost instantly through Web sites, chat rooms, e-newsletters, and social media. And because of this, fewer people are going to trade shows. We're treating each other differently these days. We're apart more, but also more in touch, and we're also learning differently.

A trade group will suggest certification for the good of the hydronics industry, but since the Great Recession, more and more people are looking out only for themselves rather than for an industry to which they can't drive or call on the phone.

Someone once described hydronics to me as a profitable, non-growth business. I smiled at that, thinking back to what my father said to me in 1970. "It's a great business, kid. You'll never be out of work because people are always going to need heat. Especially in the winter."

The people who have been most successful in this business are the ones who figured out how to stand out, and how to market themselves. They didn't sell the equipment. They sell what the equipment *does.*

My Canadian friend, Robert Bean, talks about how many different types of hydronics there are. It's so hard to pin down. "If I ask you to describe a furnace," he says, "you immediately get a picture in your head of what that looks like."

I had to agree.

"And if I said refrigerator, or fire extinguisher, or Harley Davidson motorcycle, you see pictures, don't you?"

"Yes, I do."

"Okay, what does a hydronic-heating system look like?"

I smiled at that, thinking that if we took a house and asked a hundred contractors to put a hydronic-heating system into it, there would be at least 100 ways of getting the job done. And each of those contractors would find fault with the way the other 99 planed to do it.

Which makes it a profitable, non-growth business.

Bob Villa is on the TV, looking at a hydronic-heating system, "Boy, that looks *complicated*!" he says. The contractor on the TV smiles and tries to explain it all to an audience of Americans sitting on couches, listening to the furnace run. "Boy, that looks *complicated*!"

We go out of our way to make it that way.

The number of boilers sold today in the U.S. are about the same as they were in 1970 when I jumped into the business. It never seems to grow. It just is. Profitable, and non-growth.

I love it, nonetheless.

Hydronics has taught me that's it's more about sociology than it is about engineering. It's about people.

It's also taught me that its U.S. market share may be small, but its history is large and delicious.

It's taught me that success depends on solid marketing.

It taught me that it's about community, whether that community meets in person, or online.

A concern lately, though, is the change in the way people are learning, and this is especially true of the younger people in our industry. They depend more and more on search, and do little, if any, research.

I was having dinner in Canada with some friends and we got to that point in the meal where the waitress asked about salad dressing. "What do you have?" one of the guys asked, and she recited the list like a prayer. "I'll have the balsamic vinaigrette," he said.

"That dressing played a huge role in Canadian history," I said.

"Really?"

"Yes, the French are foodies, as you probably know, and they love their salads. They used to use plain vinegar, or, as they say in France, vinaigrette, which is sort of like wine. The French also love their wine."

He was listening attentively, of course, because this is a mighty fine story, even though I was just making it all up as I went along.

"But they needed something to cut the pucker factor of the vinegar," I made that face, and continued lying like a cheap watch. "They needed balsamic, which is the perfect mellowing partner for vinaigrette." My other dinner companions, who were now hanging on my every word, all nodded. Balsamic gets a lot of respect no matter where it shows up because nobody really knows where it comes from. It's like capers.

"The problem, though," I explained, "is that there are no balsam trees in France. If you want balsam trees, you have to go to Canada. In Canada, you throw a hockey puck, you hit a balsam tree. And that's why there are so many French people in Eastern Canada. They sailed over, got the balsamic from the balsam tree bark. Balsamic is dark, right? Just like tree bark. And once they got what they needed, they saw no reason to travel further west. The English took over the west. English people don't like balsamic vinaigrette. They put vinegar on their fish and chips, but not balsamic."

One of our younger friends looked skeptical but I'm pretty good at holding a serious stare. Another friend got on his smart phone and Goggled balsam trees. He read a few words, looked at a couple of photos, passed the phone to our younger friend who saw the photo of the balsam tree for himself, smiled and said, "Wow, I never knew any of this. That's amazing!"

Behold the power of search. Oh, and of lies.

Have you noticed that when you ask someone a question nowadays (and this is especially true of younger people) the first thing they do is reach for their phones and Google for an answer. "What's the score of the game? How tall is the Empire State Building? How many Btu will that boiler put out?" Whatever the question, we have all the world's knowledge in our pockets.

But what if the answer is wrong? Who puts all that stuff in there? You think all that stuff is correct? Hey, maybe it's me talking salad dressing in there. You never know.

I'm of an age where I remember library drawers organized by Melvil Dewey's Decimal System. If I wanted to learn about heating systems, or why they speak French in Eastern Canada, or what all this fuss was about Mr. Dickens or Mr. Hemingway, or whatever interested me, I went to the library and read whole books. It was the way people my age learned. I read and grew older and developed a certain amount of perspective and a large amount of imagination. I can now tell a good story because I've read lots of books from cover to cover. That's research. Research redirects you and forces you to learn big-picture stuff. Search just answers the immediate question.

Search is veneer. Research is oak.

A young person asked me a question about a troublesome steam-heating system. I offered my best guess from my desk and some advice: Study.

"I don't have time for that," he said. "I just Google when I need an answer."

"Oh," I said. "Why are you calling me?"

"The answer I need isn't in Google yet," he said.

Before there was an Internet, I wrote, *The Lost Art of Steam Heating.* I found everything I put into that book in dozens of old and yellowed books, and in the heads of people who were much older than I was at the time. That's research. As I read, I noted how the practice of steam heating was changing through the decades. The 1880's pipe size for a certain load was not the same as for that load during the 1920s. Reading deeply and widely told me why this was.

Required system pressure also changed, as did methods of getting the condensate back into the boiler. The Dead Men were making up all of this as they went along, and they were explaining why in their books. I had to read all those books from cover to cover to understand how it all happened. I gained perspective and knowledge, and found truth. You can't find truth without research.

"Here's a good book for you to read."

"Can't you just answer my question? I don't want to learn the whole thing. I just want to get off this job and get paid."

"But how will you learn to troubleshoot, to reason, to think critically and analytically unless you approach the whole subject?"

"I just need an answer. There's no time for all of that."

"You're searching me, aren't you? I'm your mini-Google right now, aren't I?"

"I guess."

"What will you do when I'm dead?"

"I don't know (shrugs). Search someone else, I guess?"

Look at the speed at which technology is moving. Look, too, at how many old buildings we have in America. Look at how consumers are getting their information. These are forces colliding within the American heating industry. Most people in the business are searching (literally) for answers. Few are doing deep research and gaining true knowledge.

And what are the searchers searching? They're searching the stuff that the researchers put there. Push that thought forward a few generations. If few in this industry are doing research, what will be there to search in the future? You can't take out what others don't put in.

I think we're quickly heading toward a time when the people who work on the equipment - both old equipment and new - may not be able to solve the problems with those systems because, raised on search, they won't know how to think critically and analytically. There's no button for that on the smart phone.

They'll be parts replacers. And anyone can replace parts.

I get this email from a women I have never met. She finds HeatingHelp.com on the Internet, most likely through (ironically) search. She writes, "My elderly parents and my elderly aunt both have vapor-vacuum steam systems in their houses, built in 1930. It seems everyone who comes to do work says the systems have to be ripped out. Is there anyone knowledgeable about how to fine-tune these creatures? Removal isn't the best option for my elderly parents and aunt, and the systems are fantastic when they are running at their best. I am so tired of young heating guys rolling their eyes when they see these systems and telling me the only option is to totally replace the entire system."

I found her a good contractor who has done research and taught his people well. There will come a time when guys like that will have no competition. They are the true heating professionals.

The others will wonder why they don't have enough business.

Try searching *that*.

So what mattered most?

The people mattered, Erin. The people, and all that they did. The living and the dead.

But more so than that, having you, our youngest daughter, take over the family business mattered most. You mother and I could not possibly leave what we've all built in better hands than yours, Erin. Like me, you grew up in this industry. You *get it*. But more important than getting it, you like the people and find them as interesting as I do. And they like you.

You've proven yourself in so many ways, and I'm looking forward to watching where you take HeatingHelp. com in the time that I have left.

When you were very young, you said to me, "A good friend is like the Free space on a Bingo card – always there."

I will always be there for you, Erin.

So it's yours now, my daughter. Yours and your generation's. Learn from it and try your best to leave it better than you found it.

I love you.

Dad

www.ingramcontent.com/pod-product-compliance
Lightning Source LLC
Chambersburg PA
CBHW050450270326
41927CB00009B/1681